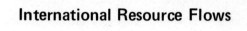

International Resource Flows

Written under the auspices of the
Center of International Studies, Princeton University

A list of other Center publications
appears at the back of this book

International
Resource
Flows

Edited by
Gerald Garvey
Lou Ann Garvey

Center for International Studies
Princeton University

Lexington Books
D.C. Heath and Company
Lexington, Massachusetts
Toronto

Library of Congress Cataloging in Publication Data

Main entry under title:
  International resource flows.

  Bibliography: p.
  1. Natural resources—Addresses, essays, lectures. 2. International economic relations—Addresses, essays, lectures. 3. International business enterprises—Addresses, essays, lectures. I. Garvey, Gerald, 1935-II. Garvey, Lou Ann.
  HC55.I57   1977   333.7   76-42172
  ISBN 0-669-01077-4

Copyright © 1977 by D.C. Heath and Company.

Published simultaneously in Canada.

Printed in the United States of America.

International Standard Book Number: 0-669-01077-4

Library of Congress Catalog Card Number: 76-42172

Contents

vi

Preface

In the past few years, resource questions have exercised an ever greater influence over foreign policy. Resource-oriented foreign policy has also become a subject riddled with value-laden assumptions and perspectives. Critical decisions—which countries should receive raw materials at what prices—involve all the old questions about who wields political power in the international order. The criteria applicable to resource distribution, particularly as they raise market-oriented assumptions as opposed to an "equity" perspective, cannot be easily selected. Yet, entire bodies of economic and social science theory depend upon such assumptions.

As more nation-states assume full responsibility for the welfare of their citizens, resource questions also come to play a larger role in domestic policy. Often inadequate information as to what raw materials will be available for distribution in the future impedes the formulation of sound resource policy. Answers by the advocates of "no-growth" economic policies conflict with the assumptions of more optimistic observers who put their faith in technological solutions to resource deprivations.

The task of developing a systematic interdisciplinary literature pertinent to the choices which lie ahead remains to be undertaken. *A fortiori*, the challenge of resource scarcity to traditional political institutions and attitudes, both national and international, is not yet adequately understood.

In response to these concerns, a group met at the Center of International Studies at Princeton University on March 20-22, 1974, to discuss "World Order Implications of Resource Availability and Use." Assisted by a subsequent grant from the Rockefeller Foundation, this group then became the core of a large consortium—including the authors represented in the present symposium volume.

On behalf of the entire group of participating practitioners and scholars in a series of conferences leading up to the completion of the essays contained herein, we extend appreciation to Dr. John Knowles, Dr. Elmore Jackson, and Dr. John Stremlau of the Rockefeller Foundation; to Professor Cyril Black, Director, Center of International Studies at Princeton; and to the entire Center staff for help in so many forms—and especially to Jean McDowall and Dorothy Dey.

As editors of the volume, we also particularly want to thank the authors themselves for their uncommonly gracious and thorough cooperation throughout the entire enterprise. Their efforts have proved a source of unfailing stimulation—and, indeed, of constructive intellectual provocation.

Gerald Garvey
Lou Ann Garvey

Princeton, New Jersey

Introduction

Scholars of international relations have directed attention to a global economy marked by two kinds of scarcity: first, shortages stemming from the physical limits of the earth's resources; second, an uneven distribution of wealth, including wealth in the form of abundant resources such as oil or arable land which are controlled by a relatively few nation-states. Population growth, rising demands for goods and services, and resulting pressures for economic development around the globe point up the threat to world order implicit in resource shortfalls. At the same time, it has become evident that scarcities do not affect the rich and poor equally. The resource problem of the 1970s has worsened the disparity between the world's "haves" and "have-nots."

The authors of this volume consider the political economy of international resource flows with particular reference to political values, institutions, and processes in a world preoccupied with scarcity and inequality. Part I addresses the problems of scarcity—and of the rumors of scarcity—with emphasis on the role of nation-states in regulating (or obstructing) the availability of vital resources. Part II deals with the multinational corporation—the institution of recent origin which has become most prominent in the actual transfer of resources across national boundaries. Together, the chapters in these parts consider the *general context* of contemporary resource transactions. The chapters in Parts III and IV then offer *partial solutions* not only to the problems of a growing distributional inequity but also to the challenge implicit in warnings of an eroding physical resource base.

In sum, the authors look neither to a lessening of anxieties over resource issues nor to a trend toward complete global resource depletion. The perspectives of cultural anthropology, law, history, and political science produce a fresh (or at least an unorthodox) viewpoint. The chapters that follow broaden the horizons of academic political economy beyond the confines of analysis in predominantly economic terms. Such a widening of approach may answer not only the interpretive needs of our present but also the intellectual demands of the future.

The sudden escalation of prices for petroleum in the 1970s, with the Arab oil embargo of 1973 as an exacerbating factor, compounded an inflationary trend in the prices for materials of all kinds.

The interpretations of the resulting "oil crisis" are often based either on analyses that relate the relatively diminishing supplies (and consequent price rises) to an exponentially-increasing demand for petroleum, or on political hypotheses that stress the struggle of Third World nations for economic equality, symbolized by the new bargaining stance of resource-rich nations such as OPEC. Fouad Ajami, in "Natives and Prospectors: Arab Oil and Competing Systems of

Legitimization," offers a more subtle explanation—a psychohistorical analysis that sets contemporary events in the perspective of the Arabs' cultural antagonism against the West. The actions of Middle Eastern nations are then explained on the basis of factors far deeper than mere dollars-and-cents calculations by OPEC technocrats. Ajami extends his analysis of the driving factor of the resource problem to the increasingly anti-Western posture of non-Arab developing nations.

Oil for the Arabs (as copper for Chile, tin for Bolivia, and so forth) has become a proxy for a deep antipathy that traces back at least to the encounter between Occident and Levant in the Crusades. Arab recollections of the power presumptuously exercised over Middle Eastern resources from the time of Napoleon onward by France, by England, and later by the United States conditioned a deep antagonism toward the West. Finally, the humiliating defeat in 1967 by Israel, a small and essentially Western adversary, hardened Arab attitudes. Six years later, these attitudes found expression in the embargo that precipitated the era of "oil politics."

Ajami reviews the responses of Western spokesmen from the policy maker Kissinger to the scholar Tucker who, espousing a "convenient morality" derived from liberal political theory, have advocated forceful intervention to restore an eroded position in the Middle East. But even concessions by Westerners to Middle Eastern demands, Ajami argues, may be suspect. By grudgingly welcoming Arabs to the circle of the "haves" in the international arena, the West could be seducing them to a position of potential conflict with the rest of the Third World. Ajami's analysis, then, offers cause for optimism only to those who would celebrate the continuation of power politics as the touchstone of the global resource system as well as of more traditional aspects of international relations (e.g., the field of war and peace policy).

Scarcities and rising fuel prices in the developed West have their more desperate counterparts in the issues of inadequate food supplies throughout the poorer nations. Lowell Dittmer focuses on these food shortages rather than limited oil supplies, yet his arguments portray an international political economy remarkably similar to that of Ajami.

In "The World Food Problem: A Political Analysis," Dittmer contends that food shortages are primarily to be explained by the logic of nation-state behavior. Although a long-term food crisis could result from a Malthusian excess of population, the outline of an immediate crisis has emerged from a changed pattern in the trade policies of the leading food-producing and exchange-bearing nations. These changes, which reflect a weakening of bloc solidarity on both sides of the Iron Curtain, tend toward the aggrandizement of particular countries and hence toward a restoration of territorially decentralized sovereignties along the lines of the classic nation-state system. (We shall find echoes of the same theme in the papers by Stephen Krasner, David Smith, and Lennart Lundquist.)

A softening of ideological considerations in the late 1960s, Dittmer argues, led both the leading Western country and the dominant Communist bloc power to rationalize their positions vis-à-vis one another along lines of national interest. The United States began to use food surpluses in the international grain trade rather than as aid to Third World nations. The resulting increase in food prices on the world market prevented poorer nations (many of them already food-deficient) from buying grain, as the shift in American policy reduced humanitarian exports in programs such as "Food for Peace."

The Nixon administration sympathized with American farmers, who despite their traditions of isolationism and militant anticommunism, now wanted to sell in profitable international markets. Following the poor harvest of 1972 in the Soviet Union, the Russians sought to maintain their domestic trend toward improved eating standards. This determination required the importation of large quantities of grain. Thus, an intensifying regard by leaders in the two most powerful states for the bread-and-butter interests of their own constituencies (rather than for now waning issues of cold war ideology) contributed to the formulation of new international resource policies. These policies had severely detrimental consequences for those who could not afford the price of admission to the subsequent bargaining sessions. Critics of the Arabs often cite the effects of oil prices on the non-resource-rich Third World. Such critics sometimes disregard certain perhaps distasteful parallels between the actions of national leaders in OPEC states on behalf of their own countrymen and the neomercantilist policies of other resource-rich nations, particularly the United States.

From what quarter, if any, might we expect a successful challenge to the trend toward a recrudescence of self-serving national power? A frequent answer in recent years has been "the multinational corporation." According to a popular thesis first proposed by Raymond Vernon—the "sovereignty at bay" thesis—the multinational corporation has begun to threaten the authority of the nation-state by reducing national control over resource supplies and pricing.

By contrast with the "sovereignty at bay" thesis, the chapters in Part II suggest that the multinationals may actually have engaged in a Schumpeterian process of creative self-destruction. True, global enterprise has contributed to the interdependencies of the late twentieth century. But the global entrepreneurs—executives of multinational corporations—failed to develop mechanisms to ensure either corporate responsiveness to consumer interests or continuous, reliable physical resource flow.

Stephen Krasner notes that with the exception of pockets of competition (as, perhaps, in markets for small plantation-based tropical agricultural products), the existence of a free international economy is a myth. In "The Quest for Stability: Structuring the International Commodities Markets," Krasner shows that the dominating characteristic of the twentieth century world economy has been its movement not toward free market price levels, but toward a condition of stability in resource flows ensured by commodity agreements, private monopolies, and cartels. On Krasner's showing, we must expect more of the same. "The Burke-Hartke Bill" writes of the narrowly defeated bill which would have fixed new import restrictions of a wide range of finished goods, "was a harbinger of things to come, not a nostalgic return to Smoot-Hawley."

Consumers have typically evidenced less interest in the prices of imported raw materials than in the uninterrupted availability of the finished products that are made from them. The rise of the multinational corporation since World War II is partly to be explained by the success with which the MNCs adapted to this desire. Through their exercise of comprehensive powers over extractive and transport industries around the world, the MNCs worked to assure a continued supply of resources to the industrial societies at reasonable (if not at free market) prices.

But in the 1960s the picture began to change. The wave of nationalizations of foreign enterprises by Third World states, supplier-state efforts at cartelization (e.g., OPEC, CUPEC), and then the Arab oil embargo shattered the pattern of the 1950s and early 1960s. Smooth delivery of materials to the industrial states is no longer assured—and, crucially, *cannot be assured* merely by the "global reach" of the MNCs. A resulting perception of instability in raw materials' supply lines has increased pressures within consumer states for intervention by politically responsible authorities. An enhanced position of the nation-state vis-à-vis the private corporation emerges as the underlying premise of the resource-exporting countries' ability to gain more favorable terms of trade, just as it is of the consuming nations' pursuit of stabilized patterns of resource transfer. Krasner discerns a twofold development: vigorous assertion of national power both by developing states on the supply side and by industrial powers on the demand side of the international resource equation. Faced with this resurgence of nationalism, it is the power of the multinational corporation, not the sovereignty of the nation-state, which is in question today.

In "Private Management of Public Interests: The Multinational Corporation's Challenge and Dilemma," Peter Gabriel pursues the issue of the confrontation between nation-state and multinational corporation. The MNC, Gabriel argues, "has attained a size . . . and influence such that its basic function can no longer be defined as the pursuit of private purposes, but must be recognized as the private management of public interests."

Gabriel challenges the usefulness of theories that assume a coterminous relationship between private and public interests, noting that the same theories tend to postulate economic efficiency as the chief means of development. Gabriel thus joins Krasner in foreseeing an explicit subordination of market (private economic) criteria to national (public and political) goals.

The ascendancy of public welfare-oriented economic development goals around the world has created a political climate hostile to the continued unquestioning acceptance of economic ideologies that call for reliance on private corporations as "engines of change." As a reinforcing factor, the need for long-range economic planning in development-oriented states probably implies an accelerating rate of transfer of decision-making authority from private business to central government.

But inconsistencies between the politically irresponsible power of global corporations and the authority of nation-states do not portend either a precipitous or an irreversible decline in the role of international private enterprise. Gabriel argues that multinational corporations succeeded through the 1950s and 1960s in part because they are *not* national, political institutions. As such, they could—and still can—serve as sources of expertise and information uncompromised by partisan or by self-serving national pressures. Instead of disappearing, the MNC will adapt to the foreseeable international context by striving to aid individual states in attaining their national development goals. That investments will have to conform to national priorities need not mean that investments will cease to be made. On the contrary, public agencies will increasingly underwrite entrepreneurial risks to ensure needed capital formation. The function of the multinationals will thus shift from risk bearing to the selling of "corporate capabilities," primarily managerial skills and access to market and technological information.

The theme of the crucial importance of technical expertise, access to information, and managerial-organizational skills provides the taking-off point for David Smith's chapter. But Smith's focus shifts from structural inconsistencies in the clash between nation-states and MNCs to issues of defects in the processes by which the poor (resource-selling) countries relate to the rich (resource-consuming) states. In "Information Sharing and Bargaining: Institutional Problems and Implications," Smith argues that nations which until recently served as resource colonies of the West must now develop practical mechanisms to recover control over the disposition of their raw materials.

As the resource concession represents the principal device for managing the actual transfer of raw materials, the needed mechanisms would look to the improvement of the concession-writing process. According to Smith, the most crucial and often determining factor in the negotiating process is the access of the contracting parties to technical and marketing information. The inequitable distribution of this knowledge is due, in part, to the corporate secrecy maintained by large multinational firms of consuming nations. Often negotiators for developing countries are not privy to the most basic information about markets, the availability of competitive resources or products, and technical innovations. Unless an international economic information center (or similar institution) is created to make scientific, marketing, and administrative information public, the less developed nations will remain disadvantaged in future contract proceedings. A tradition of information sharing among oil-producing nations throughout the 1960s, Smith notes, contributed to the success of OPEC in the 1970s. The OPEC example—dramatizing the value of exchanged data on resource prices, reserves, market opportunities, and the like—holds promise for other resource-rich nations.

The ability of developing nations to secure "fair" terms when negotiating with more experienced corporate bargainers suffers at the outset from prevailing Western conceptualizations of the bargaining process as an adversary procedure. Adversary negotiation, based as it is on a model of competitive struggle between potential winners and potential losers, conflicts with the assumption in many non-Western cultures that bargaining should proceed as a common exploration to uncover areas of mutual gain. Not only is the adversary concept jurisprudentially foreign to the negotiators of some non-Western nations, but it is of questionable practical use in resolving technical issues that require not a one-time solution as exemplified in a contract, but continuing resolution based on an assumption of an underlying common interest.

Smith recommends specific institutional innovations to help equalize the developing nations' position in concession meetings vis-à-vis their negotiating counterparts from the MNCs and industrial states. But those recommendations apply exclusively to states with raw resources to trade. In other words, a reconceptualization of the international concession arrangement to enhance the capacities of once-exploited nation-states would indeed, in the formulas advanced by Smith (and by Ajami, and probably by Krasner too), look to a more equitable distribution of global wealth. But any resulting redistribution would be only partial in its effects, since it would not reach to those countries that have neither exchange nor raw resources to sell as a means of gaining exchange. Again, the theme emerges: the idea of territorially decentralized solutions based on existing lines of national sovereignty need not frustrate, but *may complicate*, efforts to achieve equity on an international level. In the next chapter, "Managing the World's Ocean Resources: Problems of Equity and Efficiency," Lennart Lundquist presents the case for supranational—that is, for *regional*— solutions to the problem of inequity in the distribution of natural resources. In a sense, each of the first five chapters deals with aspects of the global resource problem which are inherent in the structure of an international system territorially decentralized to form a complex of sovereign power centers, the nation-states. But Lundquist argues that common exploitation of the open sea as a resource subject to no national authority also may lead to undesirable consequences. A resource that belongs to none may be abused by all, leading to the well-known "tragedy of the commons," whereby a lack of individual incentives to conserve produces the total depletion of a reserve to which all comers have free access.

Developing nations argue, on equitable grounds, for the enclosure of coastal borders along the continental shelf as national territories, thereby extending territorial seas out in some cases to the 200-mile limit. This modern maritime version of the old English enclosures movement may gain momentum as scarcities of land-based resources increase the value of oceanic resources. What is more, national enclosures, Lundquist shows, might well be *more efficient* in economic terms than is the traditional arrangement, wherein all of the ocean beyond the 3-mile (or the 12-mile) limit is treated for one purpose or another as a juridically common resource. But enclosures might prove *less equitable* in their implications for international resource distribution.

Most of the poorest states are either landlocked or have short coastlines. Even those with sizeable coastlines, such as India, have neither the technology on hand with which to exploit ocean resources nor the foreign exchange needed to import such technology. The potentially revenue-bearing oceanic resources of some twenty-five developing coastal nations might be enormously increased at a stroke through the extension of sovereignty out across the continental shelf. But ironically, the leading industrialized societies, most of them maritime states, would gain far more than would the gainers among the less developed countries. Largely in an attempt to mitigate this further inequality, Lundquist draws upon regional theory to develop a plan for the management of natural resources which improves the less developed nations' chances for equity without severely compromising the values of efficiency. The compromise of regional management, based on models of fiscal federalism, is a second-best solution to the problem of either national enclosures policies or the acceptance of a global "commons" of the sea. Poorer nations have neither the manpower nor the sophisticated technology required, for example, in the extraction of manganese nodules from the sea. By pooling skills and capital, however, the less developed nations can exploit offshore resources in a way impossible for them as single nations. (The importance of technological innovation, stressed by Lundquist, is developed further in Part IV.) There are precedents for such supranational legal and technical cooperation in the experiences of the Baltic states and in existing river basin and drainage basin agreements.

The chapters in Part IV deal with scientific and technological innovation as a means of liberating resources that would otherwise be unexploitable and thus of easing the sense of impending scarcities.

The ecological controversy of the 1960s threw into high relief certain relationships between man and the natural resource base. Underlying the ecological perspective is a holistic theory of man interacting with nature in a dynamic system, requiring balanced flows of energy and materials. The ecosystem can maintain itself as long as needed physical components of all subsystems are continuously provided. Thus, the processes of life and growth in every individual organism become metaphors for the "life processes" of an ecosystem. In his extensive writing, Lynton Keith Caldwell has forcefully expounded this view. In "Global Resource Transfers: A Scientific Perspective," Caldwell dissents from the "limits of growth" argument in its extreme form but asserts that nature will take reprisals if man persists in extravagant resource use coupled with inattention to the consequent degradation of the air, water, and biosphere generally.

To the related problems of depletion and pollution, there are no simple, utopian solutions. Adherents to the Marxist doctrine of limitless prospects for resource exploitation are as wrongly inspired as are radical conservationists who would turn man's back on technology. Technological innovations could, in some cases, liberate sources for a world preoccupied with scarcity, but such innovations are useless—and may even prove dangerous—if they are not introduced with greater sophistication by those who are responsible for the planning and implementing of technological change than has often been the case in the past. Caldwell's chapter then deals with the requirements, as he sees them, of an intelligent technological response to the problems of resource scarcity.

Only by eschewing approaches of doubtful survival value (such as ideological and religious doctrines) and by adopting a scientific perspective, Caldwell concludes, can man reconcile the ecological principles by which we must work to stabilize the natural system with the increasing demands of an industrial society. Computerized systems analysis can help men avoid some of the adverse ecological consequences of enterprise in the past and better actualize the possible benefits of technological society in the future. Caldwell's sympathy for the virtues of science—and even more anomalously, his willingness to delegate critical responsibilities for future planning to computer experts and other technocrats—bespeaks a complexity of attitude uncharacteristic of the stereotyped environmentalist.

In what specific ways might science and technology, assuming that they are properly disciplined, help ease the problems of scarcity and resource costs? In the final chapter, a guardedly optimistic analysis entitled "Technological Solutions to the Materials Problem: Some Hopes—Some Doubts," Gerald Feinberg suggests some answers. Given a willingness to undertake profound economic, social, and political changes, technological fixes may yet be brought forth for the most pressing instance of resource scarcity.

What is more, given the apparent recrudescence of nationalism among the industrial and resource-rich states, technological solutions alone may inspire confidence that the plight of the very poor can be ameliorated. Technological advances could ultimately invite a truly global redistribution of the earth's wealth rather than the merely partial redistribution achievable under the present international system, whereby a few resource-bearing states are successfully bargaining for admission to what Ajami terms the "international middle class." Technology could promise more for all, rather than merely a better deal for some. In the extreme cases considered by Feinberg, new energy sources, new extractive techniques, and new processing technologies could make for perfect autarchy even in the now resource-poor states. Hence, worldwide equity need not be a zero-sum game requiring derivation of goods from the rich so that goods can be physically transferred from citizens of affluent industrial states to those in the poor countries.

Whether any such courses of action will prove to be starters in the quest for realistic solutions, Feinberg argues, will hinge not only on man's ability to stimulate the necessary technological changes but also on mankind's capacity to adapt to uncomfortable changes in life style. The ensuing exploration into the technological-social interface is a definite and provocative contribution to ongoing research about technological man. Like Caldwell, Feinberg stresses the importance of careful, comprehensive planning if sufficient materials are to be released for the future. Alas, there may exist, in addition to the reflexive limits of the earth, limits to man's own ability to adapt socially and politically.

Part I
The Nation-State System and the Origins of Scarcity

1

Natives and Prospectors: Arab Oil and Competing Systems of Legitimization

Fouad Ajami

The temptation of trying to explain events by seeking for the obscure rather than the simple or mundane is not without dangers. Whenever we refuse to accept phenomena at face value, whenever we maintain that they relate to more complex patterns, we risk obscuring what we seek to elucidate, superimposing some of our own confusion on the argument in the bargain. Those who believe in commonsense interpretations charge that a straightforward reading of things yields a more adequate explanation than does a complex and speculative one. Often, they argue, there is no more to a particular event than meets the eye.

There are, then, risks to an unconventional probe of what is usually taken to be an economic issue. But the social scientist can hardly resist attempting to plumb the ideological, cultural, and psychological sources of the conflict over oil—a conflict that has emerged as one of the central and vexing issues of international order.

The following pages have been influenced by a view of social analysis in which, as Clifford Geertz once put it, "social actions are comments on more than themselves"; for "where an interpretation comes from does not determine where it can be impelled to go." Social actions can illuminate social reality if, in Geertz's words, the interpreter allows "small facts [to] speak to large issues, winks to epistemology."[1]

Why interpret what appears as a tangible economic issue on one level as a more elusive, complex, symbolic, and cultural concern? It is the nature of social life for humans to take symbols more seriously than the "man from Missouri" (who insists on a very obvious vision of reality) may assume. Symbols of meaning, ethical constructs, and religious beliefs form an intricate part of everyday life. Nevertheless, the reach for a symbolic explanation requires a frame of mind that concedes the limits of both raw empiricism and what some like to call "common sense." Nations bring to their encounters with one another not only realizations of material interests but also stocks of beliefs, memories, and notions of a legitimate political order. I wish to explain the way in which these artifacts structure social choices and influence human actions. In other words, I am in quest of certain psychohistorical dimensions of the clash over oil.

The oil crisis has become an occasion to reflect on the decline of the Western international order and for critics of the Arabs to invoke a notion of the inherent justness of Western imperatives. Thereby they seek to assert the precedence of their rights to world resources over those of the actual producers of primary commodities. The following pages examine this Western perspective,

3

including at the most extreme, calls by some for military intervention against the Arab oil states. This extravagant identification with a particular world order mirrors ideologies, systems of legitimization, and notions of order which lie at the core of the dissension over the allocation of the world's oil resources. Reflected are two competing systems of legitimization: (1) that of "natives" who own something and (2) that of the explorers, prospectors, and settlers—the conquistadores who really discover and therefore (in their own eyes) create the value for these resources.

The assertion by Third World states of "permanent sovereignty over natural resources" in the *Declaration and Action Programme on the Establishment of a New International Economic Order*[2] and the *Charter of Economic Rights and Duties of States*[3] reveals the developing states' deeply rooted insecurity about their rights to properties which in fact lie within their own territorial boundaries. Powerful Western states feel no need to assert their sovereignty in international forums or to ask others to respect it. This sense of security follows from the very existence of an international order which is, for the most part, of Western creation and from a preponderance of scientific-technological-military power to back this established order.

But the Western world's system of legitimization stems from more than a preoccupation with material interests backed by a readiness to defend them. It also reflects the peculiar ways in which Westerners visualize a vague (yet very real) *moral* order. In this curious order, one artifact—say, a wealthy Western world—seems natural and rational, but another—say, rich bedouins—appears anomalous, even outrageous.

A nation that defends its material interests by a combination of power and morality—as emphasized by E.H. Carr in his classic *The Twenty Years' Crisis, 1919-1939*—creates, in the process, its own "convenient morality."[4] Of course, the existence of power is easier to substantiate by empirical criteria (e.g., a nation's wealth, military force, technological superiority) than is an assertion of morality. Yet, the qualities of morality and ideology, though harder to get at than conceptions of power, exert a very real and tangible influence on a nation's actions. The oil crisis revealed some interesting shades of the "convenient morality" that accompanies power in the international system. Following an historical sketch of the Western-Arab encounter, I will try to illuminate the nuances of that convenient morality. Throughout, the issues covered have pertinence to the broader relations between the Western international system and those developing states which have been subject to Western power yet have remained marginal participants in the definition and governance of the Western world order.

The Historical Record: The Roots of Cultural Confrontation

The struggle over oil prices began to appear as a serious international issue when commodity bargaining first turned to the favor of producing governments during the early 1970s. The "Arab oil weapon," an embargo against most Western importers, was deployed in October 1973. But attempts to isolate the oil issue from seemingly more symbolic and historical concerns would prevent one from understanding the forces underlying economic and political actions of Middle Eastern nations. *Oil is, to a great extent, a proxy issue.* Old accounts and Arab grievances against the West are being settled and avenged; previous inadequacies are being compensated; the hitherto mighty are being humbled. The Algerian President Boumedienne expressed such a belief in his speech to the April 1974 U.N. Special Session on Raw Materials, when he charged that the contemporary economic order "owes its origin and substance" to colonialism.[5] The problems of oil are woven into the fabric of an international order which is in part postcolonial, yet still in the shadow of residual colonial realities.

The actors who dominate the world stage urge others not to discount the future by dwelling on the relationships of the past. But for those "others," the minor players, the past always remains relevant. And a past that cannot be obliterated today threatens to undermine the foundations of the present world order, or at least to alter its outlines radically.

Historic memories intermingle with the present, preventing Arabs and Africans, as Westerners often view it, from addressing the problems of raw materials with "common sense" and businesslike practicality. Is it so because non-Westerners irrationally race forward with their eyes transfixed on history? On the contrary, the former experiences, however painful, are useful and instrumental. Besides fulfilling purely expressive functions, Third World spokesmen and leaders invoke the past to condemn what they do not accept and to deny legitimacy to arrangements that do not favor them. Herein lies the ultimate rationality of "irrationality."

Westerners may miss the threads of continuity that connect today's international system to yesterday's empires—when merchants, missionaries, and gunboats subdued the world to Western control. That today's international institutions grow out of colonial realities, however, is a central ideological tenet in the Third World. Bernard Lewis has rightly noted that for non-Westerners, the confrontation between Arabs and the West is "far more significant and has a profounder impact than the remote and, to them, largely irrelevant rivalries between the superpowers." Of the antecedents of the present confrontation, Lewis observed:

This confrontation is the culmination of a long process which has been going on for centuries. It began with the expansion of Europe from both ends in the late 15th century, the Russians from the East, the Portuguese and other maritime nations from the West. This expansion, and the ascendancy to which it gave rise, eventually affected the whole world. It took different forms in different places. In some areas it led to direct colonial rule. In the Middle East this only happened in few places and for relatively brief periods. In most of the countries of the Middle East the impact of Western domination was indirect but nevertheless, powerful enough to shatter the old society beyond repair and to initiate a process of violent, social, economic, and political change which disrupted the traditional order, destroyed traditional loyalty and relationships, and engendered a deep resentment against the Western standard-bearers of the civilization from which these changes originated.[6]

Arab Vulnerability and the Western Challenge

Beginning with Bonaparte's invasion of Egypt in 1798, vulnerability to the West has been the central feature of political and social life in the Arab world: vulnerability to superior armies, more powerful ideas, and dominant modes of social organization. Western infidels, for centuries held in contempt, had outstripped the Muslim Arabs in political, economic, and intellectual development. The Arabs and the West, isolated from one another since the time of the Crusades, were again face to face, but the centuries had inverted the order of things: the West was now on the ascendancy, the Arabs on the decline. The encounter with the West, though not responsible for what Arabs call their "stagnation," highlighted its existence and accentuated its gravity. The thrust of Arab political life thenceforward increasingly took the form of a series of adjustments, reactions, and responses to the Western intrusion.

Muslim fundamentalists found the proper response in religious tradition itself. From the time of Muslim reformers like Muhammad Abduh in the latter half of the nineteenth century, to contemporary leaders like Qaddafi, the Islamic tradition was upheld as the ideal response—indeed, as the only genuinely indigenous one—to powerful external challenges.

Arab liberals, also concerned with the Western onslaught, reached different conclusions. For them, the remedy was to be found in a superimposition of Western institutions and modes of thinking on Arab-Islamic society. The alchemy was to consist of a bit of science, liberal political parties and elections, parliaments, and a measure of secularism and individual liberty. Moreover, a Western-style society would honor the liberals' own skills and designate them as its natural link and intermediary with the West. But the liberals failed—ideologically submerged by more radical and collectivist forces from the left and the right, and still more decisively by the military. Their failure resulted from an inability to inspire, from the inadequacy of the liberal model itself in the Arab social context, and finally—and to no mean extent—from Western policies themselves, which disillusioned the liberals and discredited them in their respective societies.

With the benefit of historical hindsight and the record of the liberals to view, Arab radicals came to see the West as their principal enemy and obstacle to a new society. But much to their discomfort, it is to the West itself that the radicals must turn for the very concepts and slogans with which they denounce it. Because radical thought is not a home-grown product, radicals—who have yet to gain mass power in Arab society—affirm the supremacy of the West at the very moment they seek to challenge it.

The initial intellectual encounter with the West was predominantly civilizational and cultural. What Ibrahim Abu Lughod has aptly called "Arab rediscovery of Europe"[7] left on the Arabs a generally favorable impression. In the latter part of the nineteenth century, Europe impressed those Arab travelers who came in contact with it. Its tolerant secularism and social organization were as much admired as were its science and technology. But liberal Europe gave way to imperialist Europe, an easy metamorphosis brilliantly described by Bertrand Russell in his work on nineteenth century Europe, *Freedom Versus Organization*.[8] The Arabs' initial fascination with the West turned bitter. Whether the Arab is selling oil or importing Western technology, his relationship with Westerners to this day reflects the resulting resentment and antagonism.

Arab folklore portrays the encounter with the West, particularly after World War I, as responsible for the culture's misery and problems, Western policies as a series of intrigues, manipulations, and betrayals.

The Sykes-Picot Treaty, the Balfour Declaration, and the postwar settlement culminating in a division of the Arab world between Britain and France changed the relationship between Arabs and the West. A cultural encounter became a political confrontation—or rather, a typical colonial confrontation between powerful outsiders and resentful but weak native populations. European colonialism lent credence to the arguments of those who had warned that Muslims must unite to reject Western artifacts or else fall prey to Western political machinations and cultural dominance.

During the interwar period, oil reflected the realities of the Arab-Western interaction. Regimes lacking political will and independence, sophistication and expertise, freely let concessions go to Western companies. A number of factors helped institutionalize an unequal bargaining relationship between foreign corporations and the Arab states: vertical integration in the industry; the political-economic vulnerability of Arab states; the support that Western governments promised the oil corporations; and most basically, the Arabs' lack of expertise. Westerners had surrounded their subject with a mystique, suggesting that oil was beyond Arab intelligence—too complicated, too intricate for the untutored native mind. Arab states were reduced to the status of recipients of royalties on a commodity controlled by companies acting as intermediaries between producers and their industrialized consumers.

Arab Nationalism: Learning the Rules of the Western Game

In 1948 Israel declared its independence. The Arab armies were defeated. And the West was assigned a considerable share of the blame.

In the aftershock of the year of the Nakba, "the Disaster," military nationalists assumed power in a number of Arab countries. The "street" became more important in political life. For nationalists, anti-Westernism became a basic motivation of (and often a sufficient condition for) political activity. Reflecting the changing fortunes of Western powers, the United States became, particularly after the 1956 Suez crisis, the principal Western adversary. America's obsession with the cold war and communism and the personalities involved—an intense reciprocal loathing between Dulles and Nasser—removed whatever advantage America might otherwise have enjoyed because, unlike the European powers, it was not hampered by a colonial past in the area.[9]

With the growth of Arab nationalism and the prominent place in it of opposition to the Western presence, oil increasingly became a point of contention between anti-Western nationalists and their more conservative rivals in the Arab world. Until Iraq joined the radical nationalist camp, and until the coming to power in Libya of a committed pan-Arabist in 1969, the map of nationalism and the map of oil had tended to be mutually exclusive. Pan-Arabism ran highest in oilless lands (Egypt, Syria). It ran lowest in Saudi Arabia and the Persian Gulf states. Cairo and Riyadh, symbols of opposing movements, groups, and ideas, competed for leadership.[10] The ideological appeal and progressivism of pan-Arabism, and of course Nasser's charisma, were matched by the Saudis' oil money. Against pan-Arabism, Riyadh stood for pan-Islamism with Saudi Arabia, home of the Prophet, as its natural capital.

Nationalists dismissed the oil-rich, conservative sheiks as stooges of the West, even while calling on them to use their strategic commodity in the cause of Arab nationalism and dignity. Was not oil a collective Arab commodity whose revenues rightly belonged to the masses, not to a handful of benighted monarchs and Western stockholders? The nationalist rhetoric called for the expropriation of Western oil properties and—in major confrontations with the West such as the Suez Crisis, and later during the 1967 war—for a boycott to plunge Western economies into crisis.

Oil-state leaders held their ground, in part as a result of the buttressing effect of conservative domestic social structures, and to a considerable degree thanks to the backing of the West. They dismissed the nationalists as both opportunistic and naive: opportunistic because, as spokesmen for poor and populous states, they were allegedly motivated by greed; naive because they misunderstood the realities of international oil. Those who saw risks in politicizing oil beyond reasonable and manageable limits recalled the fate of Iran's Mossadeq. Despite militant rhetoric, republican Iraq generally abided by the rules of the game. In doing so, the Iraqis supported the conservatives' contention that it was easier to advance radical positions on oil matters than to carry them out.

Meanwhile, most Westerners saw only three choices for the Arabs in regard to oil: drink it, sit in it, or leave it in the hands of the major private oil companies. Moderate Arab opinion by and large subscribed to, if it did not publicly embrace, this view. In this context, the Arabs' oil strategy resolved into a search for a series of incrementally more advantageous bargains. The leaders opted for a "moderate" posture, pressing for gradual increases in oil production, for maintenance of world prices, for arrangements whereby governments could share in the affairs of the industry. Despite some concessions to the producing governments, the companies by and large kept firm control. In response to a situation of persistent inequality, then, the Organization of Petroleum Exporting Countries was created in 1960. Notwithstanding its spectacular success a decade or so later, the initial OPEC strategy was defensive. Indeed, the precipitant events that gave impetus to its creation were reductions in the oil prices, which cut into the producing governments' revenues, highlighting their weakness—not their strength—vis-à-vis the companies, let alone vis-à-vis Western political powers.

After a half dozen years of regional turbulence and political upheaval, the sixties promised to be a decade of apparent security for Western interests. Egypt's union with Syria faltered; Nasser concentrated on Egyptian rather than inter-Arab politics; under the eccentric Qassem, the Iraqi "Revolution" had become firmly opposed to Nasser. When Nasser did venture forth into Yemen in support of republican forces, royalists backed by Saudi Arabia turned what was planned as a simple pan-Arab sortie into a major military fiasco. Oil money again served to frustrate the nationalists.

But it was also in the sixties that the Arab technocrats appeared. These younger Arabs sought to depoliticize oil. The Saudis had sent a generation to American universities. Educated Palestinians, the sons of refugees who had deprived themselves of necessities in order to give their children a better chance, returned to the oil states as engineers, economists, accountants, and geologists. As representatives of a new body of sophisticated opinion, and one not particularly receptive to simplistic rhetorical appeals, the technocrats proved to be a sign of changing times. More than this, they were to become a major new force in the international equation.

Such is the irony of social life: When a dynamic culture penetrates a weaker and less sophisticated one, it eventually teaches the latter the rules of the game and endows it, more unconsciously than consciously, with the means and the know-how to "make it" in the more demanding world. In this manner colonialism plants the seeds of its own destruction. Powerful outsiders, anxious to teach the "native" the virtues of metropolitan civilization, introduce him to the art of organization. Without intending to, they suggest to him that humans ought to decide their own destinies. In the early 1970s, the Arabs resolved to do just that.

The magnitude and abruptness of the 1967 defeat shocked the Arab world. Leaders had ill-prepared their people for the outcome. A few days earlier, and extolling the capabilities of their armies, they had promised victory. Yet a small state had humiliated them. As shock gave way to a more subdued search for answers, Arabs had to reassess not only their self-image but also their image of the outside world.

Israel, though not in the West, was of it. Its ideology, its world view, and its pattern of organization were all Western—*and the Arabs had to change if they were to compete.* A mood of masochistic self-criticism approximating self-hatred and hopeful previsions of an Arab renewal alternated at times and clashed at others. But in both moods, Arabs came to terms with the need for fundamental changes in practically all aspects of their society.

And nearly all Arab analysts concluded that there exists little empathy and respect in the Western international system for losers. There is very, very little utility in polemics about ethics, morality, or "right and wrong." To prevail in that system, or at least to hold one's own, required a mastery of its own rules and assumptions. The "oil crisis"—indeed, the entire contemporary global resource problem generally—rises proximately from the Arabs' acceptance of this fundamental proposition.

Between 1967 and 1973, the Palestinian Resistance Movement emerged as an important factor in inter-Arab politics, raising the banner of Palestinian nationalism and redefining the so-called Middle East conflict by interjecting new demands into the picture. Both the Left and the Right challenged middle-of-the-roadism as the policy of the regimes that lost the 1967 war. Leftists advocated radical change, and rightists recommended fundamentalist discipline and purity. The Left found support among the young and an outlet in the Popular Front for the liberation of Palestine. The fundamentalist tendency managed to find its own outlet with the coming to power in Libya of Qaddafi, who produced, just one year after assuming power, a major Arab victory by negotiating a price increase of thirty cents per barrel. Qaddafi's achievement was a turning point in the relations between producing and consuming countries.

The oil states now became financial sponsors of the "confrontation states"—Egypt, Syria, and Jordan—and of the moderate wing of the Palestinian Resistance Movement. But subsidizing war against the common enemy, Israel, required the selling of oil to the Western consumers. Hence, the moderates' position seemed more in harmony with the Arab cause than the radicals' call for embargo. Time and developments in the international system, however, were destined to favor the hard-liners. The moderate position required results, military if not diplomatic. Those who sought time to prepare for another round of fighting, while giving diplomacy its chance to produce an Israeli withdrawal, became increasingly vulnerable. The results of the June 1967 defeat were hardening into the borders of a new status quo in the Middle East. The death of Nasser in September 1970 removed the single figure who retained sufficient credibility to plead for time, to argue for the diplomatic solution, to check extremists. Sadat lacked Nasser's legitimacy and charisma. Hence, he lacked Nasser's ability to maneuver. But he had to produce tangible results in order to hold power. Sadat confronted hawkish elements at home and pressure from the pan-Arab left. Qaddafi was calling for an honorable military solution. In short, the confrontation states—and their oil-rich financial backers—had to deliver if the center, which they represented, was to hold.

On a rhetorical level, the Arab position had tended to be a maximalist one, leaving little room for maneuver. The 1967 Khortoum Summit Conference slogan ("No recognition of Israel. No negotiations. No peace.") provided Arab leaders with the appearance of a tough posture, which was fine for domestic political consumption but adverse to their image and their interests in the international context. Moreover, their inability to strike decisively against Israel or to mount a major diplomatic offensive coincided with the two superpowers' preference for the "no war, no peace" stalemate.

As long as the Arabs proved unable to translate their grievances into effective military and political action, the superpowers had little incentive to address the problems of the Middle East. America's economic interests, as well as its commitment to a militarily superior Israel, emerged intact from the 1967 war. Washington's principal Arab enemies, the Egyptians and the Bath in Syria, had suffered a devastating defeat; the Arab friends escaped the brunt of blame for Israel's victory.

The Soviet clients in the area were more dependent and less autonomous than ever, and the Soviet perspective in any case suggests little gain from rushing into a war whose outcome must be disastrous to Russian arms and prestige. The ascendancy of Sadat, both untried in leadership and known to be hostile to the Soviet Union, further committed the Soviets to a politics of immobilism in the Middle East. At any rate, the attention of the Soviet Union was elsewhere—directed to the building of a superpower condominium in a partnership offered by Nixon and Kissinger.

Arab Revenge on the West: Oil as a Weapon

Given the implications of the détente for the Middle East, two consecutive years of noise by Sadat about the "forthcoming battle," and public frustration throughout the Arab world with the post-1967 stalemate, something had to give. A near certainty that the odds in a military confrontation favored Israel dictated the decision to wage a limited war, to augment it by deploying the oil weapon, and to place Arab grievances on the agenda of the world community. The surprisingly satisfactory military results of the October War fade when compared to the events and transformations that rode on its coattails. To Western opinion shapers, the curtailing of oil production by hitherto feudal and dependent regimes, the dramatic price rise, and in general the new assertiveness of a people who had been counters in world politics rather than active movers signaled that things had gone somewhat awry. It made sense for history to be made in London, Washington, or Moscow. It made sense for Arabs to stand—or better, to hassle—at the receiving end of events forced by the whims, interests, and moods of people in these places. But there was no precedent—at least not one that had been directly experienced by those now living, or still vivid enough to have made an imprint on their consciousness—for history's setting up a capital in Riyadh or

Kuwait. There was no precedent for the disruption of lives (and profits) by bedouins turned into tribal dynasts. Had these characters from "A Thousand and One Nights" really entered the modern world? Fantasy and mythology hardly make stuff for sober individuals to take seriously.

For four decades, Western powers in the Middle East had sought to insulate the Arab oil-producing states from nationalist currents, from pressures for social changes. "Unspoiled natives"—a breed that political change had elsewhere in the world rendered nearly extinct—are easy to manage. It was a successful experiment in freezing history, a strategy desired by both the West and the dominant dynasties and made possible by a social structure that—in the Peninsula at least—had not been radicalized by the dialectic of colonialism.

The Arab oil-producing countries seemed less than *real* nation-states. They appeared as anachronistic dynastic orders, with neither the attributes nor, in retrospect, the rights that come with nationhood, Western style. Hence, the deployment of the Arab oil weapon provoked shock verging on disbelief in the West. These states, thought for a quarter of a century to have been immunized against the contagion of nationalism, in October of 1973 caught the germ. An enigmatic and hitherto fundamentalist Faisal, who had repeatedly warned against mixing petroleum and politics, cast his lot with his former rivals in the Arab world and against his former allies in the West.[11] Feudalism cuts in whichever direction the ruling dynasts may wish to tilt. Just as effectively as it had once worked to the advantage of Western interests, it was now working against them, and with ominous consequences to Western economies.

In the traditional Western world view, wealth and power look good on some but not on others. An imbalance in the distribution of world wealth is not unacceptable per se, nor is inequality in the distribution of power. And in the post-October 1973 order—Zbigniew Brzezinski notes that 1973 is as important to the Third World as is 1905, which had witnessed the defeat of Russia, a European power, by Japan[12]—wealth and power were flowing to strange places indeed.

The familiar has a way of acquiring legitimacy, of seeming to be perfectly natural. And the familiar is for the West to be in control. So long as the international system operated to the overwhelming advantage of the West, little concern was mustered over the gap between those who made it and those who did not. Indeed, laissez-faire liberalism actually endowed that gap with a patina of moral legitimacy. At any rate, the overall result—an advantaged West—reflected other inequalities that characterized the international system.

Before October 1973, it had been easy to sort out winners from losers, and just as easy to justify the results of the game. The post-1973 developments jumbled the scene, eroding its symmetry and congruence. And the Arab determination, as articulated by Sheik Ahmad Zaki Yamani in 1974, was hardening:

There were times when we were strangers to our oil wealth, when we left it to be fun and controlled by foreigners. But by the end of this year, God willing, we shall see the end of that era and the Arabs' full ownership will return to them.[13]

Two different perspectives emerged in the West—each with its own appraisal of the gravity of the crisis, each with its prescription for an appropriate foreign policy. The first perspective, limited primarily to the United States, revealed itself in a reactionary demand to restore the old order. The second, quite orthodox and liberal, suggested a "rearrangement" of that order—just enough to accommodate the rise of a new class of oil-rich states in the international system.

The Western Response I: Morality and Gunboats

In the spirit of the inevitable residuum of social Darwinism that inheres in a laissez-faire system, reactionaries have traditionally believed in inequality, in the fairness of the prevailing orders. Some sense, then, had now to be made out of the emergence of a whole new class of winners without repudiating the entire game. Unwilling to condemn inequality, unwilling to reject the legitimacy of processes that enrich some and impoverish others, reactionaries fell back to just those once-thought-descredited arguments which purported to sort out "earned wealth" from wealth that, being "unearned," is illegitimate. By such logomachy, it was possible to question the moral claims of the Arabs without questioning inequality itself.

Then, too, there was the argument that market forces had been circum-vented by an international cartel. Inequalities produced in the oil trade were therefore different from other inequalities. They represented monopoly profits extracted as a consequence of political (i.e., nonmarket) conditions and facilitated by the onset of war. Yesterday's cartel (by the major oil companies) made sense; today's (OPEC) is simply difficult to live with.

In their search for ideologies to legitimize opposition to the position of the Arab oil producers, many Western thinkers were even willing to "go Marxist." Resurrecting the labor theory of value and giving it new respectability, they argued that wealth belongs to those who sweat for it, not to indulgent sheiks who, in Paul Seabury's words, "neither sow nor reap." An advocate of military intervention against the oil states writing under the pseudonym of Miles Ignotus protested Arab receipt of windfall profits "for a product they had neither made nor found."[14] As Seabury developed the argument:

Oil producing states are essentially misnomered. They do not produce oil; rather, they remove from the ground. Western industry provides the technology, the dumps, the refineries, the shipping facilities. No toiling masses sweat in

14

subterranean mines adding the value of the harsh demeaning labor to the product (as is true for the coal industry).

To produce is to manufacture: to manufacture is, ultimately to make something by hand. Manufacturing entails labor skill, and intelligence. That technological innovation reduces the immediate presence of labor in no way affects the central issue: It takes very little production to obtain petroleum. Oil is simply pumped from the ground, and that is accomplished by western technology. Those now garnering enormous riches from this activity in fact neither sow nor reap.[15]

A hostility as old as the Crusades, rooted in a standing feud between Islam and Christendom and later given a secular overlay in the political conflict between Arab nationalists and the former colonial powers, provided ample material for an anti-Arab campaign. In the folklore which penetrates, whether we like it or not, the world of policy, the Arabs emerge as a caricature of sorts. To most Westerners, "Arab" evokes images of a fanatic and irrational people, lazy and unproductive, at once manipulative and incomprehensible. Their new success affronted Puritan ideology and deeply ingrained American attitudes about the entitlements to success.

In denying the legitimacy of Arab oil policies, the reactionaries' "convenient morality" also appealed to the precepts of globalism. The argument behind proposals to "internationalize" Arab oil—to use the euphemism which found some adherents in 1973 and 1974—was straightforward: the Western world need not respect the whims of Mother Nature; oil is simply too precious to be left under the control of irresponsible bedouins.

The marvels of ideological bias are plentiful. The human mind works its wonders when material interests are defended. No justification seems required for singling just *one* commodity out for "internationalization."

How do committed nationalists and firm believers in *Realpolitik* become staunch advocates of "internationalization" when the rights and properties of others are concerned? Consider the following passage from a book written by three prominent American academics. The temptation to dismiss the book as intellectually senseless, not to say disingenuous, must be tempered by the sobering realization that its message might very well "play in Peoria." As Friedland, Seabury, and Wildavsky expressed it in *The Great Detente Disaster*, the seizing of Arab oil would really show the old concern for world welfare:

Like other aggressors, the United States could claim that it is acting not only in its own interest, though that is sure, but for world welfare as well. It could set up an international consortium to sell oil at $6 a barrel, with $4 a barrel going to the exporters and $2 a barrel set up as an immense development fund to be allocated in lump sums through the World Bank, the United Nations Development Fund or any other agency set up by recipient countries.[16]

Robert W. Tucker appeals to the same morality. His widely discussed scenario for military intervention would have Americans occupy Arab oil fields, then devise a system of allocation and a reasonable cost-plus-pricing arrangement. The benevolent United States would thus intervene to protect, in addition to its own interests, those of "political eunuchs" such as Western Europe and Japan. Resource-poor Fourth World countries would view such intervention with nothing "but relief, however disguised."[17]

Despite changes in the international order, colonial assumptions and beliefs linger. The image of the "unspoiled native"—uncorrupted by ideology, unmoved by nationalism, unwilling to defend his rights, and very much a part of the old colonial tradition—is revealed by reactionary rhetoric about intervention in the Middle East. In the scenarios offered by most advocates of military intervention, the natives were hardly worth putting on the chessboard. Portraying the entire matter as an easy and cheap expedition, almost an outing, Tucker refused to believe that oil-state natives could, as threatened, destroy their oil facilities:

It is the anticipated destruction of the oil facilities that has been insistently raised by those who have dismissed the technical feasibility of employing military power in the Persian Gulf. Intervention would prove self-defeating, the argument runs, if only because we would inherit a shambles that might well take eight or nine months to repair ... The kind and scope of the destruction commonly envisaged evokes the thoroughness of the destruction wrought by German forces during World War II as they withdrew from the Middle East. Would the Arabs match this record? There is little in their past behavior to suppose that they would.[18]

Tucker even suggested a harking-back to the "invisible native" who just happens to be there but is remembered mostly as an afterthought: "There is, it is true, a modest number of people who live and work in this territory. But they would be free to stay or leave as they pleased. The probability is that almost all would stay, particularly if they were treated with care and respect."[19]

The perception of material interest always comes suffused with deeply felt beliefs about the ought and the good. Hence, the traditionally privileged—and for that matter, all humans but the weak who lack the ability to defend a competing notion of order—give their own interests universal claim. The erosion of Western power—underscored by the waving of deference by Third World leaders—became an occasion for what James Reston aptly called the "calamity howlers"[20] to conjure up apocalyptic images of the end of civilization. Friedland and company saw events as a crisis that affects "not just how we live but whether we and others will subsequently live."[21] Tucker viewed the same events as a manifestation of impending chaos,[22] and Walter Laqueur depicted the coming of a new dark age.[23]

Irving Kristol, an influential conservative thinker—once billed as Nixon's favorite philosopher—wrote that "Insignificant nations, like insignificant people, can quickly experience delusions of significance." It is, of course, up to the powerful to see to it that they are stripped of such delusions. Hence, keep the gunboats ready, for they are "as necessary for international order as police cars are for domestic order."[24]

The Western Response II: Accommodating Arab Membership in the Western System

In contradistinction to the purveyors of doom and their reactionary nostalgia, an important segment of American analysts and policy makers, though willing, in the words of one of their foremost spokesmen, to recognize the crisis of the international system,[25] still believed that America's hegemony could be salvaged by accommodating the *nouveaux riches*. Whereas the language and the discussions of the reactionaries revolved around the decline of the West—Spengler's name managed to become a household word—the advocates of restructuring, a group that comprises prominent liberal academics and businessmen, offered a different set of labels and code words. They "recognized a turning point" in North-South relations; they urged a "great transcontinental bargain" between developed and developing countries; they called for a "mutual survival pact" to protect the interests of both.[26]

But under the new labels lies an old premise: the stability of a social system, as the liberals see it, depends upon a viable middle class. The advocates of restructuring the international system were offering middle class status to the oil producers—admittedly a late offer, but certainly more attractive than the dispatching of gunboats.

Enfranchising a middle class in the international system is, of course, not a new idea. But—and this is a point of considerable importance—the basis on which the invitation is issued, and the consequent opportunity afforded a society to join the middle layer of the international system, has traditionally not depended on the possession of abundant raw materials. When present at all, favorable resource endowments helped but were not primary attributes of the middle class states. They tended to be secondary to factors such as the political and cultural links of a particular society with one or more of the principal industrial societies, its stage of social mobilization, and its ability and desire to absorb metropolitan tastes, techniques, and preferences. Brazil, Taiwan, and South Korea are prototypes of middle class states in the international system. The Arab oil states never really qualified under the old rules; when their policies plunged the international capitalist system into a serious crisis, middle class status became theirs for the asking.

Though my own perspective differs from his, and though the circumstances under which the invitation to the Arabs is being extended are unique and hence present obstacles to generalization, I find great merit in Immanual Wallerstein's suggestion that the existence of buffer states (he calls them semiperiphery countries) separating metropolitan center countries from periphery countries has always been essential to the "systemic survival" of the world capitalist system. Wallerstein identifies three major mechanisms that enable a world capitalist system to survive: (1) military strength; (2) "the ideological commitment to the system as a whole"; and (3) the creation of a middle stratum in the system. Of the last mechanism, he writes:

> But neither force nor the ideological commitment of the staff would suffice were it not for the division of the majority into a large lower stratum and a small middle stratum. . . . This semi-periphery is then assigned as it were a specific economic role, but the reason is less economic than political. That is to say, one might make a good case that the world economy as an economy would function every bit as well without a semi-periphery. But it would mean a polarized world-system. The existence of the third category [semi-periphery] means precisely that the uppper stratum is not faced with the unified opposition of all the others because the middle stratum is both exploited and exploiter.[27]

The magnitude and severity of the oil producers' challenge, and the unique circumstances under which an attempt to restructure the international system is being launched, raise problems which Wallerstein's perspective cannot adequately explain. But his perspective is not totally irrelevant either.

Restructuring the international system by accommodating the oil states is, in part, an attempt to undermine the solidarity of the Third World by bringing actively into the international system those who have that single commodity which presents, when embargoed or highly priced, problems that other commodities exported by less fortunate Third World states simply do not.

The reordered status of nations is being proposed at a time when the Pax Americana is not as preponderant as it used to be. Restructuring promises to contract new alliances on slightly more "egalitarian" foundations, with rising centers of regional power—what C. Fred Bergsten describes as local leviathans[28] —such as Iran, Saudi Arabia, and Brazil. The benefits of international stratification would have to be distributed over a greater number of players. And while that signals an erosion of the United States' power position, additional players also lower the costs of maintaining international stratification—perhaps a welcome relief and adequate compensation for a nation deeply scarred by its Vietnam involvement.

The Western roots of the international system are too strong to be cut with a single stroke. Stronger still are the roots of contemporary inequality—and the mentality which allows humans and societies to justify boundaries of moral exclusion, enabling them to empathize with some peoples and neglect others. The rebellion of the oil producers did not remake the international system. But neither can the Arabs' stroke be dismissed as a fluke. Even if the OPEC nations' challenge of Western dominance is temporarily overwhelmed and defeated in a powerful backlash, the events of the midseventies' challenge enter the stock of human knowledge and memory. They suggest to the previously unassertive (in Kristol's words, the "insignificant") that power can be challenged, that structures of dominance are not unassailable. Newly powerful nations today weave pretensions, visions of grandeur, whims and world views, into the fabric of order that only yesterday had been tailored to the desires of Western nations.

The oil crisis highlighted the connection—implying an essential oneness—that Westerners make between the West on one hand and civilization and world order on the other. It also precipitated a massive transfer of wealth, plus a healthy transfer of dignity and power, to oil-rich nations. Just as yesterday's order accommodated the can-do American liberals, today's accommodates the imperial dreams of the Shah of Iran and the whims of the King of Saudi Arabia. And though these changes occurred with the parameters of the present world order, the incident reminded once-complacent "great powers" that orders are artifacts, not products of nature. They are changing rather than eternal.

Notes

1. Clifford Geertz, *The Interpretation of Cultures* (New York: Basic Books, 1973), p. 23. My analysis here is influenced by the reading of Geertz's work. See in particular his essay "Ethos, World View, and the Analysis of Sacred Symbols" in *The Interpretation of Cultures*, pp. 126-41.

2. United Nations, General Assembly, Sixth Special Session on Raw Materials and Development, (U.N. doc. A/RES/3201 [S-VI]), May 1974.

3. Adopted by the United Nations, General Assembly, December 1974.

4. (New York: Harper and Row, 1964).

5. Boumedienne's speech, delivered on April 10, 1974, p. VIII of test.

6. Bernard Lewis, "The Palestinians and the PLO," *Commentary* 59 (January 1975): 41-42. Reprinted from *Commentary*, by permission; copyright © 1976 by the American Jewish Committee.

7. In the book of that title (Princeton, N.J.: Princeton University Press, 1963).

8. (New York: Norton, 1962), particularly Chapter XXXI.

9. See my essay "On Nasser and Legacy," *Journal of Peace Research*, nos. 1-2 (1974): 41-49.

10. See Malcolm Kerr's study of this period, *The Arab Cold War* (New York: Oxford University Press, 1971).

11. On Faisal's cautious oil policy see Arnold Hottinger, "King Faisal and Arab Oil Policy," *Swiss Review of World Affairs* (June 1973): 8-9.

12. "Recognizing the Crisis," *Foreign Policy*, no. 17 (Winter 1974-75): 65.

13. *The New York Times*, 1 December 1974, p. 17 © 1974 by The New York Times Company. Reprinted by permission.

14. "Seizing Arab Oil," *Harper's*, March 1975, p. 45.

15. Excerpts from Paul Seabury's two essays in *The New Leader*, "Thinking About an Oil War" (November 11, 1974) and "The Moral Issue" (February 17, 1975), pp. 7 and 13 respectively.

16. (New York: Basic Books, 1975), p. 189.

17. "Oil: The Issue of American Intervention," *Commentary* 59 (January 1975): 28.

18. Ibid, p. 26. Reprinted from *Commentary*, by permission; copyright ©1975 by the American Jewish Committee.

19. Robert W. Tucker, "Further Reflections on Oil and Force," *Commentary* 59 (March 1975): 53.

20. *The New York Times*, 1 December 1974, p. 15.

21. *The Great Detente Disaster* (New York: Basic Books, 1975), p. 3.

22. See Tucker's "A New International Order?" *Commentary* 59 (February 1975): 35-50.

23. "The Next Ten Years," *Harper's*, December 1974.

24. "Where Have All the Gunboats Gone?" *The Wall Street Journal*, 13 December 1973.

25. "Recognizing the Crisis," Foreign Policy, no. 17 (Winter 1974-75): 65.

26. See Hollis Chenery, "Restructuring the World Economy," *Foreign Affairs* 53 (January 1975); also The Trilateral Commission's report, "A Turning Point in North-South Economic Relations," New York, 1974.

27. Immanual Wallerstein, "The Rise and Future Demise of the World Capitalist System," *Comparative Studies in Society and History* 16 (September 1974): 387. Reprinted by permission of Cambridge University Press.

28. "The Response to the Third World," *Foreign Policy*, no. 17 (Winter 1974-75): 4.

2

The World Food Problem: A Political Analysis

Lowell Dittmer

The prospect of a world food crisis has been periodically invoked since 1798, when Malthus predicted that population growth would increase geometrically while food production increased arithmetically. In the late 1940s and early 1950s, the alarm again sounded. The newly constituted Food and Agriculture Organization reinforced Malthus's predictions with evidence that the introduction of modern medicine tended to accelerate birthrates well before the commercialization of agriculture could increase food production.[1] The initial successes of the Green Revolution in the late 1960s temporarily dissipated public concern about a world food problem. However, a world grain deficit of 7 to 11 million tons existed by the time of the World Food Conference held in Rome in November 1974.[2] Again, food shortages became a major issue of world discussion, if not of world politics. One pessimistic study by Eduard Pestel and Mijailo Mesarovic projected that even if the birthrate in South Asia should drop to the level of the death rate within the next fifty years, the population would still grow to such an extent that 500 million children would probably starve to death within that period.[3] The Pestel and Mesarovic study is based on the same Malthusian assumption of the ultimate incompatibility between population growth and food production and thus falls easily within the tradition of crisis literature on food problems.[4]

But this literature tends to focus on historical, global trends of food-population relationships and on redistributive or technical solutions to the food problem. Such perspectives ignore the political context which may influence food availability, and not surprisingly, this inattention to politics is reflected in inappropriate agricultural policies. The failure of officials to distinguish between physical and political-economic and between long-term and short-term causes of food shortages results in policy recommendations that confuse stop-gap humanitarian undertakings (neither economically ample nor politically feasible over the long term)[5] with basic structural reforms. The purpose of this chapter is to place the natural or long-term tendencies within the political-economic context. I shall argue specifically that the food crisis of the early 1970s arose as a result of the conjunction of long-term demographic and physical factors with certain political decisions—particularly the U.S. policy of détente. Because the economic implications of détente and the political ramifications of agricultural policy are ignored in most analyses of the food crises, these influences will receive my primary attention.

For their helpful comments and criticisms, I wish to thank Clark Murdock, Glenn Snyder, Gerald Garvey, Herbert Roth, Hiroshi Sato, and Phil Speser.

21

Demographic and Physical Adversity

Low per capita income regions already contain roughly two-thirds of the world's 3.7 billion people.[6] From 1959 to 1964, population in Latin America increased by 11.5 percent, while food production increased by only 6.5 percent; in the Far East, population increased by 10 percent, food production by only 8.5 percent. The years 1964-74 have seen no alteration in this trend.[7] This population increase has made the balance between food and people so delicate that minor climatic changes can easily upset it. For example, a shift in the average temperature in the Soviet Union of only one degree centigrade will measurably affect nearly one-half the Soviet agricultural system.[8] Unfavorable weather resulting in a 19.6 million-ton shortfall in the 1972 Soviet wheat harvest contributed to the first absolute decline in world agricultural production in more than twenty years.[9] According to some forecasts, unfavorable weather will recur in the future with increasing frequency as the earth cools.[10] Other basic difficulties undermining food production include a shortage of investment capital in the agrarian sector, traditional land tenure arrangements that fail to reward peasants for innovating, poor communications systems, and storage and distribution systems inadequate to accumulate a surplus to ensure against poor harvests. The Green Revolution appeared to have run its course by the late 1960s, causing per capita growth of agricultural production to slacken.[11]

The recent food problems of the wealthy, industrial First World are quite different from those of the Third World. Shortages in the former are caused by inflation, rising living standards, and temporary market imbalances, while deficits in poorer countries are traceable to unrestricted population growth and low per capita productivity. Thus, reforms proposed in one context (or nation) do not necessarily contribute to improvement in another, quite different one. Rising living standards and a long-standing cultural preference for meat protein have, for instance, resulted in a shift from range- to grain-fed livestock, first in the United States and prospectively in the Soviet Union and Japan. The world's cattle presently consume as much grain as 8.7 million people.[12]

A number of solutions have been proposed for the aforementioned adverse trends: wide-spread dissemination of family planning information and birth control techniques; structural reform of traditional tenure systems; infusions of capital and credit into Third World agricultural sectors; provision for some form of international food reserve and early warning system; and in affluent regions, excise taxes or rationing to reduce meat consumption.

As serious as demographic and physical adversities are, and as commendable these proposals for their solution, political factors bear a much larger share of responsibility for the immediate crisis than is usually recognized. If world population doubled between 1750 and 1900 and again between 1900 and 1960, it should also be noted that world food production more than doubled between 1750 and 1900, and once again more than doubled in the subsequent sixty years.[13] During the early 1960s, the United States was accumulating a large and expensive grain surplus, and the Green Revolution bade to make India and other developing countries self-sufficient in food production.[14] Whereas the present crisis is thus not necessarily a harbinger of doom, neither is it a mere epiphenomenon of the poor harvest of 1972. The bumper harvests since 1972 have not resulted in rebuilding of the world's depleted grain reserves, indicating the problem transcends the matter of one year's short harvest.[15]

Politics and the Food Crisis

I would argue that the single most important political-economic factor contributing to the current food crisis was the emergence in the early 1970s of a more free and internationally-oriented agricultural commodity market in the United States, a development that paralleled and soon became closely linked with American détente policy. The liberalization of the market was undertaken by the Nixon administration, partly on the basis of traditional Republican economic ideology and partly to help redress the $2 billion balance of trade deficit that appeared in 1971 and increased to $6.5 billion the following year.[16] To improve the terms of U.S. trade, the dollar was devalued in December 1971 and then again in the Smithsonian Agreement of February 1973, following President Nixon's failure to force adequate revaluation of European currencies. Secretary of Agriculture Butz hailed the Agricultural Act of 1970 as an "historic turning point in the philosophy of farm programs in the United States." The government eliminated commodity-by-commodity acreage restrictions on wheat, feed grains, and cotton; grain stocks previously controlled by the government were returned to the open market; and all export-subsidy programs were gradually terminated or suspended. In the summer of 1973, Congress adopted a four-year farm law that extended these provisions, eliminating planting controls and high subsidies and urging farmers into all-out production to meet world food demand. Secretary Butz saw a "long term movement away from controls and towards greater reliance on market forces,"[17] implemented in conjunction with a campaign to persuade other nations to lower their import restrictions against U.S. commodities.

By the late 1960s, however, it had become increasingly difficult to protect any one nation's agricultural export markets, for other nations were also increasing their production and export of similar farm products.[18] Of the total international trade in food and raw materials, the developed countries contributed 57 percent in 1955 and 62.4 percent in 1966.[19] Thus, the developed countries, which at the beginning of the postwar period already held a large share in the world export market for food and raw materials, were yet more strongly competing in it.

Even more momentous in its impact on world commodity markets has been the inclusion of members of the socialist bloc in the international markets as an economic side payment to promote détente. During the cold war era, when American foreign policy was informed by such ideas as containment and the domino theory, the United States blockaded exports to the socialist countries and at the same time contributed large subsidies to developing nations in order to forestall revolutionaries from rising to power on a tide of mass protest against poverty and hunger.[20] The "Food for Peace" program (Public Law 480), which subsidized American producers while selling food surpluses at concessional prices to developing nations, was passed in 1954 and remained in operation through the 1960s, during which the United States provided 96 percent of all food and nearly 60 percent of the world's total bilateral aid (about 57 percent of it in food) to developing countries.[21]

In the late 1960s the Nixon-Kissinger regime fundamentally reoriented the international system. Key to this reorientation was a rapprochement with the Soviet Union and the People's Republic of China. In the new international order, a diplomatic concert among three to five "superpowers" would negotiate mutually acceptable spheres of influence. The consequent withdrawal of obtrusive superpower presence from much of the Third World, permitting relatively autonomous and stable regional subsystems to emerge, would at the same time deprive smaller client states of much of the leverage they had formerly been able to exert against their jealous patrons.[22] The deideologization of politics would allow national interest to reemerge as a dominant criterion for international behavior, placing interstate relations on a more pragmatic and flexible footing.

Economic Implications of the Nixon-Kissinger
Reorientation

Freeing the commodity market from political restrictions and expanding its clientele resulted in unexpectedly intense competition within an expanded and ideologically neutralized international market, while encouraging the developing nations to fend for themselves. The new market reflected a spurt in foreign demand, an improvement in American trade balance, inflated food prices, and a general volatility of supply and demand. The sudden increase in foreign demand may be attributed principally to the participation of the socialist nations in the market.

The intergovernmental agreement reached in Washington in October 1972 provided for tripling of Soviet-American trade from the $500 million of the 1969-71 period to at least $1.5 billion in 1972-74. This optimistic trade provision was quickly superseded by trade activity itself. In 1973 alone, Soviet-American trade totalled $1.4 billion, more than double the $640 million 1972 level. A sizeable proportion of these purchases were agricultural. Following the poor harvest of 1972, the Soviets bought 40 million tons of grain abroad—and cornered one-fourth of the U.S. wheat crop—rather than reneging on a Five-Year Plan commitment to increase domestic protein consumption. Even following a record Soviet grain harvest in 1973 and a 1974 crop officially described as the second highest in the nation's history, the Soviets continued to place orders for American wheat and corn. President Ford authorized a smaller-than-intended purchase amounting to $380 million in 1974.[23]

Sales of U.S. agricultural commodities to the People's Republic of China, under political embargo prior to 1972, exceeded $175 million in fiscal 1973. Total Sino-American trade was projected to reach $1.25 billion by the end of 1974, an increase of $500 million over 1973. Altogether, agricultural sales to the socialist bloc in fiscal 1973 totalled nearly $2 billion, about 20 percent of all U.S. commodity exports. Meanwhile, demand by traditional customers also continued to wax. Japan, already at the limits of expansion of domestic agricultural production, bought $2.3 billion in U.S. agricultural commodities in fiscal 1973 (almost double the amount purchased the previous year) and in the first half of fiscal 1974 imported $1.5 billion worth of American farm products—an amount 91 percent higher than that purchased during the corresponding period of 1973.[24] Alone among major traditional U.S. customers, Western Europe did not increase its food imports, for reasons to be discussed later.

"Doing business with the Communists" improved the American trade balance, since the Russians and Chinese both bought much more than they were able to sell, partly because neither nation enjoyed most-favored-nation status (the Jackson-Vanik amendment to the trade bill precluded this, ostensibly on behalf of more liberal Jewish emigration policies—though the exclusion of China from most-favored-nation status on the same basis is a non sequitur). In 1972, when the Soviet Union ran a world trade deficit exceeding $1 billion, her first since World War II, the Soviet-American balance of trade favored the United States by a ratio of five or six to one, though by 1974 the gap had narrowed to two to one. In Sino-American trade, the United States in 1974 held better than a ten-to-one advantage.[25] In all, agricultural exports contributed $4-5 billion in 1960-69, $8 billion in 1972, $9.3 billion in 1973, and $10 billion in 1974.[26]

In 1973, world prices nearly doubled for wheat, soybeans and soybean meal. Corn prices rose about 75 percent. At their peak in September 1973, cotton prices attained levels not reached since the Civil War.[27] Thus, the increase in foreign demand escalated food prices for those who could still afford it and withheld it from those who could not. These repercussions were international in scope, since the United States exports such a large proportion of world agricultural commodities.[28] Although total agricultural exports for fiscal 1974 were $20 billion, higher prices accounted for about 90 percent of this increase. The higher prices of commodity exports, in turn, enabled the United States to pay for the quadrupling of cost of imported oil.[29]

The more volatile character of the fluctuations on an already unpredictable commodity market may turn out to be a more enduring consequence of the liberalization and internationalization of the market than the price increases. Previously, the market had been cushioned by the presence of a large grain surplus. "Carryover" stocks, retrospectively justified as a reserve, began accumulating in the United States from the early 1950s through purchases of the government-owned Commodity Credit Corporation. By 1961, feed grain carryover had built up to nearly 85 million tons, and wheat stocks to more than 1.4 billion bushels. These stocks, combined with the potential grain on cropland held idle by Department of Agriculture farm programs, represented the equivalent of ninety-five days of world food consumption.[30]

By 1974, these reserves had declined to twenty-six days. This depletion has been widely ascribed to socialist grain purchases, but the purchases themselves were a consequence of deliberate American policy decisions. Butz has repeatedly emphasized that the existence of stockpiles tended to depress prices and thus reduce production incentives. In the 1960s, it was costing the Department of Agriculture more than $1 million a day just to store and maintain surplus farm stocks, a figure that intimidated even supporters of a reserve. In legislation passed in 1973, Congress rejected the idea of government stocks in anything more than token amounts.[31]

Although the absence of a surplus to cushion sudden increases in demand makes the market more unstable, both future traders and commodity producers have discovered an interest in market volatility. Traders stand to profit whether prices move up or down, so long as they fluctuate. And farmers, who have themselves started holding crops from the market while observing such fluctuations, anticipate that a reserve might stabilize the market, but at a low level.[32]

Perhaps the most significant factor contributing to the disequilibration of the market was the inclusion of the socialist bloc. The Russians (unlike the Chinese) were not barred from the American market before 1971 and, in fact, made limited grain purchases following the Cuban missile crisis of 1963. However, neither the international environment nor Soviet internal politics facilitated large Soviet purchases of grain on the world market.[33] The Russians and the Chinese alike proved shrewd and somewhat furtive buyers within the American grain market, which in no way distinguishes them from many capitalists. The unsettling influence of these two nations is magnified by the fact that they purchase grain without advance warning, buy in enormous quantities, and sometimes casually violate prior trade agreements.[34]

International Repercussions of Liberalized
Food Trade

Food prices in market systems fluctuate with the prices of other goods and services, reflecting general inflationary pressures. An increasing fraction of the value added to the final product reflects processing and marketing costs, with the result that retail prices tend to inflate although farm prices may hold constant or even decline. New food products that are convenient (and more expensive), such as freeze-dried and deep-frozen items, make it possible to accommodate a rising living standard with increasingly costly services, without substantially increasing actual food consumption. Indeed, per capita caloric consumption in the United States reached a peak in 1910 from which it has been declining ever since.[35] Thus, general inflationary pressures have contributed significantly to the overall rise in recent American food prices. But the increase in foreign demand indicated by a single Soviet purchase had an immediate panic effect on the future market that sent a strong inflationary ripple through the economy, resulting in the sharpest one-month increase in food prices in twenty-two years in January 1973, and amounting to an increase of more than 20 percent by the end of the year.

The Soviet agricultural plight that promoted this purchase was serious but not disastrous. During the Khrushchev era, the government expanded wheat production to make bread but killed livestock when the harvest was poor. In the Brezhnev-Kosygin era, the nation grows wheat not only to make bread but to feed livestock, and rather than foreclose on its livestock program when production is poor, the government will import vast amounts of wheat for both bread and livestock. The leadership was able to redress a shortfall in the 1972 wheat harvest by importing 11 million tons of wheat from the United States and 7.55 million tons from Canada and Australia.[36]

Western Europe's inflation owes more to OPEC oil price increases than to imports of high-priced American food. Although Europe has traditionally been the largest customer of American agricultural commodities, the European Economic Community has erected high import tariffs and granted subsidies to its own relatively inefficient food producers. By 1973, Europe had been displaced by the Far East as the leading growth market for American farm products.[37] The poor harvest of the summer of 1975 may reverse this trend, but probably only temporarily.

Japan probably has the most implacable food problem in the industrialized world. Despite an increased living standard, average daily per capita caloric intake has remained substantially lower than in any other developed country, even including such marginally developed countries as Spain and Venezuela. Yet, the food factor in Japan's cost of living was 43 percent in 1973, against a corresponding figure for the United States of 22 percent. Domestic agricultural production and cultivable cropland have been shrinking since the mid-1950s, and Japanese dependence on imports has increased proportionately. As of 1972, the country imported about 46 percent of its food needs (compared with 19 percent in 1957). Thirty-two percent of these imports came from the United States, making Japan by far the largest single market for American farm products, accounting for some 11 percent of the total.[38]

Yet, since 1971, Japan has been subjected to a series of economic "shocks." In August of that year the Nixon administration announced a temporary 10 percent surcharge on imports; in October, the administration gave Japan an ultimatum on trade in cotton textiles, forcing the Sato regime to impose an export surtax; and in 1973, the United States suddenly imposed an export embargo on soybean products (Japan at that time purchased 92 percent of her soybeans from the United States). While these policies helped to relieve the American trade imbalance—nearly three-fourths of which accrued to Japan in 1972—they proved disastrous to Japan. By the end of 1973, Japan's balance of trade changed from a surplus of $4.7 billion to her first payments' deficit in six years, and inflation rose to the highest in the industrialized world. The nation's real G.N.P. declined by an estimated 3.25 percent in 1974. The 1975 G.N.P. projections suggested a recovery increase of only 2 percent, signaling Japan's deepest slump since the postwar years.[39]

The Japanese have taken steps away from their extreme economic and political dependence on the United States. A "develop and import" policy designed to diversify sources of food supply has already resulted in increased purchases of grain from Australia and soybeans from China. The Southeast Asian nations can provide markets for Japanese manufactures while exporting foodstuffs and primary products. If qualms about Japanese economic domination can be overcome, something like a demilitarized "Greater East Asian Coprosperity Sphere" may yet emerge. Politically, the Japanese have recognized the People's Republic of China, negotiated with the Soviet Union and China concerning joint development of Siberian and offshore Chinese petroleum resources, and refused to join the American condemnation of the Arab oil boycott.[40] If the American nuclear umbrella is seen to be as unreliable as her international trade policy, Japanese assertions of autonomy may extend to the military sphere as well.

Most seriously hurt by the rise in demand for American agricultural products were countries in South Asia and sub-Saharan Africa, which experienced a simultaneous decline in domestic sources of supply. As the increase in commercial sales drastically reduced food aid from the United States, the increase in demand drove the market price up. Thus, foodstuffs previously distributed through government aid channels were diverted to the commercial market to meet the rising demand. Although gross U.S. agricultural exports increased from about $7 billion to more than $12 billion in 1972, the quantity allocated to P.L. 480 aid programs dropped to the lowest level since the start of the program. Thus, only a few days after President Ford approved the 1974 sale of 2.2 million tons of wheat to the Soviet Union, Secretary of State Kissinger reportedly informed Indian officials that the United States would be able to supply only about 500,000 tons of reduced-price grain.[41] The 4.2 million tons of food aid shipped in 1973 was less than one-fourth of that annually made available in the 1960s.[42]

Thus, owing to the success of a series of détente-related negotiations aimed at defining mutually acceptable spheres of influence and at circumscribing the resort to force, the developing nations were on the one hand assured of relief from competitive superpower penetration. On the other hand, it no longer seemed so necessary for superpowers to insure client states against seduction by the opposing bloc through the distribution of largesse. Only those countries on the margins between different spheres of influence—countries such as Vietnam—could claim such attention. The other major impact of the events of the early 1970s on the Third World was the increase in world food prices, which by 1974 had risen 100 percent above 1968-70 levels.[43] Because among the poor the income elasticity of demand for food is very high, food price inflation tends more directly and severely to affect an underdeveloped than an industrial economy.[44] The inflation of food prices must nevertheless be seen as part of a worldwide commodity inflation, reversing the postwar trend in which commodity prices remained low while the prices of manufactures continually rose.[45] The increased price of raw materials was of benefit to those developing countries which export food commodities or extractive products such as petroleum. But those nations which export neither often must import both, and this requires that they defer development projects (with possibly serious long-term consequences) and redirect investment funds to purchase the needed food or fertilizer.[46]

Politics and Food: Difference at the Margin

I have suggested that although the ultimate relationship between population growth and food production is a complicated one, the difference at the margin between starvation and survival at any given time has more to do with the immediate political-economic context than with long-term demographic or physical adversities. In point is the process by which American agricultural and trade policy, though independently conceived, came to dovetail with concurrent American détente policy, giving substance to détente, while at the same time undermining the economic infrastructure of the old containment policy.

The Nixon-Ford détente policy was seemingly based on assumptions similar to those espoused by functionalist theorists such as David Mitrany and Ernst Haas:[47] If trade can be facilitated between two blocs, an interpenetration of interests will ensue, making warfare increasingly unlikely and possibly creating a momentum toward further convergence. "Intractable" political issues may, paradoxically, be resolved by recognizing the legitimacy of the status quo, since mutual recognition of the status quo will reduce tensions, and socialist systems inherently require higher tension levels than do pluralist systems. Without the threat of a surrounding capitalist bloc, it would no longer be possible to legitimate political repression. The forces of nationalism could assert themselves in Eastern Europe, or even among Soviet minority nationalities.[48]

Recognition of the status quo implied a tacit forfeiture of the universalistic, eschatological claims inherent in both Western and socialist ideologies, and once the ideologies had been so comprised, nation-states tended to revive a nationalism more consonant with the *Realpolitik* implicit in détente. The revival of nationalism affected international economics as well, in the form of an emerging neomercantilism. Various national governments would intercede in the market on behalf of the export-import sector of their economies.[49] These factors corroded intrabloc solidarity on both sides. If the bloc leader acted in terms of national interests rather than in terms of the ideology upon which bloc unity had been premised, no practical basis remained to distinguish one bloc from another. Equal political and economic relationships by each nation-state with all nation-states became feasible.

The politics of food in the postwar era, then, arose in the context of the cold war. Because of the disproportionate political influence of the agricultural sector in a still gerrymandered Congress, a system of price supports was instituted, resulting in the accumulation of a large agricultural surplus. It was in the national interest to dispose of this surplus through nonmarket channels in order to avoid depressing commodity prices. Containment ideology legitimized such a channel: The surplus should be distributed to new Third World countries which now stood in danger of take-over by Communist-affiliated insurgents. A relationship of political symbiosis arose between client and patron states. If the client violated this relationship of mutual obligation and responsibility, the patron state would cut off aid (and perhaps even send in an expeditionary force to compel more filial behavior). If the patron failed to satisfy client needs, the latter might (perhaps involuntarily) realign with the opposing bloc.

Under the impact of the "new philosophy of foreign policy" introduced by Nixon and Kissinger, ideological commitments of this kind seem to have atrophied. The two major superpowers, in behaving more like collusive than competitive duopolists, have thereby mitigated the benefits as well as the hazards that the Third World derived from their competition. The reaction of the Third World to the American rescission of food aid programs seems one of intensified resentment—particularly of the United States, perhaps because neither the Soviet Union nor the People's Republic of China ever participated in an organized way in food aid programs. From this perspective, détente seemed to signify an era of political and economic collusion among the superpowers leading to abandonment of the Third World and giving rise to a new international configuration of north against south.

Third World hostility toward the superpowers has become audible in a series of well-publicized international conferences: the U.N. General Assembly's votes to admit the People's Republic of China to the Security Council, to expel the Union of South Africa, and to recognize the Palestine Liberation Organization; and the international conventions on the human environment (Stockholm, 1972), world population (Bucharest, 1974), and food (Rome, 1974). The "world countryside"—the Third World—is, however, dependent on the "world cities" for much of its food as well as for most of its manufactures. With the most prominent exception of the oil countries, the present relationship of the "world countryside" to the "world cities" is still largely appellative, and the sanctions available to the former against an increasingly self-absorbed First World are limited to the threat of embarrassment in international forums and world public opinion.

Notes

1. Leroy L. Blakeslee, Earl O. Heady, and Charles F. Framingham, *World Food Production, Demand, and Trade* (Ames, Iowa: Iowa State University Press, 1973), pp. 5-10.

2. *New York Times* (hereafter *NYT*), 8 November 1974.

3. Eduard C. Pestel and Mijailo Mesarovic, *Mankind at the Turning Point* (New York: E. P. Dutton, 1974), pp. 115-30.

4. Cf. William and Paul Paddock, *Famine—1975! America's Decision—Who Will Survive?* (Boston: Little, Brown, 1967); D.S. Halacy, Jr., *The Geometry of Hunger* (New York: Harper and Row, 1972); Paul and Arthur Simon, *The Politics of World Hunger: Grassroots Politics and World Poverty* (New York: Harper and Row, 1973); Jorgen Randers and Erich K.O. Zahn, "Agricultural Sector," in *Dynamics of Growth in a Finite World*, Dennis L. Meadows et al., eds. (Cambridge, Mass.: Wright Allen Press, 1974), pp. 257-369.

5. All food surpluses on hand in the world as of 1970 would not solve the needs of the food-deficient countries for more than two to three months, and since 1970, food surpluses have declined substantially. Robert G. Stanley, *Food for Peace: Hope and Reality of U.S. Food Aid* (New York: Gordon and Breach, 1973), p. 46.

6. Douglas N. Ross, *Food and Population: The Next Crisis* (New York: The Conference Board, 1974), pp. 1-16.

7. Stanley, *Food for Peace*, p. 43.

8. Ross, *Food and Population*, p. 16.

9. Because of the Soviet shortfall, combined with reduced harvests in Southeast Asia and Australia, world output of wheat, rice, and coarse grains declined by 33 million tons in 1972. Since output must expand at the rate of 25 million tons annually just to remain abreast of current population growth, the pressure of a 58 million ton deficit was felt. *NYT*, 5 November 1974, pp. 1, 14.

10. Kenzo Hemmi, "Nogyo to Keizai" [Changing World Food Situation], *Mainichi Shimbun Sha* (Tokyo), 10 September 1973, pp. 4-10.

11. United States, Department of Agriculture (USDA), *Handbook of*

Agricultural Charts, Agricultural Handbook no. 455 (Washington, D.C., October 1973), p. 51.

12. Ross, *Food and Population*, pp. 1-4. Brown estimates that the annual availability of grain per person in the poor countries is only about 400 pounds per year, nearly all consumed directly, while in the U.S. and Canada, per capita grain utilization is approaching one ton per year, only about 150 pounds directly consumed. Lester Brown, "Population and Affluence" (Overseas Development Council, paper no. 15, September 1973). The most common indirect consumption is through meat consumption, which depends on substantial grain inputs; in the case of beef, for example, 12 pounds of grain must be fed to provide one pound of usable protein.

13. D. Gale Johnson, *The Struggle Against World Hunger* (The Foreign Policy Association, the Headline Series, no. 184, August 1967). See also K.L.R. Pavitt, "Malthus and Other Economists: Some Doomsdays Revisited," in *Models of Doom: A Critique of the Limits of Growth*, ed. H.S. Cole et al. (New York: Universe Books, 1973), pp. 217-24.

14. During the 1950s and 1960s, the developing countries as a group raised their overall agricultural production at an average rate of nearly 3 percent per year—a more rapid expansion than had been achieved by most industrial countries at comparable periods in their own development. Thomas W. Wilson, Jr., *World Food: The Political Dimension* (Washington, D.C.: Aspen Institute for Humanistic Studies, 1974), p. 14. See also Pauline K. Marstrand and K.L.R. Pavitt, "The Agricultural Subsystem," in *Models of Doom*, pp. 56-66.

15. Lester Brown, "The Politics of Food," *Foreign Politics* 14 (Spring 1974): 30-35. The 1973 harvest was bountiful, but the 1974 harvest actually fell 16-18 percent behind projection.

16. Since 1820, the U.S. has annually exported 21-30 percent of its agricultural output, although the percentage of the labor force producing this food has decreased from 70 percent of the population to less than 9 percent. Despite the decrease in farm manpower and the increased volume of industrial manufacturing, farm products have maintained about the same proportion of the U.S. export market and consistently contribute the largest trade surplus to the balance of payments. Stanley, *Food for Peace*, p. 3.

17. Earl Butz, "Talk Delivered in Paris to the Agricultural Ministers of the World's Major Countries," April 11, 1973, released by the Office of the Secretary, USDA.

18. USDA, *International Trade Press Kit*, (1973).

19. Colin Clark, *Starvation or Plenty?* (New York: Taplinger, 1970), pp. 128-43.

20. Cf. Franz Schurmann, *The Logic of World Power: An Inquiry into the Origins, Currents, and Contradictions of World Politics*, Part I (New York: Pantheon Books, 1974). As John F. Kennedy's Task Force on Foreign Economic

Assistance noted: "The controlling fact is that the need of the underdeveloped world for investment capital (and for other resources as well) can be met in only two ways: by extraordinary external aid or by forced savings. These alternatives are inescapable. The first alternative leaves the way open for the evolution of a free society. The second requires a totalitarian political system." Quoted in Seyom Brown, *The Faces of Power* (New York, 1968), p. 203.

21. Stanley, *Food for Peace*, p. 7. In the mid-1960s, the U.S. annually exported a total of about $6.5 billion in farm products, 28 percent of which were shipments under P.L. 480. This included 78 percent of the wheat exported, 54 percent of the vegetable oils, 53 percent of the rice exports, and 33 percent of the cotton. Cf. Robert M. Stern, "Agricultural Surplus Disposal and U.S. Economic Policies," *World Politics* 12, no. 3 (April 1960): 422-34.

22. Cf. Donald C. Hellmann, *Japan and East Asia: The New International Order* (New York: Praeger, 1972).

23. *NYT*, 18 November 1974.

24. *NYT*, 4 June 1974, pp. 1, 9; USDA, *International Trade Press Kit*, (1973); and Economic Research Service (ERS), USDA, *Outlook for U.S. Agricultural Exports* (February 21, 1974).

25. *NYT*, 4 June 1974, pp. 1, 9; 30 May 1973, p. 51; 16 January 1975, p. 18.

26. USDA, *Handbook of Agricultural Charts* (October 1973); Stephen S. Rosenfeld, "The Politics of Food," *Foreign Politics* 14 (Spring 1974): 17-30.

27. H. Christine Collins, "Price Developments During 1973," *Foreign Agricultural Trade of the U.S. (FATUS)* (March 1974): 15-22.

28. Since the 1960s, with only about 7 percent of the world's surface and 6 percent of its population, the U.S. has supplied about 42 percent of its total wheat exports, 50 percent of all feed grain exports (corn, barley, sorghum, and oats), 21 percent of all cotton exports, and 90 percent of world soybean exports. The products of 29 percent of all U.S. farmlands were harvested for export, an absolute increase from 47 million acres in 1955 to 85 million acres in 1972 (while total crop acreage declined from 340 million acres to 296 million acres during the same period). Stanley, *Food for Peace*, pp. 3-6; *Handbook of Agricultural Charts*, (October 1973).

29. In 1973 the U.S. exported $14.1 million worth of agricultural products. While the price of U.S. fuel imports increased 22 percent, the price of U.S. food exports increased by 55 percent. Ross, *Food and Population*, pp. 1-16.

30. ERS, USDA, *Grain Stocks, Issues and Alternatives: A Progress Report* (February 1974).

31. *NYT*, 15 September 1974, IV, p. 6; 5 July 1974, p. 1; Rosenfeld, "The Politics of Food," p. 19; *Grain Stocks, Issues and Alternatives*, (February 1974).

32. *Aberdeen American News*, Aberdeen, South Dakota, 31 July 1973. By

1975, however, a strong array of farm organizations had reversed their position and lobbied in favor of the higher income guarantees and price supports included in the 1975 farm bill. *NYT*, 16 March 1975, IV, p. 4; 30 March 1975, IV, p. 3.

33. Soviet purchases were also facilitated by certain international monetary changes, such as the increased value of gold.

34. When the contract price is higher than the market price, purchasers may cancel—as the U.S.S.R. did in January 1975, when its purchase price was at $5.50 at the time the market price had dropped to $4.00. In the case of customers like the U.S.S.R., penalty charges may not be enforced. Cheryl Christenson, "Dynamics of Food Transactions" (Paper presented to the Annual Meeting of the International Studies Association, Washington, D.C., February 21, 1975).

35. *The Formation of Food Prices and Their Behavior in Times of Inflation* (Paris: Organization for Economic Cooperation and Development, 1973), passim; Joseph R. Barse, *Japan's Food Demand and 1985 Grain Import Prospects*, ERS, USDA, Foreign Agricultural Economic Report no. 53 (1969).

36. *NYT*, 18 November 1974.

37. *U.S. International Trade Press Kit*, (1973); Butz, "Talk to Agricultural Ministers," April 11, 1973.

38. ERS, USDA, *Agricultural Policies in the Far East and Oceania*, Foreign Agricultural Economic Report no. 37 (November 1967); *NYT*, 15 September 1974, IV, p. 6; Barse, *Japan's Food Demand*, p. 11 ff. Japan is currently one of the most import-dependent nations in the world. The United Kingdom has succeeded in raising its degree of self-sufficiency from 55 percent to 65 percent over the past ten years. Japan's record of 53 percent is the lowest degree of self-sufficiency among developed countries. Lyle P. Schertz, "World Food: Prices and the Poor," *Foreign Affairs* 52-53, (April 1974): 511-38.

39. *Grain Stocks, Issues and Alternatives* (1974); ERS, USDA, *Japan's Farm Commodity Market: A View of U.S.-Australian Competition*, Foreign Agricultural Economic Report no. 289 (1970); Kazuo Sato, "Trade Relations Between the U.S. and Japan: The Past and the Future" (Paper presented at the East Asia Symposium, Pembroke State University, N. Carolina, April 7, 1973); J. Rey Maino, "Japan 1973: The End of an Era?" *Asian Survey* 14, no. 1 (January 22, 1974): 1 ff.; *NYT*, 12 June 1974, pp. 61, 67; 23 December 1974, p. 43.

40. Stockpiling is also taking place under the administrative regulation of the Japanese government. *NYT*, 1 July 1973, III, p. 1; Bruce J. Greenshields and Linda B. Schneider, "Diplomatic Ties May Benefit Chinese-Japanese Farm Trade," *Foreign Agriculture* 11, no. 2 (January 8, 1973): 2-5; Barse, *Japan's Food Demand*; and John M. Maki, "Japan and World Politics in the 1970s," *Pacific Affairs* 46, no. 2 (Summer 1973): 289-98.

41. *Grain Stocks, Issues and Alternatives*; Schertz, "World Food," pp. 511-38. In March 1975, Washington and New Delhi signed an agreement for the

supply of 800,000 tons of wheat to India on concessional terms, the first such agreement since termination of P.L. 480 shipments in 1971. Although Indian food officials welcomed the agreement with relief, the quantity pledged is probably but one-fourth of what the government will have to import by commercial purchases in 1975. *NYT*, 24 March 1975.

42. *NYT*, 8 November 1974; 23 January 1975, p. 33. The big drop showed itself in the 1973-74 figures. Wheat exports under Title I of P.L. 480 (under which surplus food is sold for long-term loans in dollars or convertible currencies at low interest rates) dropped from 4.5 million tons in 1972 to ca. 1 million tons in 1974; corn, grain, and sorghum exports dropped from 1.2 to 0.5 million tons. Under Title II (direct grants to governments or to international agencies such as CARE), wheat dropped from 1.6 million tons to 700,000 tons, rice from 0.25 million to zero; vegetable oils from 190,000 tons to slightly more than 50,000. The cuts meant that some 20 million of the world's poorest people who received food from the U.S. in 1972 received none in 1974.

43. Hollis B. Chenery, "Restructuring the World Economy," *Foreign Affairs* 53, no. 2 (January 1975): 242-64.

44. See E.M. Ojala, *Agriculture and Economic Progress* (London: 1952), p. 89.

45. The exporting countries had to sell 53 percent more primary produce to buy the same quantities of manufactures in 1967 as in 1950. Clark, *Starvation or Plenty*, pp. 128-43. It has been estimated that over the ten years since 1957, the change in the terms of trade has involved a gain to the industrialized countries of some $7,000 million a year from lower prices for their imports and a further gain of $3,000-4,000 million from higher prices for their exports, which would be equivalent to the whole of Western aid according to its broadest definition. Sarah Child, *Poverty and Affluence: An Introduction to the International Relations of Rich and Poor Economies* (London: Hamish Hamilton, 1968), p. 117.

46. Vigorously denouncing the Arab oil embargo, the U.S. in October 1973 suspended export sales of petroleum-based fertilizer, thus making a major contribution to the 1.5 million ton fertilizer shortfall in the developing countries, which was projected to cost 15 million tons in lost grain production in 1974. *NYT*, 3 November 1974.

47. David Mitrany, *A Working Peace System* (Chicago: Quadrangle Books, 1966); Ernst B. Haas, *Beyond the Nation-State: Functionalism and International Organization* (Stanford, Calif,: Stanford University Press, 1964).

48. Hisahiko Okazaki, *A Japanese View of Détente* (Lexington, Mass.: D.C. Heath, 1974), *passim*.

49. Cf. Richard N. Cooper, "Trade Policy Is Foreign Policy," *Foreign Policy* 9 (Winter 1972-73): 18-37.

**Part II
The Multinational
Corporation at Bay?**

3 The Quest for Stability: Structuring the International Commodities Markets

Stephen Krasner

During the last fifty years, raw materials (products drawn from nature through simple technical processes without the addition of other materials or further fabrication) have entered global trade through a wide variety of structures: competitive markets; private and public monopolies; private, quasi-private, and public cartels; bilateral state trading arrangements; and international commodity agreements. But competitive markets, which would maximize global welfare at least in a static sense, have played the least important role. Virtually every major raw materials flow has been subject to one variety or another of explicit control.

The absence of competitive behavior reflects the desire of multinational corporations and consuming states for stability and security rather than price minimization. Although exporting state governments have strong incentives to maximize foreign exchange earnings, even they value stability.

Since World War II, large corporations have been the principal organizers of world markets in all natural resource industries with important economics of scale. This includes virtually all minerals with the exception of tin, as well as agricultural products that are grown on large plantations. Fundamental political and economic developments are, however, now altering the international system. Private companies will no longer be able to assure stable and secure supplies. This will lead not to greater competition, but to more extensive state intervention. The challenge is to order intervention so as to assure the orderly development of supplies—a political as well as an economic task.

The relative absence of competitive behavior in raw materials markets reflects the desire of all major actors—multinational corporations, importing states, and exporting states—for stability. The noncompetitive behavior of multinational corporations stems from a relatively high degree of concentration in most mineral industries, and from the incentive structure that confronts the managers of large, complex, publicly owned companies. The petroleum, copper, aluminum, lead, zinc, iron ore, magnesium, nickel, mercury, and other materials markets are oligopolistic: decision makers in one firm realize that their actions will affect the behavior of other firms. Their awareness is particularly sharp because generally high ratios of fixed to marginal costs make price cutting attractive in the face of falling demand. But such price cutting can lead to competitive behavior in which all producers sell below full costs. Thus, actions that undermine established collusive practices can have short-run benefits but are likely to result in long-term losses.

Confronted with such a situation, managers are likely to follow conservative policies. Risky behavior may at times offer higher returns to the corporation but does not promise commensurate benefits for its managers. With the separation of ownership and management, dismissal is only likely to result from a dramatic decline in the corporation's fortunes—the very kind of decline likely to result from destroying an established pattern of oligopoly behavior. Various incentive payments for superior performance are unlikely to offset this personal risk confronted by managers contemplating competitive policies. Both the structure of materials industries and the position of their managers, then, encourage a search for stability.[1]

There are also compelling reasons for public actors to be concerned with the security and stability of raw materials markets. For less developed exporting states, foreign sales are usually the major sources of government revenues.[2] Political leaders, interested in maximizing their international earnings, are more likely than are the other major actors involved in raw materials markets to engage in risky behavior. But even for the leaders of Third World States, stability can be important. Fluctuations in price or loss of markets can severely strain the ability of a state apparatus to meet social demands encouraged during temporary periods of high earnings and expansive public expenditure.

For the governments of more developed exporting states, the desire to avoid instability is even stronger—much stronger. No fiscal incentive exists to maximize export earnings, but there are pressures to meet the demands of powerful economic groups. Such pressures are more easily dealt with in a stable situation than an unstable one. Farmers or mineral companies are not likely to be politically satisfied by international markets in which their past expectations are continually upset by changes in price levels or sales patterns.

For importing states, raw materials are an important component in the production of a wide variety of goods, but their cost is often a small percentage of the final selling price. Petroleum represents the only important exception to this generalization. While crude oil accounts for 85 percent of the total selling price of heavy oil, 55 percent of that of home heating oil, and 40 percent of that of gasoline, wheat accounts for only 18 percent of the price of bread, iron ore for 9 percent of the cost of steel, and bauxite 7 percent of the cost of aluminum.[3]

For political leaders in advanced importing states, the basic objective of raw materials policy is to avoid the unexpected, not to maximize economic welfare through perfect competition. Economic dislocations caused by abrupt changes in prices or availabilities can create local or even national political discontent, while economic well being achieved by minimizing prices is not likely to engender an equally strong positive voter response.[4]

In sum, stronger incentives exist for political leaders in industrial states, and for managers of multinational corporations, to avoid instability in raw materials markets than to maximize economic welfare or corporate profits. While exporters and exporting states are interested in maximizing their returns, they too have incentives to establish stable markets.

**Forms and Consequences of Intervention in
Raw Materials Markets**

There have been some commodities in which relatively little action has been taken to control international markets. These are mainly tropical agricultural products, such as cocoa, and various fats and oils, in which economies of scale and vertical integration are unimportant. During the colonial era, imperial regimes saw little incentive in raising the costs of raw materials used by home country manufacturers. And since independence, dispersed production patterns and political difficulties have prevented effective state intervention.[5] Only during wartime has the pattern of trade and price for tropical foodstuffs grown primarily on small plots been extensively regulated at the international level.

Competition has occurred at times in all other materials markets, but it has been bounded by public or private intervention. It would be helpful to survey some of the forms of such intervention.

Exporter State Intervention

Prior to World War II, there were several efforts at state intervention in raw materials markets in which production was controlled by a single state or concentrated in a few areas. Brazil first intervened in the coffee market in 1906. During the 1920s, Cuba attempted to influence the world market for sugar, Chile for nitrates, Mexico for sisal, and Britain (through her colonies in Asia) for natural rubber. During the depression, joint efforts were undertaken by governments in exporting areas to control the price of rubber, quebracho (a tanning agent), nitrates, and mercury. But between World War II and the actions by OPEC in the early 1970s, there were no effective market interventions by producing states.[6] In sum, exporter state control took place mainly in the 1920s and 1930s.

International Commodity Agreements

To date, international commodity agreements, whose memberships include both importing and exporting state governments, have been a more important form of public intervention than have exporter state monopolies or cartels. International commodity agreements were first developed as a response to the economic chaos of the 1930s. During that decade, arrangements were concluded for coffee, sugar, tin, wheat, and tea. Since World War II, there have been agreements for coffee (first signed in 1962), for cotton textiles (also in 1962), for tin (1953), for cocoa (1972), and for wheat (1949).

Private Monopolies and Cartels

By far the most important form of institutional intervention in raw materials markets has come from private corporations. In natural resources in which significant economies can be achieved through large-scale and vertical integration, corporations have been the dominant actors. Thus, international trade patterns in petroleum, copper, magnesium, aluminum, lead, zinc, cobalt, iron ore, bananas, diamonds, quinine, phosphates, and other natural resources have been at least partially determined by the decisions of the managers of large, complex, private corporations. Markets have occasionally slipped from their grasps. But by and large, they have been enormously effective. Corporations operating in oligopolistic situations have been able to agree on stable prices that are above competitive levels but below short-term and often medium-term, monopolistic ones. They have been able to integrate new sources of supply smoothly, because of their ability to operate across national boundaries. Before World War II, companies generally organized markets through explicit cartels. Since then, with more vigorous antitrust action in Europe as well as the United States, tacit collusion has become the dominant mode of coordination. This has, however, been a change of form, not of substance.[7]

Market intervention, then, has been widespread. Its impact remains to be evaluated. Three factors need to be examined: the effect of intervention on the level of prices, the pattern of trade, and the stability of prices.

Price Levels

Evaluating the impact of market intervention on price levels requires some effort at estimating levels that would have prevailed under perfectly competitive conditions. Given the lengthy record of intervention which has existed for some raw materials (e.g., petroleum and aluminum), there is no empirical base for making such calculations. However, one attempt to classify a number of materials cartels as "efficient" or "inefficient"—on the basis of whether they were able to raise prices at least 200 percent above the unit costs of production and distribution—concluded that only nineteen out of fifty-three cartel organizations studied had achieved this degree of control.[8]

Still, some spectacular examples of success occur. During the postwar period, the major oil companies kept world crude prices well above what they would have been under competitive conditions, even before the price increases imposed by oil-exporting states in 1973. Intergovernmental commodity agreements have almost certainly helped to maintain prices above what they would have been in a free market, if only because the effect of such arrangements is asymmetrical. Quotas and buffer stock purchases can maintain an effective floor on prices during cyclical downturns, although price ceilings cannot be held during upturns unless new supplies are available to replenish buffer stocks or to meet higher quotas.

However, intervention can also have a degressing long-run effect on prices. A collusive agreement invariably increases the supply of the commodity covered. If the price elasticity of supply is high, this increase can result in a new equilibrium price lower than the one which would have existed if intervention had not occurred in the first place. During the 1920s, for instance, Brazil's accumulation of large coffee stocks resulted in increased domestic and foreign production and ultimately contributed to an 80 percent decline in coffee prices during the 1930s. In sum, market intervention has probably had a positive effect on prices, but the available evidence does not allow a systematic and thorough appraisal.

Trade Patterns

Nonprice factors, in particular market intervention and political blocs, have had an important impact on the pattern of trade. The most extensive recent work on world mineral trade patterns has been conducted by John E. Tilton of Pennsylvania State University. In a study of trade patterns for copper, lead, zinc, and aluminum, Tilton concluded that ownership, political blocs, and traditional trading ties were more important determinants of the pattern of trade than were distance or total share of world exports and imports.[9] In a more recent study of the aluminum industry, Tilton and Andre Dorr found that for the years 1950, 1955, 1960, 1965, and 1970, ownership ties were the most important determinant of the world pattern of trade in bauxite and aluminum, with long-term contracts having an important impact for 1965 and 1970.[10] Unfortunately, similar information is not available for other commodities.

A simpler measure, akin to Savage and Deutsch's "relative acceptance indicator,"[11] does suggest that nonprice factors are very important for trade in other commodities as well. The matrices in Table 3-1 show trade patterns for six major commodities not studied by Tilton. Five major importing states head each column; the four to six largest exporting states designate each row. The values in the matrices are equal to the percent of i's total exports which are sent to j, minus the percent of j's share of the total imports of major advanced market economies, divided by j's share of imports, where i is the exporting country and j the importing country. That is, the entry is equal to

$$\frac{\dfrac{X_{ij}}{X_i} - \dfrac{M_{ji}}{M_i}}{\dfrac{M_{ji}}{M_j}}.$$

Table 3-1
Trade Patterns among Major Producers and Consumers of Six Commodities, 1972[a]

	Italy	United States	Japan	France	Germany	United Kingdom
1. Cocoa *(SITC #072.1)*						
Ghana		+0.14	+1.72	−0.84	−0.45	+0.37
Ivory Coast		−0.27	−1.00	+2.88	+0.90	−0.95
Nigeria		−0.65	−0.54	−0.96	−0.22	+2.19
Brazil		+2.26	−1.00	−1.00	−0.97	−1.00
Cameroon		−0.98	−1.00	−0.45	+0.72	−1.00
2. Coffee *(SITC #071.1)*						
Colombia		+0.05	−0.33	−0.78	+0.72	+0.79
Ivory Coast		−0.02	+1.33	+4.61	−0.58	−1.00
Kenya		−0.73	+0.05	−0.94	+1.16	+2.03
Uganda		−0.04	+1.43	−0.15	−0.23	+6.09
Brazil		−0.11	−0.14	−0.31	−0.56	−0.09
3. Tea *(SITC #074.1)*						
India		−0.44	−0.58	0.00	+1.14	+0.31
Ceylon		+0.23	−0.25	+0.75	+0.11	−0.23
Indonesia		+0.67	−−	−1.00	−0.09	−0.59
Kenya		−0.04	−0.95	−0.90	−0.77	+0.49
4. Tin *(SITC #283.6* *and #687.1)*						
Malaysia		+0.32	+0.71	−0.26	+1.18	−0.94
Indonesia		−0.47	−0.59	+1.19	+2.07	−1.00
Bolivia		−0.18	−0.90	−0.73	−0.09	+3.61
Nigeria		−0.90	−1.00	−0.94	−0.17	+5.67
Thailand		+0.84	−0.15	−0.76	+0.43	−1.00
5. Natural Rubber *(SITC #231.1)*						
Nigeria	−0.94	−0.18	−0.89	−0.92	+0.32	+3.84
Liberia	−0.26	+1.78	−1.00	−0.45	−0.59	−0.78
Malaysia	+0.36	+0.19	−0.49	+0.19	+0.16	−0.01
Indonesia	−0.11	+0.83	−0.53	−0.50	+0.59	−0.38
Thailand	−0.63	−0.60	+4.49	−0.85	−0.87	−0.94

Table 3-1 (cont.)

	Italy	United States	Japan	France	Germany	United Kingdom
6. *Iron Ore* *(SITC #281.01)*						
Liberia		−0.32	−0.73	+0.45	+1.15	−0.60
Brazil		−0.76	−0.34	+1.33	+0.78	+0.02
Canada		+3.72	−0.84	−0.95	−0.56	+0.78
Venezuela		+3.36	−1.00	−0.79	+0.24	+0.24
Australia		−0.89	+1.10	−0.69	−0.78	−0.70
India		−1.00	+1.42	−1.00	−0.99	−1.00

[a]The matrices are derived from figures in United Nations, *World Trade Annual, 1972* (New York: Walker and Co., 1974). The statistics in this volume are generated from those reported by twenty-four major market economies. If all states were included, some figures would be smaller since some of the X_{ij}s would be smaller.

The value of this indicator ranges from plus infinity to minus one. A value of zero indicates that trade is proportional to the relative share of imports and exports of a particular pair of countries. The higher or lower the value, the greater the deviation from the pattern that would obtain if countries traded equally with each other according to their relative shares of trade. High or low values strongly suggest that nonprice factors are at work.

Nearly one-third of all the entries in the matrices are either very low or very high. Thirty of the 150 entries are equal to or less than −0.90, indicating very minimal or no trade. Eighteen are equal to or greater than 1.00, indicating that the exporting country is sending twice as much or more to the importing country as would be predicted by their relative market shares. Only 24 of the entries fall between −0.25 and +0.25, the range of values in which trade between two states is more or less proportional to market shares. These figures suggest something other than perfect markets even for commodities such as cocoa, coffee, tea, tin, and rubber, where vertically integrated companies are unimportant.

Price Stability

The postwar record of price stability for major raw materials suggests that market control has had an impact.

Table 3-2 indicates the average annual percentage change in price for the indicated commodity for the years 1949-50 through 1973-74. In each case, the

Table 3-2
Price Stability of Major Commodities in World Trade, 1949-50 to 1973-74[a]

Stability	Commodity	Average Annual Percentage Change in Price
Very Stable	Bananas	4.4
	Petroleum	4.6
	Wheat	5.6
	Sugar	6.8
Stable	Tea	8.1
	Quebracho	8.2
	Lead	9.6
	Burlap	10.5
	Zinc	10.8
	Coffee	11.7
	Lamb	13.2
	Copper	13.6
	Tin	13.6
Unstable	Coconut Oil	20.1
	Rubber	21.1
	Cocoa	26.5

[a]These figures are taken from various issues of International Monetary Fund, *International Financial Statistics*. The figures are derived from spot prices for major producers. The figure for sugar is derived from the Philippine price series. It exaggerates the stability of sugar prices because the Philippines were part of the American preferential sugar system and thus sold little on the volatile world sugar market, which accounted for perhaps 15 percent of sugar sales. The figures for nonferrous metals are spot prices in Montreal and probably exaggerate the volatility of price changes in these minerals because they do not take into account long-term contracts which governed a significant percentage of postwar sales for these products.

single highest figure has been dropped. The commodities reported on in Table 3-2 have been divided into three groups: very stable, stable, and unstable, with divisions at points of significant discontinuities in average annual percentage price changes. Hence, the distinction between stable and very stable is admittedly arbitrary. All commodities in the "very stable" group have been subject to extensive private or public control. Bananas have been a virtual private monopoly for most of the postwar period, oil was effectively controlled by a private ologopoly until 1973, and wheat and sugar by extensive domestic regulations as well as by international commodity agreements. All three commodities in the unstable group—coconut oil, rubber, and cocoa—are agricultural products exported from less developed areas which have been subject to no extensive public or private regulation.[1,2]

The market structure of commodities in the middle group is varied. Tea and burlap have had little international regulation. Coffee was governed by an international commodity agreement between 1962 and 1972, although prices were less stable under the agreement than they were for the previous decade. Since 1953, International Tin Agreements have attempted to stabilize prices through the use of buffer stocks. New Zealand lamb has entered the world market primarily through special sterling area trading arrangements. Since at least the 1920s, quebracho has been under the control of Argentine and Uruguayan authorities. Lead, zinc, and copper have been subject to tacit collusion by major international corporations.

It is possible that underlying supply-and-demand functions account for the observed degrees of price stability. Still, this would hardly seem to be the whole story. There is no clear rank order division between minerals and agricultural goods, although, given the vagaries of weather, one might have expected the latter to demonstrate consistently less stable price movements. While the three commodities with the least stable prices are all tropical farm products, so is the most stable. Correlation is not causation, but market intervention appears to have had an important impact on the price stability of major traded commodities during the postwar period.

What can be concluded from this brief review of postwar raw materials development? First, public or private collusion probably has exerted an upward pressure on commodity price levels. However, until the recent precipitous rise in crude oil prices, the difference between actual prices and those that would have existed under competitive conditions had not caused major market disruptions. Second, nonprice factors have largely determined the international trade patterns of raw materials. Third, public and private intervention has helped to stabilize prices for most major commodities.

Recent Developments: The End of an Era

Developments in recent years suggest that the postwar pattern is at an end. The evidence, though sketchy and of recent vintage, is cumulatively suggestive. The general price increases of 1973 and 1974, sharply increased bauxite and crude oil prices, the oil embargo, a wave of nationalizations, and Third World exporting states' efforts to establish cartels all indicate that *existing institutional mechanisms for stabilizing raw materials markets are no longer effective.* In particular, they suggest that *multinational corporations are losing control over minerals markets.*

The price increases of 1973 and 1974 were unprecedented for the postwar era. Table 3-3 was computed from the price changes for the sixteen commodities shown in Table 3-2. For each year signs were taken into account, and the highest and lowest figures were dropped from the calculation. No attempt was made to

Table 3-3
Mean Annual Price Change for Sixteen Commodities Excluding High and Low Values[a]

1948		1959	+1.1	1970	+9.9
1949	−10.5	1960	−2.3	1971	−3.9
1950	+27.8	1961	−5.9	1972	+6.6
1951	+20.6	1962	−0.2	1973	+34.2
1952	−5.7	1963	+4.8	1974	+58.4
1953	−1.3	1964	+5.3		
1954	+7.1	1965	+4.3		
1955	+1.1	1966	+0.6		
1956	−0.6	1967	+0.4		
1957	−2.9	1968	+1.2		
1958	−3.9	1969	+8.1		

[a]The sixteen commodities are those represented in Table 3-1.

weight prices by total value, since this would have given a few materials—particularly crude oil—too decisive an influence. Rather, the following figures give some indication of the general price trend for a large number of raw materials markets. The price increases in 1950-51 and 1973-74 both reflected general inflationary pressures, but the magnitude of the latter was far greater. Two major commodities, wheat and oil, were virtually unaffected during the earlier period, while the prices of all sixteen commodities listed in Table 3-1 increased by more than 10 percent in either 1973 or 1974.

A second development, and one directly related to the continued viability of market stabilization by private companies, is the wave of nationalizations that has swept the Third World. All major oil-exporting states have announced plans for assuming formal ownership. Between 1970 and 1974, Guinea, Guyana, Jamaica, and Surinam assumed at least majority control of their bauxite mines. Since 1970, nationalizations of iron ore facilities have taken place in Chile, Gabon, Mauritania, and Venezuela. Copper nationalizations have occurred in Chile, Zaire, Zambia, and Peru.[13]

Formal ownership has not necessarily meant fully effective control. The very concept of participation agreements in the petroleum industry was developed by the Saudis to rationalize the continued involvement of private companies in crude exploitation.[14] Eighty-five percent of world petroleum trade moves through the facilities of the seven majors, and through preferential access agreements, private corporations still maintain an important role in marketing other commodities. Nevertheless, there is an undeniable thrust toward less autonomy for international corporations. Though their discretion over pricing and allocation has not disappeared, it is waning.

A third development suggesting the possibility of instability in international raw materials markets is the attempt by less developed exporting states to establish cartels. Prior to the 1973 oil price increases, these states had been unable cooperatively to intervene for the purpose of raising prices on international markets, except in some commodities of minor importance such as quebracho. Since 1973, coffee, copper, bauxite, cocoa, iron ore, and other commodities exporters have intimated or actually implemented efforts at market control. Such efforts are not likely to endure, but they can have important short-term effects.

Many potential groupings of raw materials exporters lack one critical resource possessed by a number of the oil-producing states—excess wealth. The surfeit reserves held by the Gulf Shiekdoms, Kuwait, Libya, and most importantly Saudi Arabia mitigate the internal temptation to cheat, which has bedeviled past control efforts by less developed states. In addition, a central group of oil producers share a common international enemy in Israel. Still, these differences are unlikely to deter other groups of exporting states from at least attempting to intervene in world markets. Opportunities for price gouging exist in many commodities; producers can, at least for a short while, demand and get higher prices even without controlling production. Efforts to support prices through export or production cuts can dislocate world markets before they collapse because of internal dissension, development of new supplies, or reductions in demand.[15]

A final development—one likely to be *sui generis*, but which cannot be ignored by prudent governments—is the structural significance of the Arab oil embargo against the United States, South Africa, and the Netherlands. This action violated one of the cardinal principles of postwar materials trade: equal access and free movement of materials.[16] Although the major oil companies coped brilliantly with this problem by diverting oil in such a way as to render the embargo ineffective, the action of Arab states is but one more indication that the postwar structure is changing.[17]

Long-Term Trends: The Decline of the MNC

It seems unlikely that price fluctuations, nationalizations, the oil embargo, and putative exporting state cartels represent mere temporary departures from a stable situation. A number of secular trends are undermining the international economic order that existed since World War II. The relative economic strength of the United States is declining, and with it the policy commitment to the free movement of goods and factors. The bargaining power of host country governments relative to multinational corporations is increasing. The development of politically safe, new sources of supply requires very large capital expenditures and is economically risky. These developments suggest that private companies will no longer be able to stabilize international materials markets.

The ability of MNCs to meet rapidly growing demand for many major minerals without supply or price disruption depended in part upon the broader international economic structure within which they operated. This structure was sustained by the power of the United States and by a common policy commitment to the free movement of goods and capital, as well as to a low level of government interference in the private sector. The Bretton Woods Agreement, which provided guidelines for the international monetary system, was basically an American project.[18] Although a system of convertible currencies related to each other through fixed exchange rates was not established until the late 1950s, American dollars provided the liquidity for the rapid expansion in international trade which took place after the war. The United States pressed for a more open trading system, supported guidelines for international behavior that were institutionalized in the General Agreement on Tariff and Trade, and backed the postwar multilateral negotiations which dramatically reduced tariffs.[19]

More directly relevant in an analysis of raw materials markets was the support given by the American government for direct investment. After World War II, when many American firms were leery of foreign commitments, the United States introduced investment guarantees, negotiated treaties to prevent double taxation and the discriminatory treatment of subsidiaries, supported the creation of national and international lending agencies to ensure a flow of capital for foreign ventures, and introduced tax measures that made foreign investment attractive.[20]

American policy reflected national as well as private interests. For a hegemonic economic power—a state whose economy is relatively more developed and much larger than that of its trading partners—an open international system is beneficial in a number of ways. An expanded international market helps underwrite economies of scale for domestic industries. The opportunity costs of closure are less for a large state than for its smaller trading partners, and this enhances, at least potentially, its political power.[21] The potential costs of social instability produced by exposing the national economy to the vagaries of the world market are small for a hegemonic state, because its large size and diverse economy mean that only a modest proportion of its economy will directly depend on world trade.[22]

The declining economic size and relative level of development of the United States has led some powerful domestic interest groups to favor a more closed and protectionist foreign economic policy for investment as well as for trade. The Burke-Hartke Bill[23] was a harbinger of things to come, not a nostalgic return to Smoot-Hawley. The social disruption caused by the open flow of goods and capital has made the American labor movement increasingly skeptical of the benefits of the existing system. Various domestic industries—steel and textiles, for example—have secured either "voluntary" or more formal agreements that protect them from foreign competition. Export controls imposed by the American government, such as those on soybeans in 1973 and closer monitoring of all grain exports since October 1974,[24] indicate that central decision makers at times find the exigencies of domestic needs such as inflation more pressing than those of maintaining an open international economic structure. The 1975 tax bill[25] deprives large multinational oil companies of depletion allowances, while extending such tax deductions for smaller, primarily domestic corporations. The same bill also made modest changes in the tax treatment of foreign earnings. These measures are unlikely to have dramatic consequences for MNCs, but they do reflect a change away from unquestioned belief in the unmixed blessings of direct investment.

With the waning of American commitment to an open structure, it will no longer be possible for multinational corporations to exercise the kind of discretion that they have enjoyed in the past. State controls will increase. The transfer pricing policies of the companies will be subject to greater scrutiny.[26] Antitrust actions will become more extensive, and greater strictures will be placed on personnel policies. Invidious distinctions will be made in the treatment of foreign subsidiaries and local firms.[27]

These developments are almost certain, since restrictive actions by one state will in themselves create the incentive and temptation for others to follow suit. Such demonstration effects, coupled with growing nationalist pressures, will make it politically attractive for many regimes to put pressure on the MNCs. States may find that they can protect their own fiscal and supply needs only by countering restrictions imposed by other states.

A second development is the rising power of less developed states in relation to exploiting companies' raw materials. Raymond Vernon and others have described at some length what they have called the obsolescing bargain.[28] When private corporations first broach the possibility of developing raw materials to a regime in an underdeveloped country, they enjoy great power. They offer the prospective host country capital, technical skill, and access to the world market. For the state, anything that comes of a successful venture is an unexpected bonanza. As a consequence, initial concession terms, particularly those let in the past, have been extremely attractive to the foreign investor. Tax payments were not high; exploitation rights were granted for periods of up to ninety-nine years.

But once a successful discovery is made or a plantation developed, the bargaining power of the foreign corporation declines. Capital expenditures can be made from internally generated funds; the privileged access that MNCs offer to international sources of finance is no longer necessary. As nationals of the host country are brought into the operations of the firm, they acquire technical skill and market knowledge. Even if such learning processes are slow, the increasing diffusion of knowledge about raw materials industries enables host countries to hire independent advisors. The power of the government increases. With this shift, Vernon argues, come demands for the renegotiation of concession terms. The logical conclusion of the increased ability of host countries to operate extractive industries is nationalization, and eventually the assumption of actual managerial control.

This bargaining process has been reinforced by political developments in most Third World states. Foreign-owned industries have become symbols of subservience. Demonstrations of independence from advanced states and from the multinational corporations which manifest these states' power and interests can be valuable assets for a political regime. Thus, the first major act of the Peruvian military upon taking power in 1967 was to announce the nationalization of the International Petroleum Corporation, a subsidiary of Exxon. Indeed, the fact that the Belaunde government had failed to resolve the long-festering IPC dispute satisfactorily was actually offered as the rationale for the coup.[29] Again, when the military seized power in Bolivia in 1968, one of its first acts was to nationalize the facilities of the Gulf Oil Corporation—even though there was, in fact, no outstanding disagreement between the government and the company. The regime's ultimate failure to carry off this exercise, which finally resulted in Gulf's reentering the country through its Spanish subsidiary, contributed to its downfall. Thus, regardless of the particular distribution of capital, technical skill, and market knowledge between MNCs and host countries, there exist strong incentives for political leaders to nationalize the assets of large, salient foreign holdings.

A third development, largely following from the second, is the increasing costs associated with the development of politically secure new sources of supply. Those areas which have already been most heavily explored are the same ones where breaches of contract and nationalizations are least likely. Discovering new deposits in these countries is becoming costlier. For instance, the ratio of the value of metals discovered for each dollar of exploration expenditure has dropped from 80 in 1955-59 to 45 in 1965-69 for the western part of the United States, and from 160 in 1951-55 to 55 in 1966-70 in Canada for nonferrous metals.[30] More importantly, it is the development of new deposits which most often requires unconventional technology involving very high nonfungible capital expenditures. Estimates of the cost for the now-abandoned first project for extracting petroleum from shale deposits in Wyoming ranged up to $1 billion.[31] Work on the Athabasca tar sands is proceeding with the impetus given by the Canadian government's provision of $1.4 billion to save the project.[32] Exploitation of the North Slope field required unusual engineering feats, including the construction of the Alaskan pipeline at a cost of $6 billion.

Uncertainty about the availability of cheaper sources of supply complicates private companies' difficulties. This problem is particularly acute in the petroleum industry. The cost of oil in the Middle East is something less than ten cents per barrel. The projected cost of crude extracted from shale is seven to eleven dollars per barrel. If the oil cartel should collapse in the next five or ten years, and the world market were not controlled, investments in expensive alternative sources would be completely lost. A similar situation could develop in the aluminum industry if projects to use clays instead of bauxite are implemented. Corporations are unlikely to assume such risks even if they can procure the capital necessary for development. Without explicit state intervention, either through the investment of capital or the control of markets, the orderly provision of new supplies, which private corporations have handled with relative smoothness in the past, will not take place in the future.

In summary, the reduction of American power and consequent changes in the international economic structure, the changing relationship between host country governments in the Third World and multinational corporations, and the costs and risks of developing new supplies in politically safe areas have undermined the ability of private corporations to manage international raw materials markets. Answering to pressures for stability, particularly in consuming states, public intervention will replace or supplement private action. The question confronting decision makers in advanced industrial states is not whether this intervention should take place, but how.

Future Options

The institutional options open to dealing with the instability imminent in existing international raw materials markets can be distinguished along two axes: (1) whether action is taken by one or more than one country, and (2) whether both importing and exporting states are involved. Monopoly control alone can be ignored, since there is no major commodity (except diamonds) where intervention would be profitable for a single exporting state. The other four options shown in Table 3-4 are possible and not mutually exclusive.

What kind of action is most likely for those industries in which multinational corporations have ordered markets in the past but are unlikely to be able to do so in the future?

The easiest policies for importing states are unilateral. The simplest are emergency preparedness plans that can be implemented if unexpected shortages do develop. Stockpiling is another alternative, but it can involve heavy carrying costs, particularly for agricultural commodities. Mandatory consumption con-

Table 3-4
Institutional Options for Dealing with Potential Market Instabilities

	One State	*Two or More States*
Exporters	Monopoly control	Producer cartels
Importers	Stockpiling Trade controls Consumption controls	Coordinated stockpiling and trade controls
Importers and Exporters		Bilateral and multilateral arrangements

trols are unlikely to be imposed without clear evidence of a threat to the nation's economic well-being. The effectiveness of such unilateral action will vary with the state's level of dependence on foreign supplies and the size of its national market. The United States—a net exporter of food, and 70 percent or more self-sufficient in phosphate rock, copper, vanadium, and iron ore—is in a relatively secure position. Only for cobalt, manganese, chromite, tin, and bauxite is the United States more than one-third dependent on supplies from lesser developed countries.[33] American stockpiling would not only be a guarantee against unexpected supply constraints but could also regulate international markets. For smaller states, stockpiles of one to two years of consumption could insulate their own economies but would not be large enough to affect external structures.

Prospects for any kind of multilateral endeavor, whether by exporters, importers, or both, are far less predictable. Least likely would be a series of successful cartels by less developed exporting states. Given their need to maximize short-term revenue, and the development of new supplies and alternative consumption patterns, such cartels are likely to be undermined—internally by cheating, and externally by the erosion of their market share.[34]

Nor does cooperation among consuming states seem likely. In this area as in others, oil may be the exception. Oil has elicited a modest common response with the creation of an International Energy Agency, vague commitments on minimum price, emergency allocations, and a financial safety net. But no other commodity is as important, either financially or economically; hence, no other commodity is likely to present consumers with so serious a common threat. In the absence of such a threat, consuming nations are unlikely to overcome differences stemming from different levels of import dependence, customary patterns of trade, commitments to internal economic groups, and divergent international political objectives.

Unilateral action, or agreements among consumers if they are concluded, is unlikely to be perceived as entirely satisfactory. Efforts will be made to reach agreements with producing states, for only they can ultimately guarantee stability of supply. Exporters among lesser developed nations have made such arrangements a major plank in their platform for changing the international economic order.

However, exporter-importer agreements pose both economic and political difficulties. The economic objections are familiar. By artificially raising prices, such agreements can encourage overproduction and substitution. They can perpetuate high-cost production. They can involve expensive buffer stock operations. Most of these problems can be resolved if wealthier states are prepared to commit a level of resources sufficient to maintain buffer stocks, ease adjustment for inefficient producers, and perhaps mitigate distortions by providing compensatory financing at least partly as a substitute for higher prices.

The political problems of international commodity arrangements are more treacherous. International commodity councils could exacerbate tensions and increase instability of supply if they become but one more forum for less developed countries to voice their ideological dissatisfaction with the existing international order. Such actions are not simply manifestations of pique, but rather reflect the desire of Third World leaders to take advantage of symbolic instruments of power where their advantage vis-à-vis the industrialized world is greatest. The behavior of producing states is likely to depend primarily upon their economic prospects. Those that are enjoying substantial growth are more likely to regard commodity agreements as tools to further their economic ends; those that find their development efforts frustrating are more likely to turn to ideological objectives.

A second source of difficulty arises from domestic politics in consuming states. Formal commodity agreements, subject to legislative approval, can be used by domestic pressure groups to frustrate public purposes. This is particularly true in the United States, where political power is fragmented and decentralized. Congressional renewal of the International Coffee Agreement, for instance, was delayed for two years in the late 1960s because of General Food's concern about the import of instant coffee from Brazil. Only when the State Department found a solution acceptable to the company did the House Ways and Means Committee act on the necessary legislation. Exporting states are not likely to be familiar with the intricacies of the American political system. If the U.S. government is forced to follow narrow and obstructionist policies in international commodity councils, the frustration felt by producing states could lead to actions that exaggerate rather than dampen market instability.

As a general policy, the greater the danger of politicizing a particular commodity market, the wiser it is to search for loose and ill-defined bilateral and possibly regional arrangements. Universal agreements are only likely to be successful if producing countries experience economic progress and domestic pressure groups in consuming countries are satisfied.

Notes

1. Stephen D. Krasner, "Business Government Relations: The Case of the International Coffee Agreement," *International Organization* 27 (Fall 1973): 497-501; and literature on the behavioral theory of the firm, such as Richard M. Cyert and James G. March, *A Behavioral Theory of the Firm* (Englewood Cliffs, N.J.: Prentice-Hall, 1964), and Oliver E. Williamson, *The Economics of Discretionary Behavior: Managerial Objectives in a Theory of the Firm* (Englewood Cliffs, N.J.: Prentice-Hall, 1964).

2. Harley C. Hinrichs, *A General Theory of Tax Structure Change During Economic Development* (Cambridge, Mass.: The Law School of Harvard University, 1966).

3. United States, Council on International Economic Policy, Special Report, *Critical Imported Materials* (Washington, D.C.: Government Printing Office, 1974), p. 25.

4. Howard S. Bloom and H. Douglas Price, "Voter Response to Short-Run Economic Conditions: The Asymmetric Effects of Prosperity and Recession," *American Political Science Review* 68 (December 1975). The literature on relative deprivation suggests exactly the same response. People are more dissatisfied by a decline from an existing level of rewards than they are satisfied by an unexpected improvement upon their present lot. See, for instance, Ted Robert Gurr, *Why Men Rebel* (Princeton: Princeton University Press, 1970) and James C. Davis, "Toward a Theory of Revolution," *American Sociological Review* 27 (1962). See also James Q. Wilson, "The Politics of Regulation," in James W. McKie, ed., *Social Responsibility and the Business Predicament* (Washington: Brookings, 1974), p. 139 for other arguments leading to the same conclusion.

5. Stephen D. Krasner, "Oil is the Exception," *Foreign Policy* 14 (Spring 1974).

6. States exporting coffee during the late 1950s and states exporting cocoa in 1964-65 attempted to control their international markets. Both efforts failed.

7. Ervin Hexner, *International Cartels* (Chapel Hill: University of North Carolina Press, 1945); George W. Stocking and Myron C. Watkins, *Cartels in Action* (New York: The Twentieth Century Fund, 1946); Heinrich Kronstein, *The Law of International Cartels* (Ithaca: Cornell University Press, 1973); James C. Burrows, *Testimony of Dr. James C. Burrows Before the Subcommittee on Economic Growth of the Joint Economic Committee of the Congress of the United States*, July 22, 1974 (Cambridge, Mass.: Charles River Associates, n.d.).

8. Paul MacAvoy et al., "Basic Documentary Materials on Cartels." (Unpublished paper, Massachusetts Institute of Technology, Oct. 3, 1974).

9. John E. Tilton, "The Choice of Trading Partners: An Analysis of International Trade in Aluminum, Bauxite, Copper, Lead, Manganese, Tin and Zinc," *Yale Economic Essays* 6 (1966).

10. John E. Tilton and Andre L. Dorr, "An Econometric Model of Metal Trade Patterns," in William A. Vogely, ed., *Non-Fuel Minerals Modelling* (Baltimore: Johns Hopkins University Press, forthcoming).

11. Richard I. Savage and Karl W. Deutsch, "A Statistical Model of the Gross Analysis of Transaction Flows," *Econometrica* 28, no. 3 (July 1960).

12. The International Cocoa Agreement, negotiated in 1972, was not in operation long enough to affect these calculations.

13. United Nations, Economic and Social Council, Committee on Natural Resources, *Permanent Sovereignty over Natural Resources* (E/C. 7/53), January 31, 1975.

14. M.A. Adelman, "Is the Oil Shortage Real?" *Foreign Policy* 9 (Winter 1972-73): 83-84.

15. Zuhayr Mikdashi, "Collusion Could Work," *Foreign Policy* 14 (Spring 1974); Stephen Krasner, "Oil is the Exception," *Foreign Policy* 14 (Spring 1974); C. Fred Bergsten, "The Threat is Real," *Foreign Policy* 14 (Spring 1974); Bension Varon and Kenji Takeuchi, "Developing Countries and Non-Fuel Minerals," *Foreign Affairs* 52 (April 1974); C. Fred Bergsten, "The New Era in World Commodity Markets," *Challenge* 17 (September-October 1974); Raymond F. Mikesell, "More Third World Cartels Ahead?" *Challenge* 17 (November-December 1974); and particularly John E. Tilton, "Cartels in Metal Industries," *Earth and Mineral Sciences* 44 (March 1975).

16. This principle has hardly been inviolable. The United States had contradicted it in 1956 when it threatened to deny Venezuelan oil to the British and the French as part of its effort to end their occupation of Suez. But, Arab action was by far the most blatant and threatening denial of the principle of equal access.

17. See the testimony of Robert B. Stobaugh in U.S., Congress, Senate, Committee on Foreign Relations, Subcommittee on Multinational Corporations, *Hearings on Multinational Oil Companies and Foreign Policy*, Part 9, 93d Cong., 2d Sess., pp. 167-91.

18. Richard Gardner, *Sterling Dollar Diplomacy* (Oxford: Clarendon Press, 1956).

19. For discussions of the relationship between American power and policy and the postwar economic system, see Raymond Aron, *The Imperial Republic: The United States and the World 1945-1973* (Englewood Cliffs, N.J.: Prentice Hall, 1974), Part II; David P. Calleo and Benjamin M. Rowland, *America and the World Political Economy* (Bloomington, Ind.: Indiana University Press, 1973); and Robert Gilpin, *U.S. Power and the Multinational Corporation: the Political Economy of Foreign Direct Investment* (New York: Basic Books, 1975).

20. Mira Wilkins, *The Making of Multinational Enterprise* (Cambridge, Mass.: Harvard University Press, 1974), p. 288.

21. For explications of this argument, see Albert Hirschman, *National Power and the Structure of Foreign Trade* (Berkeley: University of California Press, 1946); and Kenneth W. Waltz, "The Myth of Interdependence," in Charles P. Kindleberger, ed., *The International Corporations* (Cambridge, Mass.: M.I.T. Press, 1970).

22. Robert Gilpin, *U.S. Power and the Multinational Corporation: the Political Economy of Foreign Direct Investment* (New York: Basic Books, 1975).

23. The Burke-Hartke Bill, introduced by Congressman Burke of Massachusetts and Senator Hartke of Indiana, called for quantitative import restrictions and new taxes and other restrictions on MNCs. It was not passed. For the text, see the *Congressional Record*, September 28, 1971 (S15142), vol. 117, no. 142.

24. *New York Times*, 10 October 1974, p. 45, c.3; *New York Times*, 20 October 1974, p. 1, c.2; *Barron's*, 14 October 1974, p. 36.

25. *New York Times*, 30 March 1975, III, p. 1, c.5.

26. *Wall Street Journal*, 19 December 1974, p. 1, c.6.

27. C. Fred Bergsten, "Coming Investment Wars?" *Foreign Affairs* 53 (October 1974).

28. Raymond Vernon, "Conflict and Resolution Between Foreign Direct Investors and Less Developed Countries," *Public Policy* 17 (Fall 1968); Raymond Vernon, *Sovereignty at Bay: The Multinational Spread of U.S. Enterprises* (New York: Basic Books, 1971), Chapter 2; Theodore H. Moran, "The Theory of International Exploitation in Large Natural Resource Investments," in Steven Rosen and James R. Kurth, eds., *Testing Theories of Economic Imperialism* (Lexington, Mass.: D.C. Heath, 1974).

29. John P. Powelson, "International Lending Agencies," in Daniel A. Sharp, ed., *U.S. Foreign Policy and Peru* (Austin: University of Texas Press, 1972).

30. National Academy of Sciences, *Mineral Resources and the Environment* (Washington, D.C.: 1975), p. 16.

31. *Wall Street Journal*, 7 October 1974, p. 7, c.1.

32. *New York Times*, 5 February 1975, p. 1, c.7.

33. Council on International Economic Policy, *Critical Imported Materials*, p. 5.

34. See note 15.

4 The Multinational Corporation in the New International Economic Order

Peter P. Gabriel

Next to the disappearance of Europe's colonial empires and the emergence of the United States and the Soviet Union as the two dominant, political powers in the world, the most important development of the three decades following World War II has been a historically unparalleled upsurge in international trade and investment and, as a result, in the economic interdependence among nation-states. In turn, the prime agent in this extraordinary increase in international resource flows has been the multinational corporation.[1]

But the influence of the multinational corporation (MNC) has gone far beyond its direct participation in international trade and investment. As the latest transmutation of the large national business enterprise, the MNC plays a determinant role in the allocation and use of the world's resources—regardless of whether or not it controls their flow through international trade and investment channels. It plays this role through the conception of new products and services; through the development of new ways for their manufacture, supply, and distribution; and through the creation or stimulation of demand for them. Current rates of energy consumption, for example, would be unthinkable without the role of large corporations in the development and expansion of the automobile and electric appliance industries and in the supply of the fuel and power required for the operation of their products.

Thus, the patterns and pace of industrialization typified by today's capitalist economies have been largely determined by and continue to be dependent on the business enterprises we call MNCs. Therefore, any major change in the flow and utilization of world resources, and hence in the basis of a country's industrial development, will significantly affect the future of these companies. Conversely, maintenance of the MNC's traditional mode of operation—the uninhibited management of global enterprise systems by criteria of private benefit maximization—is likely to extend current patterns of world resource distribution and use.

If this is true, several questions suggest themselves. What is the power of MNCs to influence resource flows and utilization likely to be in the future? What will be the future role of these companies if pressures for a major reallocation of world resources result in significant constraints on MNC operations? What institutions might assume whatever functions MNCs are forced to relinquish?

An earlier version of this essay was published under the title, "The Multinational Corporation and the Management of Public Interests" in *Journal of World Trade Law* 11, no. 1 (January-February 1977).

How will such changes affect the efficiency of resource use? Evidence now at hand or clearly perceptible trends permit some speculative answers to these questions.

I

One approach to conjecturing about the future is to analyze the conditions underlying past and current trends and to assess the prospects of their continuation into the future. While this approach does not necessarily suggest the precise scenarios that will actually occur, it does eliminate highly improbable trends from consideration. It also serves as a corrective to the human proclivity for straightline extrapolation from the past.[2]

Most analyses of the MNCs ascribe their past growth to a number of factors *inherent in the nature* of these enterprises: their ability to sense production and market opportunities on a worldwide scale; to mobilize and assemble the factors of production necessary to capitalize on these opportunities; and generally to apply the company's unique technological, organizational, and other resources in those parts of the world where they earn the highest return.[3] The enormous expansion of multinational corporate operations has also been attributed to the faculty of these companies to take advantage of international differentials in capital and labor costs; to avoid—through operating in the interstices of different national jurisdictions—irksome government regulation; to minimize taxes through the use of intracorporate transfer pricing and other devices; and to gain competitive advantages through extending scale economies across national boundaries.[4]

A contributing—and perhaps decisive—factor often ignored in analyses of the postwar rise of the MNC (and in prognoses of its future) is the extraordinarily favorable environment in which this expansion occurred. Almost all of the industrialized countries and many of the less developed countries experienced unprecedented rates of sustained economic growth in the 1950s and 1960s, precisely the period during which the MNC achieved its position of dominance in the world. Clearly, entry into new markets and their development are easier, and less likely to meet with opposition, in rapidly expanding economies than in relatively stagnant ones—especially for a foreign company.

Equally favorable to the spread of multinational enterprise were certain circumstances quite unique to the two decades, roughly, following the end of the Second World War. Some of these circumstances were specifically relevant to the foreign operations of American companies. Specifically:

1. The nearly prostrate condition of most European industrial firms at the end of the war and their consequent difficulty to venture abroad, compared to the unimpaired vibrance of their American counterparts.

2. The undeniable superiority, at least into the 1960s, of American management skills (a result of longer experience with large-scale enterprise and more vigorous competition in the United States), which contributed to making the first waves of U.S. direct investment abroad highly successful and encouraged their emulation by other American direct investors.
3. The increasingly overvalued condition of the U.S. dollar and the resulting incentives for American corporate investors to acquire foreign productive assets both for serving foreign markets and for supplying domestic corporate needs for finished products and semimanufactures from abroad.
4. The reality of United States political and economic hegemony, which—effectively enduring at least through the Eisenhower years—enabled American corporations to exploit all of the foregoing advantages to the hilt, whether consciously or otherwise.

By the late 1950s, with postwar reconstruction largely completed, American multinationals were joined by European companies on the international direct investment scene. The Japanese soon followed. The Europeans and Japanese had quickly absorbed much of the managerial skill of the American companies and at the same time developed highly competitive technologies of their own. With regard to third countries, mostly in the less developed world, they soon came to share with American multinational corporations the advantages of size, superior technical and organizational capabilities, international sourcing and distribution networks, ready access to capital markets all over the globe, and all the other competitive strengths peculiar to the large corporation of worldwide scope. Far from replacing the operations of the early entrants, the new arrivals further widened investment and market opportunities for all multinationals.

The largely unrestricted use of these resources and skills in the continuous spread of multinational enterprise was facilitated by a highly propitious, ideological climate. In the home countries of these companies, challenges to the concept and power of the large corporation were still (that is, in the 1950s and early 1960s) relatively muted and largely ineffective. The notion of corporate social responsibility could still be preempted by public relations gestures. It had yet to constrain corporate action to any significant degree. Issues like pollution, the "export of jobs," impending resource scarcities, and indeed the whole economic growth controversy were just beginning to progress from academic journals to popular literature, with legislative and regulatory concern still years away.

In the European host countries, which received the vast bulk of the initial waves of new foreign investment (mostly from the United States), the full economic effect of this investment had yet to be felt. Its immediate benefits from the transfer of entrepreneurship, management, and technology were too apparent, and local commitment to the freedom of private enterprise too strong to produce effective measures against the continuous widening and deepening of the foreign corporate presence. De Gaulle's France, it must be acknowledged, was a notable exception. But the economic integration under the European Common Market blunted the potential effectiveness of the checks he sought to impose on American multinationals. In fact, as Jean Jacques Servan-Schreiber argued in his widely read *Le Défi Américain* (published by Atheneum in 1968 as *The American Challenge*), American multinationals decisively accelerated European economic integration.

No less favorable to the multinationals during the first two decades following World War II was the climate in the less developed countries. Economic dependence was still perceived as being coextensive with political dependence. International institutions like the United Nations and its progeny the World Bank and the International Monetary Fund, were dominated by the industrial countries, if not the United States. All of these institutions, in concert with official foreign-aid agencies and almost the entire academic establishment of the West, including universities, research institutes, and their foundation sponsors, were urging less developed countries to adopt strategies and forms of economic development based essentially on the experience and patterns of industrialization in Western economies.

Under this political and philosophical umbrella, the MNC flourished. Foreign-aid agencies tended to make their dispensations contingent on host country respect for private foreign direct investment. The investors—almost all of them MNCs—were widely celebrated as "engines of growth," purveyors of "better standards of living," essential "agents of change."[5]

The worldwide drive for economic development produced its own performance cult. Conventional growth standards not only measured success but also highlighted relative failure. More often than not, the laggards in the growth race could be singled out as countries which had restricted the inflow of foreign private investment. While the cause-and-effect relationships at work here were the object of a great deal of controversy, the view generally prevailed that the influence of MNCs on economic growth as conventionally defined was positive in most of the countries where the scope of their operations was significant.

II

To recall, in 1976, the conditions and forces which encouraged and facilitated the rise of the MNC in the 1950s and 1960s is to bring to mind how dramatically they have changed. American multinationals as a group have lost most of the advantages they once possessed relative to their European and Japanese competitors. Disparities of size and technical capability have narrowed, if not disappeared altogether. Similarly, United States dominance of the politics and economics in the nonsocialist world lives on only in the wistful rhetoric of Washington officials, while the world is seeking to replace the defunct *Pax*

Americana with a new order that takes into account the continued standoff between the U.S. and Soviet superpowers, the resurgence of Europe and Japan, and the failure of force as a means to protect or pursue Western interests in Third World countries—a failure that first became manifest in the ill-fated attempt to thwart Egypt's seizure of the Suez Canal in 1956 and culminated in the Vietnam disaster.

No less significant have been the changes in the ideological climate for the MNC. In its home countries, emergence of new standards of socially permissible corporate conduct has been accompanied by more and more active government intervention. Popular acquiescence in the single minded pursuit of corporate profit and growth objectives has waned. So has the traditionally tacit popular support of the legitimacy of the corporation as such.[6]

Again, desire for the benefits of economic growth has become tempered by preoccupation about its negative effects on the quality of the environment and social life in general. Efficiency criteria in the organization and conduct of economic affairs have to compete today increasingly with equity criteria relating to the distribution of benefits as well as with concern about the sociopolitical implications of the continued trend toward ever greater concentration of corporate power. As a result, there is mounting "confusion on the part of business as to the proper goals of the large corporation,"[7] and the proper means of achieving them. "The corporate institution is undergoing attack from without and suffering lack of confidence within. The ideological foundations of the business society are being severely shaken."[8]

While many of the changes in the ideological climate for the large corporation in the industrialized countries have been subtle and latent, with their full impact yet to be realized, the changes affecting the MNC in the less developed countries have been harsh, overt, and of immediate effect. Nationalism, coupled with mounting political assertiveness toward the rich countries (encouraged by the stalemate between the superpowers); a pronounced shift to the Left or to populism in most parts of the Third World; the very process of economic and social development itself, with its continuous, upward push to popular expectations and its attendant political instability—all of these factors combined to cause a steady, marked deterioration of the MNC's acceptance in the less developed countries.

The impact on MNCs of these political trends was reinforced and accelerated by the emergence of new schools of thought (or the updating and broadened popularity of older theories, depending on one's interpretation) concerning the process of development in general and the role played in it by the foreign corporation. One of these schools, essentially based on Marxist theory, holds that the integration of less developed countries into the world capitalist system through the operations of the MNCs exacerbates rather than lessens relative underdevelopment. It does so by, *inter alia*, maintaining inequalities in income distribution, failing to incorporate in the productive process the large majority of low-skilled and unskilled labor, and encouraging—through the introduction of the life styles of the rich countries—private and public consumption at the expense of essential saving and local capital formation.[9]

Generally related to this theory and arriving at many of the same conclusions is another school of thought questioning the effects of foreign direct investment. Its central argument is more technical than philosophical. Mainly associated with the work of the United Nations Commission for Latin America (ECLA) and most prominently with the Chilean economist Osvaldo Sunkel, this so-called "dependencia" school reasons that the process of economic development in Latin America (and other parts of the less developed world) has been influenced more by economic and institutional links to external centers of dominant, economic power than by internal needs for structural transformation.

... the phase of import-substituting industrialization in Latin America, like the period of primary export growth that preceded it, constitutes a new form of integration of the underdeveloped and developed economies in the international economic system.

This new system is essentially based on the giant multinational corporation.... A new international division of labor seems to be growing.... The multinational corporation develops in the central economies (where its headquarters are located) both new products and new ways of producing these products, as well as the capital equipment to produce them. In strong contrast to previous policies, the underdeveloped countries are now encouraged to industrialize and modernize. The central economies even grant aid and extend public and private financing for industrial development, and foreign private enterprise assists through measures such as the installation of branch plants or subsidiaries, association with local firms, and the selling of patents and licenses. All this enables the underdeveloped countries to industrialize and produce the manufactures developed in the central economies, utilizing imported machinery, inputs, technology, financing, human resources, etc. This new international setting within which development and underdevelopment proceed has critically affected the structure of the Latin American economy.[10]

In effect, the proponents of the "dependencia" school argue, the orientation of foreign direct investment to the global needs and interests of MNCs—and the companion, similar orientation of large segments of local enterprise and infrastructures in the host economics—has prevented structural changes that would lead to better utilization of local factor availabilities (particularly surplus labor), reduce dependence on foreign inputs, improve the distribution of wealth and income, and create truly indigenous stimuli to development.

This new intellectual rationale (as distinct from essentially emotional pressures of far longer standing) for the sharp curtailment of the freedom of private foreign direct investors gained wide currency in the host countries at the same time that the political trends noted above were gathering force. The inevitable result has been increasingly strident individual and collective assertion by Third World countries of sovereignty over their own resources and the manner in which these are being exploited; insistence on developing their own industries; and consequently a nearly universal drastic change of the former permissiveness of these countries vis-à-vis the multinational corporation. This change is reflected in the revocation of concession agreements in the extractive industries, the nationalization of foreign investments in basic industries like public utilities, the divestment rules—covering all foreign-controlled enterprises—being implemented by the Andean Pact nations, and the general subordination of MNC operations to host-country economic development plans.

By far the clearest indication of the final demise of the era of MNC dominance in the Third World is the United Nations resolution entitled "The Charter of Economic Rights and Duties of States," which was voted by the General Assembly in December 1974 with 120 nations in favor, 6 opposed (the United States, the United Kingdom, the German Federal Republic, Denmark, Belgium, and Luxemburg), and 10 abstentions. Among other things, the resolution seeks to legitimate what virtually every less developed country had been practicing in one way or another for the last ten years or so: the abrogation of all agreements and international obligations protecting the interests of the foreign investor, whenever such action is perceived to be in the interest of the host country. Obviously encouraged by the extraordinary success of the Organization of Petroleum Exporting Countries, the sponsors of the United Nations resolution set out to proclaim a new international economic order.

Indeed, the growing acceptance of the need for a new international order has been one of the most important consequences of the "energy crisis." To be sure, the situation precipitated by OPEC's actions with respect to oil was not the first major crisis provoking serious doubts about the system which the unprecedented rates of sustained growth experienced by the Western economies and many of the less developed countries during the 1950s and 1960s seemed to have vindicated. But neither the gradual collapse between 1968 and 1972 of the Bretton Woods arrangements for international monetary affairs, nor the sudden acceleration in 1972-73 of worldwide inflation, nor the emergence of food shortages and other resource scarcities, nor mounting awareness of the explosive potential of the steadily widening gulf between the rich and the poor countries, nor widespread concern about the manifest inability of policy makers to deal with these problems within existing frameworks of economic cooperation could accomplish what OPEC's successful quadrupling of oil prices achieved: recognition that the time for a fundamental reordering of international economic relations has finally come.

III

How, then, will a new order affect the multinational corporation? Although it is not yet possible to predict what the precise outlines of the new international arrangements presently in the making will be, one thing can be foretold with assurance: the multinational corporation will continue to perform a vital function in them. For with all of the far-reaching and profound changes that have occurred in its political and ideological environment, the inherent strengths that the MNC derives from its condition of large-scale private enterprise remain unimpaired and, what is more important, unequalled. For any relevant future, the particular capabilities—technological, managerial, entrepreneurial, and logistical—on which modern industry rests will continue in decisive degree to be in the possession of the private corporate sector in which most of them originated, in which they were developed to today's levels of efficiency, and in which the store of existing industrial knowledge and techniques is continuously being refined and expanded through innovation.

In fact, the central imperative of today's technological society, let alone tomorrow's, is the large organization. Only the large organization affords the indispensable economies and efficiencies of large-scale operations and specialization in the development, production, distribution, and delivery of the goods and services on which societies (both industrialized and industrializing) have come to depend.[11]

International economic integration, formal and *de facto*, has added the dimension of *inter*dependence among nation-states, with the MNC constituting the institutional linchpin through which interdependence becomes effective. The economic linkages which the MNC has deepened and largely sustains are of three kinds: access to markets as both supplier and seller of raw materials, intermediate goods, and finished products; access to the latest generation of technology (in the broadest sense of this term); and international specialization of production through intracorporate, vertical integration across national boundaries.

Given the essentiality of large-scale operations to the efficiency of production and distribution in most segments of modern industry, the question is not whether the multinational corporation will survive as a centrally managed, global institution, but how and under what kinds of control it will continue to perform its unique economic functions.

The complex of issues to which the MNC gives rise on the international scene is closely related to the prospective position of these companies in their home countries. The United States, as the largest and most highly developed industrial nation, may well become the first in which the issue of private corporate power versus the public interest is joined. As Blumberg writes:

The concentration of economic power in the megacorporations and of potential control in the leading financial institutions inter-connected as a result of multiple or interlocking directorships presents serious questions for the nation. These questions are all the more important because of the far-ranging reach of corporate power. The scope of corporate decision-making has widened markedly and increasingly involves major questions of public policy concern. Corporate decisions affect many groups, communities, and even the nation in major respects. Corporate influence, moreover, transcends economic matters and has important political and social dimensions as well.

The concentration of power goes beyond the more limited question of the antitrust laws. . . . It goes to the nature of society itself. The fundamental question is the relation between size and liberty. To what extent does the compounded concentration of economic power and control threaten the primacy of political decision-making by democratic institutions and the maintenance of social and political controls over the major centers of power, which are essential components of a free democratic society?[12]

Viewed in this light, the large corporation (which, as we have seen, is for present and most other purposes synonymous with the MNC) is potentially as beleaguered by its home-country constituencies as by its host countries. There is little conceptual difference between, for example, public interest groups in the United States calling for drastic, legal and regulatory reforms in order to make large corporations "more accountable" and foreign host governments seeking to restrict the freedom of MNCs operating within their borders. The essential motivations are highly similar—even though, in the nature of the case, governments have been more successful in their endeavors than public interest groups have so far proved to be.

Conceptually, then, albeit glossing over many important intercountry differences and nuances, we can simplify the issue of the MNC in the future political economy of world resource flows in the following terms: The MNC, as an ostensibly private institution, has attained a size, and its operations a reach and influence, such that its basic function can no longer be defined as the pursuit of private purposes but must be recognized as the private management of public interests. In Blumberg's phrase, "business has become a *public institution*, and business leadership increasingly involves issues of public policy concern. The forces influencing the conduct of business are in many ways increasingly analogous to the conduct of *public organizations*." (Emphasis added.)[13]

If this is true of national enterprises, it is doubly true of corporations whose reach is global. The addition of foreign constituencies aggravates an already complex problem. It does not change its fundamental nature.

IV

According to classical economic theory, the conflict between private and public interests is more apparent than real. In this view, the rational pursuit of private corporate benefit within reasonably free markets will allocate resources wherever they yield the highest return. Assuming, among many other things, that relative rates of return on resource commitments are proportional to relative scarcities of such resources in the area (geographic and/or industrial) where they are invested, the economist can prove with mathematical rigor that this process leads to "optimal" resource allocation in the sense of maximizing world output and hence "world welfare." By this reasoning, the interests of the private corporation and those of the public are coterminous. The most effective way of promoting the latter is to support the former.

The trouble with this proposition is that it rests exclusively on the criterion of *efficiency*. Quite aside from the increasingly pressing issue of "externalities" (the social and environmental effects, negative or positive, of business activity), it has nothing to say—as far as the present context is concerned—about the *distribution* of world income.

In a world of almost grotesquely unequal resource endowments (including the capacity to absorb and make use of new productive investment), the efficiency criterion inevitably has led MNC investments to favor the rich countries and neglect the poor. Of the more than $130 billion of private foreign direct investment in place by 1973, barely one-third was in less developed countries, with petroleum and mining industries accounting for almost half of this portion. This distribution of MNC investments may well have increased "world welfare" (viewed as the sum of all output, worldwide) more than it would have been had the distribution been skewed the other way. But it is a matter of record that the rich got richer and the poor got poorer as a result. The remarkable solidarity with OPEC's intransigence of virtually the entire Third World bloc, including the countries most seriously affected by the explosion of oil prices, is one of many signs that the less developed world is simply no longer willing to accept this dispensation.

Yet not only in the context of the distribution (both global and national) of income and privilege has the notion been challenged that the private interests of business enterprises (large corporations in particular) are identical with the public interest. In country after country, purely market-based criteria of resource allocation and use are being subordinated to socioeconomic goals and priorities conceived through political processes and translated into national plans and budgets. These increasingly constrain the operating freedom of the private corporation. In the battle—typically waged in ideological terms—between the advocates of the market mechanism and the proponents of at least *some* measure of resource allocation through central planning, the latter are steadily gaining ground. Two practical reasons account for this trend.

One is the possible, if not certain, prospect that recent secular patterns and rates of economic growth may change and slow down significantly because of relative or absolute resource scarcities. Such a change or slowdown seems bound to give public intervention ascendancy over private business decision making as the different claimants on national income compete more and more aggressively for their respective slices of a stagnant or shrinking product.

The other reason for the spread of political interference with the market system is the inexorably growing interdependence among economic sectors, as indeed among nations, caused to a significant degree by the very agglomeration of power which the extraordinary success of the large corporation has engendered. This interdependence gives many private corporate decisions a scope and impact well beyond those the decision maker intended. The novelty of the contemporary setting lies not in the nature but in the *scale* of these decisions (as, for example, in the massive MNC-induced movements of short-term funds during the international monetary crises of the early 1970s) and in their concentration in relatively few companies. Similarly, the basic problem of the large corporation, especially the MNC, lies not in irresponsible or socially insensitive behavior on the part of individual managements, but in the total impact of their *aggregate* actions on the constituencies affected. (The results are compounded by the frequently concerted nature of these actions, due in turn not necessarily to collusion, but to the use of identical sources of information and uniform patterns of response.)

In any case, most governments (whatever their ideological texture) are no longer able or willing to abide passively the political and social effects of private corporate decisions in such interrelated areas as employment, prices, the development and location of industrial activity, industrial research and innovation, environmental protection, the country's balance of payments, its competitive position in foreign markets, and its dependence on foreign resources. These and related concerns are leading in more and more countries to the implementation of legislative, regulatory, and national planning devices which affect decision-making in the private corporation substantially—in fact, are beginning to transform the latter into an executive organ of public policy. Far from exempting the MNCs from this trend, their extraterritoriality makes them its first object. The 1974 United Nations Charter of Economic Rights and Duties of States illustrates the intent:

Each State has the right ... to regulate and supervise the activities of transnational corporations within its national jurisdiction and take measures to ensure that such activities comply with its laws, rules and regulations and conform with its economic and social policies. . . . (Chapter II, Article 2.b.)

V

But despite all of the political, ideological, and social pressures besieging the large corporation, at home as much as abroad, it still retains the decisive trump card noted earlier: the unique possession of the skills and capabilities which are vital both to the maintenance and continuous development of existing industrial structures as well as to the creation of new ones. More than one thousand agreements between Western companies and socialist economies—from simple "turnkey" contracts to complex "coproduction" arrangements and even joint ventures in third countries with multinationals—suggest that even Communist countries see no institutional alternative to the Western private corporation (at least not in the relevant future) as the supplier of superior technological and managerial skills, international sourcing and distribution systems, and all the other competitive strengths associated with large-scale private enterprise.

It is essentially these unique assets, not the highly fungible *financial* resources that conventionally recognize and statistically measure private foreign direct investment flows,[14] around which bargains are being struck between MNCs and the governments of countries restricting the freedom of the foreign corporate presence (i.e., most of the less developed countries, but also industrial states like Australia, Canada, France, and Japan). In an analysis of some years ago, I described this bargaining process as follows:

In the international investment market, foreign corporations compete for investment opportunities, access to which host governments control. These in turn compete for foreign private investments, i.e., for the benefits that only such investments can supply. . . . The price which the receiving country will ultimately pay is a function of (1) the number of foreign firms independently competing for the investment opportunity; (2) the recognized measure of uniqueness of the foreign contribution (as against its possible provision by local entrepreneurship, public or private); (3) the perceived degree of domestic need for the contribution. The terms the foreign investor will accept, on the other hand, depend on (1) his general need for an investment outlet; (2) the attractiveness of the specific investment opportunity offered by the host country, compared to similar or other opportunities in other countries; (3) the extent of prior commitment to the country concerned (e.g., an established market position).[15]

It is evident that conditions in this international investment market have turned rather drastically in favor of the host countries. While more and more countries are becoming dependent on technology from abroad which only the large multinationals possess, the MNCs are becoming more and more dependent on outlets for it. Even in such highly specialized areas as aircraft, nuclear reactors, and computers, host countries can shop around for the terms they perceive to be most favorable to them.

Thus, when the United States government denied Allende's Chile credit for the acquisition of Boeing 727s, France offered Caravelles and Russia Ilyushins. When Westinghouse Electric Corporation proved unable to overcome U.S. restrictions on the export of nuclear fuel processing technology, Brazil signed a $4.5 billion contract with Kraftwerk-Union and other West German firms. When IBM refused to enter into joint ventures with European companies, Control Data proved more adaptable.

This shift in bargaining power has been proceeding for a sufficient length of time to indicate the characteristics of certain trends. These, in turn, suggest some of the aspects of the future framework within which the MNC will perform its unique function. Among these trends, the following appear to be particularly significant:

1. The extent of traditional kinds of foreign ownership in individual companies and/or key industries is being limited to minority positions, if not proscribed entirely. (E.g., Canada, Japan; most less developed countries. Current opposition in industrial countries to potential OPEC investments will probably foster this tendency.)
2. New projects undertaken with MNC management or other forms of MNC participation are being conceived and executed increasingly within the context of host-government national development plans, as opposed to being identified and developed by conventional, market-oriented, cost-benefit criteria (which is not at all to suggest that the former always and necessarily exclude the latter)—a trend perceptible in most of the less developed countries.
3. The entrepreneurial (financial) risks of such projects are being assumed increasingly by host governments and other public agencies rather than private investors.
4. The basic function of the MNC is shifting from the mobilization of capital, in which the company's reward is an entrepreneurial one for risks taken, to the sale of its corporate capabilities, in which its reward is a managerial one for services rendered.

If continued, these trends will extend and deepen two sets of effects already clearly visible:

1. Changes in the locus or the availability of "economic rents" within the MNC's worldwide network of operations, and consequent changes in the structure of profit incentives; these largely determine the design of international corporate systems which, in turn, affect national cost and price structures.
2. The transfer of decision making, governing a significant and rising volume of international resource flows and allocations, from private corporations to governments and hence a shift from decision making informed by private markets (whatever their kind and structure) to decision making informed by considerations essentially or ultimately political in character.

Even though the initial stimuli for these changes tend to be local (their incidence certainly no longer being limited to less developed countries), the very nature of the MNC makes for their rapid, if not instantaneous, transmission from their points of origin to other countries covered by the company's global system.

Changes in the locus of the MNC's economic rent, and their secondary and tertiary effects, are most apparent in the international oil and other extractive industries. In oil, historically, the industry's primary source of profits was in low-cost crude production, chiefly from the countries forming the OPEC. In order to sell the crude oil, the companies built worldwide refining and marketing (or "downstream") facilities through which they moved the finished product at little or no gain, being amply compensated by the huge profits realized "upstream." Successive increases in royalties and taxes levied by producer countries and their recently initiated complete take-over of ownership of producing operations have removed the essential incentive for "downstream" subsidization and are forcing the companies to reexamine the practicability of continuing vertical integration.[16]

But host government inroads into multinational corporate decision making related to the design of worldwide systems of production, supply, and distribution are increasing in other industries as well. In manufacturing, some countries are requiring MNC subsidiaries to produce for export in exchange for permission to produce for local markets. Others are insisting on local establishment of research and development facilities, the effective transfer of technology to local competitors, the creation of labor-intensive plants, or the production of only marginally profitable products required for national development.[17] These and similar measures clearly affect not only the profitability of different components of the MNC network but also their essential kind, location, and development; the international flow of the inputs they need and the outputs they produce; and the associated internal and external costs and prices.

The most important implication of these trends is the transfer of basic, resource-allocative decisions from private corporate managers to government policy makers. With a rapidly diminishing number of exceptions (the United States and West Germany being the most significant left), governments all over the world have come to reject the classical doctrine of comparative advantage which, in its modern incarnation, subjects the international movement of investment, extractive, manufacturing, sales, and procurement activities—as well as the development of the requisite technologies—to a major extent to centrally perceived, private dictates of the optimum division of multinational corporate labor. Instead, as suggested before, governments are insistent on promoting industrialization and economic growth in accordance with their own development plans and priorities—and on making the operations of multinationals subservient to them.

Viewing the MNC's situation from the perspective of the year 1976, it must be acknowledged that these trends have not been affecting all MNCs alike. There remains a wide spectrum of corporate susceptibility to government interference with the traditional form of foreign direct investment. This spectrum ranges from oil and other extractive industries at one extreme to high-technology companies like IBM at the other, and from the pervasively restrictive policies in the less developed states (as well as in some industrial economies like Canada, Australia, and Japan) to liberal countries like Germany. But developments over the past few years indicate that there is considerably more likelihood of MNC-managed industries subject to highly restrictive regulation setting a pattern for industries still relatively less regulated, and of countries implementing tight controls over foreign investment setting a pattern for countries still relatively liberal, than the reverse. As a consequence, the role of the corporation in the international area is shifting—much more perceptibly than its domestic role—from the pursuit of privately determined purposes to the management of public interests defined not by the "invisible hand of the market," much less by multinational corporate officials, but by national political will expressed through government action.

VI

This change in the concept of its role presents the MNC with both formidable challenges and profound dilemmas. The challenges lie in the task of adapting worldwide strategies and the interdependent components of global corporate systems to the requirements and constraints of national political goals and economic plans, and to the new institutional arrangements (like joint ventures and contractual relationships of expressly limited or uncertain time horizons), which are rendering the traditional mode of foreign direct investment progressively irrelevant—together with its essential assumptions: complete, long-term control; the freedom to locate facilities and activities wherever most convenient; the ability to take full advantage of intercountry cost, tax, market-price, and currency differentials through centrally designed and managed, interaffiliate financial arrangements and transfer-pricing systems.

As the steadily growing number of innovative devices for the commitment of foreign corporate capabilities in the less developed and Eastern socialist countries shows, this challenge of institutional or technical adaptation is very probably surmountable. But in measure as these devices prove successful and spread, the MNCs will face a far more complex dilemma. Having become captives of their host countries, they become instruments of the widely discrepant—indeed, in many cases, irreconcilable—policies of both host and home governments. How can an MNC deal, without creating conflict, with one country's prohibition against exporting jobs and another country's insistence on job creation through exporting labor-intensive goods to the former? Or, in the strictly political sphere, with the Arab-Israeli conflict or the likes of the U.S. Trading-with-the-Enemy Act? Whose jurisdiction should a company like IBM—which operates in 126 countries overseas, has 23 plants in 13 countries, and 8 development laboratories in as many countries—recognize?

In the halcyon years of the MNC's postwar growth, the implicit answer to this question could be, in effect, "none—or whatever national jurisdiction most favors the company's interests." Governments were either too weak or dependent to challenge the power of the MNCs or too little aware of the impact of their operations. It was in this setting that the central headquarters of multinationals not only significantly influenced national economic policy in many host countries but also functioned as surrogates for world government with respect to the international allocation of a steadily increasing portion of the world's resources, including technology. If the international power constellation existing today, with its conscious assertion of national sovereignties had obtained immediately following World War II, it is unlikely that the multinationals would have reached the dominant position they did achieve. Arguably, international trade and investment would have lagged far behind the levels that the MNCs fostered—as would have economic growth, viewed in global terms.

In actuality, benefiting from the political umbrella of U.S. hegemony, Third World impotence, and governmental inexperience in dealing with their operations, the multinationals facilitated a degree of global economic integration which probably could not have been brought about by political means. In so doing, they could avoid, until recently, the issue of how to reconcile the divergent aspirations of different national constituencies affected by their activities. And they could point to the manifest efficiency of these activities in terms of expanding world product as vindication of their claim to legitimacy.[18]

This twin issue of the jurisdictional authority of the large corporation's multinational constituencies and the relevance of the efficiency criterion as the legitimizing factor of supranational corporate power has now become paramount. As was suggested earlier, the position of the MNC vis-à-vis its home and its many host constituencies is part and parcel of the larger issue of the private corporation in modern society. The issue, both nationally and internationally, is whether corporations should continue to determine patterns of economic growth, resource allocation, income distribution, and a country's degree of dependence on foreign resources and markets—based on the premise that the market choices of amorphous multitudes of consumers ultimately express their social preferences—or whether political decisions should intervene. At its root, it is the conflict between maximizing efficiency alone and maximizing a wide variety of social goals of which efficiency is only one, and not necessarily the most important one.

In the context of the current debate in the United States on national economic planning, Senator Jacob Javits quotes from an editorial in the *Wall Street Journal* which summarizes the prevalent business position on this question:

Unlike corporate planning, which generally leads to decisions with an eye to maximizing efficiency and profits, government economic planning is dictated by political goals that are often inimical to efficiency.[19]

In Javit's view, the argument is not convincing:

It is true that political goals may sometimes be inimical to efficiency but efficiency is neither the exclusive property of private enterprise nor necessarily the highest virtue in our society. Ours is not yet a corporate state.

It just may be that one source of our current economic difficulty is too great a concern with "efficiency" in government. In the name of efficiency millions of Americans would be consigned to the scrap heap of endemic unemployment in order to try to shave some mathematical fractions from the rate of inflation. Even if the trade-off works, our society has larger, more humane goals than efficiency alone.[20]

Included in the "larger goals" of nations are purposes—like the achievement of political status, social autonomy, and self-determination of national welfare priorities (including the distribution of income and economic opportunity)—that are or can easily become directly antithetical to the unfettered optimization of global economic efficiency through international specialization and central management of production, on which the MNC has traditionally founded its primary claim to legitimacy.[21] To the extent that the claim of *supranational efficiency* no longer suffices, the MNC must prove its legitimacy through demonstrated effectiveness in contributing to the accomplishment of *national goals*. But since the goals of one country frequently conflict with those of another, the MNC—as their actual or perceived instrument—can gain acceptance in the former country only at the expense of losing it in the latter.

The oil industry once again provides a recent illustration. According to testimony before the United States Senate Subcommittee on Multinational Corporations at its 1974 hearings, the international oil companies clearly chose (or were forced) to abet OPEC's 1973-74 quadrupling of crude oil prices and to take pro-Arab positions in the Mideast conflict (including the publication in the U.S. press by some companies of advertisements favoring the Arab point of view).[22] While these actions may have extended the companies' life expectancy in the producer countries, they certainly fueled political pressures in the United States for major government intervention in the oil industry. Similarly, acquiescence on the part of MNCs generally in host country insistence on the transfer of manufacturing from home to host countries has strengthened the efforts of organized labor in MNC home countries toward government regulation of the companies' international operations.

In fact, long-standing, popular demands in the MNC's home countries, particularly the United States, for increased public regulation of the activities of large corporations in general are being decisively strengthened by growing, public awareness of the international operations of these companies and their domestic repercussions. (The recent revelations of corporate participation in political subversion overseas,[23] involvement in large-scale bribery, and the use of foreign subsidiaries to conceal illegal domestic activities have been grist for the anti-corporate mill.)

In an article on the possible role of the U.S. government in the nationalization of the international oil companies in Venezuela, *The New York Times* quotes Melvin A. Conant, an Assistant Administrator of the Federal Energy Administration, in these terms:

It's still the case that most of the international oil executives grew up in a system in which *they* determined the level of supply, price, what investments would be made, and government—any government—played a supporting role when called upon but did not intervene. . . . [This is] beginning to change at an accelerating rate, and nowadays decisions on investments or the construction of a refinery or of tankers, or levels of production are all matters in which *government* decisions determine the course of action of the companies. (Emphasis added.)[24]

While most conspicuous in the current case of oil, "government determination of the course of action of the companies" is increasingly apparent in the operations of multinationals generally. The larger the corporation becomes in an absolute sense, or the larger it is in relation to its host environment, the more likely is the prospect of it becoming the manager or agent of public interests defined by government policy rather than private corporate objectives. Left to their own devices and guided solely by standards of globally efficient production, MNCs would not now be building petrochemical manufacturing capacities in OPEC states (almost certainly affecting the expansion possibilities of the companies' home installations), nor steel plants in Africa, nor nuclear reactors in Brazil, nor a diesel engine plant in Colombia. All of these projects are underwritten or sponsored by governments; none were initiated by MNCs. All of them obviously serve national goals and purposes perceived to be more important than the maximization of efficiency in international resource utilization.

The steadily expanding intervention of governments in the decision-making process of multinationals is leading to renewed calls for international agreements to regulate the actions of both companies and governments. But the prospects of such agreements being negotiated conclusively, much less of their being actually observed by their signatories, do not appear promising. There is too much diversity in the political and economic interests of today's nation-states, too much disparity in their relative stages of economic and social development, too much divergence in their relative dependence on the different kinds of benefits MNCs can provide and in their relative willingness to assume the economic and political costs associated with these benefits, and above all, there is too much change in the relative bargaining power of both host and home countries and in their perception of self-interest for such agreements to be likely to assume the force of effective international law.[25]

The more likely prospect is for continued bilateral relationships between MNCs and the governments in whose jurisdiction they function. Individual companies (probably with growing involvement of home governments) will continue to bargain with host governments for investment outlets, access to markets, and assets already committed. Individual host governments will continue to bargain with multinationals (and increasingly with their respective home governments) for the resources and capabilities these have to offer.[26]

The transfer of private corporate functions of entrepreneurship and risk taking to public institutions not directly subject to "the discipline of the market" will no doubt produce some of the worst results prophesied by conservative economists and MNC spokesmen alike. There will be less efficiency in resource use. In fact, there will be—as there already has been—significant resource *waste*. But the costs of such waste must be seen in perspective. It is at least arguable that governmental control, particularly by host governments, over MNC investments and operations is more likely over the long run to expand the effective transfer of real resources and technology where they are most needed (simply by making the MNC both more acceptable and more accountable within the individual country), and that this situation is more likely to avoid further international polarization (especially between rich and poor countries) than the MNC's traditional mode of operation has proved to be. To the extent that this is true, the costs of resource "suboptimization" or "misallocation" (by the economist's criterion), or even outright resource waste, will be a small price indeed for helping prevent political and social tensions from exploding into war, either civil or international. The argument is not that the presently evolving environment with its new institutional arrangements for multinational corporate operations will safeguard the world from national or international strife. The argument is the far more modest one that the new arrangements are less likely to deteriorate into a *casus belli* than the traditional form of foreign investment.

A reputation, or at least notoriety, is often achieved by positing extremes. Thus, most of the better known speculations about the world's future either give rise to fears of apocalypse or nurture hopes for millenium, with few alternatives in between. As for the multinational corporation, the two views most often belabored are that these companies represent consummate good—in the lyrical terms of Courtney Brown, "a new world symphony . . . the hoped-for force that will eventually provide a means for unifying and reconciling the aspirations of mankind"—or, to the contrary, that they constitute the ultimate evil of international capitalist exploitation. Not surprisingly, the first view predicts for the MNCs continued, robust growth until a few score corporate behemoths control the lion's share of world production (presumably "unifying and reconciling mankind" along the way), while the second view urges the MNC's dismemberment.

Neither of these views has much to commend it. The first is supported by little evidence. The second ignores the imperative need—imposed by modern technology and societal interdependence—for the capabilities that, at least over the reasonably foreseeable future, only the large corporation can supply. What is required is more objective and dispassionate recognition of both the essentiality of the large corporate institution *and* the legitimacy of popular objections to it. Satisfying all of the latter will not remove the former. Both sides have to accept their respective realities.

To this end, particularly in the international sphere, more research is needed on what the minimum conditions are for the large corporation to be able and willing to mobilize and deploy its unique capabilities. On the one hand, on such issues as the need for ownership and long-term control of foreign operations, apparent corporate willingness to enter into novel arrangements has belied, time and again, prior MNC claims as to their "impossibility" or "unattractiveness." On the other hand, far too little is known about the range of applicability or appropriateness of these new arrangements, both from the standpoint of the resource supplier and from that of the resource recipient, which only systematic inquiry into actual experience with them can reveal.

Similarly, a large research agenda remains in the area of MNC-government and intergovernment interactions as related to MNC operations generally and, in particular, the performance of specific functions in the planning and execution of new forms of foreign corporate resource commitments, as well as the transformation of existing investments. How are opportunities identified, resource suppliers selected, appropriate institutional arrangements conceived, responsibilities divided, performance evaluated, and disputes settled? How do incentives vary among industries, countries, and types of projects? What accounts for such variances? On what basis do MNCs "price" the supply of technology and proprietary skills and capabilities. What accounts for success or failure in their implantation in the receiving environment? To what extent and how do different home governments intervene in MNC interactions with host governments? What factors determine the degree and type of such intervention?

These are but a small number of the questions on which a great deal of empirical research remains to be undertaken.[27] The current emphasis in United Nations agencies on improving the availability of information on multinational corporate activities will undoubtedly aid in finding the necessary sponsorship. The results, in turn, are likely to lead to better insights and more effective concepts for shaping the future of the multinational corporation.

Such research may also, and more generally, foster the development of new theory that more realistically reconciles the economics of efficiency with the politics of distribution.

Notes

1. The literature on the growth of the multinational corporation has become vast. A sampling should include: John H. Dunning, ed., *The Multinational Enterprise* (New York: Praeger, 1971); Charles P. Kindleberger, ed., *The International Corporation* (Cambridge, Mass.: MIT Press, 1970); Christopher Tugendhat, *The Multinationals* (London: Eyre & Spottiswoode, 1971); Raymond Vernon, *Sovereignty at Bay: The Multinational Spread of U.S. Enterprises* (New York: Basic Books, 1971); Mira Wilkins, *The Maturing of Multinational Enterprise: American Business Abroad from 1914-1970* (Cambridge, Mass.: Harvard University Press, 1974).

2. It seems to have been this kind of straight-line extrapolation that informed predictions, in vogue until recently, that the growth of the MNCs will persist unabated until, by the 1980s, some 250-300 multinational giants will account for three-fourths of world product and dominate the international economic scene. (See, e.g., Howard V. Perlmutter, "Some Management Problems in Spaceship Earth: The Megafirm and the Global Industrial Estate," *Academy of Management Proceedings*, August 1969).

3. See Sidney E. Rolfe, *The International Corporation* (Paris: International Chamber of Commerce, 1969).

4. A far more critical exposition of the reasons for the success of the multinationals, and of their effects, is given in Richard J. Barnet and Ronald E. Müller, *Global Reach: The Power of the Multinational Corporations* (New York: Simon and Schuster, 1974).

5. For a representative summary of these views, see Council of the Americas, *The Effects of United States and Other Foreign Investment in Latin America* (New York: January 1970).

6. Professor Blumberg cites "a 1974 poll of the Opinion Research Corporation" which "showed that only 11% of the American public believed that the performance of business was good." (Philip I. Blumberg, *The Megacorporation in American Society* [Englewood Cliffs, N.J.: Prentice Hall, 1975] p. 177.) Because of the great concentration of business activity in the large corporations, popular attitudes toward "business" tend to be synonymous with attitudes toward the large corporation. The relevant statistics are revealing. "In 1973 the 1000 largest industrials (ranked according to sales) accounted for about 72% of the sales, 86% of the employees, and 85% of the profits of all American industrial corporations. Within this group, the 200 largest . . . represent . . . about three-quarters of the total sales, assets, employees, and profits of the entire group. . . . (Ibid., p. 174.)

7. Ibid., p. 177.

8. Ibid.

9. A summary statement of this line of reasoning is presented in Thomas E. Weisskopf, "Capitalism, Underdevelopment, and the Future of the Poor Countries," in J.N. Bhagwati, ed., *Economics and World Order* (New York: Macmillan, 1972).

10. Osvaldo Sunkel, "Underdevelopment in Latin America: Toward the Year 2000," in J.N. Bhagwati, ed., *Economics and World Order*, pp. 207-208.

11. E.F. Schumacher, in *Small is Beautiful* (London: Blond & Briggs, 1973) argues a different view. See pp. 57-68 and *passim*.

12. Philip I. Blumberg, *The Megacorporation in American Society*, p. 177.

13. Ibid., p. 14.

14. A more complete discussion of this point is in Peter P. Gabriel, *The International Transfer of Corporate Skills* (Boston: Harvard Business School, Division of Research, 1967), pp. 84-85 and ff.

15. Peter P. Gabriel, "The Investment in the LDC: Asset with a Fixed Maturity," *Columbia Journal of World Business* 1, no. 3 (Summer 1966): 114. Reprinted with permission.

16. See "The Oil Industry Retrenches," *Business Week*, July 14, 1975, pp. 140-146.

17. For some recent examples, see "Multinationals Find the Going Rougher," ibid., pp. 64-69.

18. A representative cross-section of these views is found in Courtney Brown, ed., *World Business: Promise and Problems* (New York: Macmillan, 1970).

19. Jacob K. Javits, "The Need for National Planning," *The Wall Street Journal*, July 8, 1975. Reprinted with permission.

20. Ibid.

21. An excellent analysis of the origins and ramifications of these political conflicts is Joseph S. Nye, Jr.'s "Multinational Corporations and World Order," in George W. Ball, ed., *Global Companies: The Political Economy of World Business* (New York: Prentice-Hall, 1975), pp. 122-147.

22. See *Multinational Corporations and United States Foreign Policy*, Hearings before the Subcommittee on Multinational Corporations of the Committee on Foreign Relations, United States Senate; First and Second Sessions on "Multinational Petroleum Companies and Foreign Policy," Part 5 (Washington: U.S. Government Printing Office, 1974).

23. Extensive documentation of some of the major cases of overseas political activities on the part of American multinationals can be found in *Multinational Corporations and United States Foreign Policy*, Hearings before the Subcommittee on Multinational Corporations of the Committee on Foreign Relations, United States Senate; First Session on "Political Contributions to Foreign Governments," Part 12 (Washington: U.S. Government Printing Office, 1976).

24. Robert M. Smith, "Ambassador Urged U.S. Take Role in Venezuelan Oil Talks," *The New York Times*, June 30, 1975. © 1975 by The New York Times Company. Reprinted by permission.

25. For a review of recent proposals and a discussion of several interesting new alternatives, see Eugene V. Rostow, Joseph S. Nye, Jr., and George W. Ball, *Global Companies*, pp. 156-173.

26. The outcome of this bargaining process will be determined, as it has been throughout the recent history of private foreign direct investment, by the relative dependence of the parties on the benefits they respectively associate with the objectives they seek to attain and their relative willingness to do without them. Given the multipolarity or policentricity in the current concert of nations, and the evident competition among multinationals of all countries for almost any major opportunity anywhere in the world, the tensions inevitably

arising from this process are, in my judgment, more likely to be successively alleviated by striking as effective bargains than by hardening into the "investment wars" feared by some observers. (For a different view on this and related issues, see C. Fred Bergsten "Coming Investment Wars?" *Foreign Affairs* 53 [October 1974].)

27. Professor Streeten, in a remarkable recent article, offers some poignant observations on how, where, and by whom such research, to the extent that it involves the less developed countries, might usefully be undertaken and why so much research on economic development, in which I would include the present subject, has not been overly helpful to at least some of its objects. (Paul P. Streeten, "Social Science Research on Development: Some Problems in the Use and Transfer of an Intellectual Technology," *Journal of Economic Literature* 12, no. 4 [December 1974].)

Part III
The Solutions to Scarcity I:
An Equitable Sharing of
Resources

5 Information Sharing and Bargaining: Institutional Problems and Implications

David N. Smith

Within the mineral-producing countries of the Third World, there is a growing consciousness that the information base which should serve as the foundation for bilateral negotiations with foreign enterprises has been, with few exceptions, the monopoly of the foreign companies themselves. Hence, access to crucial data is coming to be regarded as crucial in adjusting the balance of power in mineral development arrangements between host country governments and foreign firms.[1]

The OPEC successes of the post-1972 period have led a number of observers to conclude that there has been a dramatic shift in bargaining power from the producing companies to the producing countries, not only in oil but throughout the minerals industries generally.[2] Such a generalization from the oil example, however, seems premature. As of mid-1975, the evidence hardly confirms that "sovereignty is no longer at bay in host countries."[3] Thus, it remains unclear if the newly formed cartel and commodity groups will be able to raise prices and limit supplies arbitrarily.[4] Indeed, it even remains to be shown that member states of these groups can establish the sort of community of interests which alone will permit them to take the more modest step of effectively pooling the information needed to negotiate with foreign investors.

Over the long run, the information-sharing role of OPEC may turn out to be the function most amenable to emulation and perhaps the *most important* to emulate. For the ten years prior to 1973, the data-sharing and collective bargaining function of OPEC distinguished the negotiation and administration of petroleum production agreements from the less successful contractual ventures of developing countries in other industries.[5]

It is true, of course, that there have been some dramatic shifts in bargaining power between foreign investors and host countries in industries other than oil. The nationalizations of copper mining operations in Zaire and Chile, of iron ore operations in Venezuela, and of bauxite operations in Guyana, for example, undoubtedly reflect such a shift. But in most natural resource industries—and most developing countries generally—the bargaining picture has not changed drastically from the situation of, say, a decade ago.[6]

The questions of concern in this chapter relate to the type and quality of information that representatives of developing countries bring to negotiations with foreign firms. They relate to the data base from which various host countries were operating when, for example, in 1974 Peru negotiated a copper development agreement with the Mitsubishi and the Homestead Mining Companies; Niger negotiated a uranium development agreement with the French Commissariat à l'Énergie Atomique and Continental Oil; Lesotho negotiated a diamond mining agreement with De Beers Mining Corporation; and Bolivia negotiated a lead, silver, tin, copper, bismuth, and antimony mining agreement with the French Bureau de Recherches Geólogiques et Minières. Of concern too are the information sources that were available, for example, to the Liberian government when it renegotiated its iron ore development agreement with the Liberian-American-Swedish Minerals Company in 1974, or to the Papua-New Guinea government when it renegotiated its copper development agreement with the Bougainville Copper, Ltd., in the same year.[7] And do any of these countries have adequate information for *administering* these agreements?

Toward a Dynamic Bargaining Model of the Concession Arrangement

As a first step in an analysis of the role of information in the transfer of resources through "concession contracts,"[8] it is essential to distinguish *bargaining power* from *negotiating power*, and further to distinguish negotiating techniques and skills from the *information base* to which these skills are applied. Even when bargaining relationships have, in fact, changed in a particular resource industry to the extent that the positions of the producing companies, and perhaps also of the consuming countries, have weakened, critical questions remain: Does the host country know that the bargaining situation has shifted? If so, does it have the information needed to negotiate terms that reflect the new power? In many cases, lack of such knowledge in the host country means that the theoretical shift in bargaining power has little operational significance.

The distinction between bargaining power, negotiating skills, and the information base for negotiation is critical. Proposals to improve the position of developing nations vis-à-vis foreign firms from developed nations often focus on improving the skills of representatives of the poor nations to make them more effective negotiators.[9] Theoretical analyses of the company-host country exchange process often focus on strategy, tactics, and skill, as well as on negotiating factors such as "impatience" and "reciprocal demand intensity."[10] But an improvement in negotiating techniques is likely to be of only marginal significance in improving the position of developing nations in their relations with foreign firms if the information-poor party lacks the information critically needed to assess its own bargaining power and the economic and business context in which it is bargaining. Preparation for negotiation (of which access to information is a central element) is, in many respects, more important than the negotiation itself.

To understand the role of information in relationships between the governments of less developed countries and foreign firms, it is necessary to understand the bargaining and negotiating model that characterizes these relationships. Until recently, arrangements between these governments and private companies have been viewed by the parties, as well as by outside observers, in isolation from economic, social, political, and bureaucratic forces, as if they were little more than simple commercial contracts between private parties for the sale of goods. This view of the concession arrangement—this "static bargaining model"[11] in which a fixed set of rewards is divided in a single set of negotiations between two parties—is descriptively inappropriate.

The history of contractual revisions, particularly over the last decade, suggests that "negotiation" is not an isolated act, but a continuing process. And this same history informs us that the rewards are not necessarily fixed. Not only can financial relations between the parties change over time, but the benefits to both parties can often be increased by charging higher costs to consuming countries. Finally, other "parties" may affect the outcome of initial and ongoing negotiations: consuming countries may alter demand patterns, and other producing countries may provide assistance to a particular producing country or may compete with it in offering inducements to attract foreign investment. Thus, it is more useful to view the concession arrangement as an ongoing "process" than as a "contract." In this dynamic bargaining model, access to information becomes critical not only at the stage of first contract negotiation but throughout the life of the relationship. And as other parties begin to exert influence on the arrangement, these parties may be seen as potential sources of information not previously available.

Nevertheless, the fact that the arrangement takes a "contractual" form has a profound influence on the ultimate sharing of benefits from the developing country's natural resources. Negotiations proceed in an adversary setting in which each party, in theory, advances his own case through a bargaining process that assumes equal negotiating power on both sides. Spokesmen in developing countries have recently argued that their international economic relationships are carried forward under rules and institutions devised within the countries of the industrialized world.[12] Adversary bargaining is one such "rule of the game." The adversary theory of bargaining, largely a Western concept, has been imported into the concessions process by the lawyers who represent Western firms.

The contract traditions of many parts of the Third World, where many of the economically valuable natural resources exist, have not been adversary in nature. Bargaining in a number of these societies—Indonesia is a major example— has assumed that both parties will proceed on a basis of goodwill and compromise[13] aimed at furthering mutual interests. In some instances, differing societal views of the nature of contract bargaining have led to situations in which the two parties proceed on quite different premises.

The primary factor making the adversary relationship inappropriate has been the foreign firm's near-monopoly of critical information. The lack of information among developing countries is so severe that in many instances very little bargaining or negotiation actually occurs. It is not uncommon for a host government either to accept a contract as proposed by the investor, with no pretense of host country input, or to use negotiating sessions merely for altering grammar in the contract or else as a forum for political maneuvering among different agencies of the host government.[14]

In the United States, it has long been recognized in judicial dispute settlement that the adversary process falls far short of the theoretical standard. The individual in civil or criminal litigation is often handicapped by inadequate legal counsel and insufficient fact-gathering resources. In civil litigation between private parties, the richer, better represented litigant may overwhelm the poorer through superior know-how. Steps have been taken to begin to remedy this problem: provision of skilled counsel through third party sources; removal of certain kinds of disputes from the strictly adversary process;[15] and various measures to increase the access of each party to critical information through pretrial disclosure proceedings.[16] These new conceptualizations of the adversary process in dispute resolution in the United States suggest a need to rethink the international bargaining relationships where one party is likely to be permanently disadvantaged by inadequate access to relevant information.

Institutional reshaping of the relationship between the foreign investor and the developing country would involve two major changes in the basic structure of the relationship: (1) provision for greater access to critical information by the host country, and (2) removal of the exchange relationship from a strictly adversarial setting. The first proposal would provide for, and make explicit, the role of third parties—other producing countries, the investor's home country, international organizations—in the relationship. The second proposal attacks the basic assumption concerning what the two-party relationship should be.

Information Critically Needed by Host Countries

In the initial bargaining stages, the host government needs information on the extent and value of its resources; the nature and structure of the industry; the role of the firm in that industry structure; the demand, marketing, and trade patterns that affect the industry; and terms of agreements negotiated by other countries.

Traditionally, developing countries have not had the most basic information on these various subjects. For example, agreements negotiated by other countries were notoriously unavailable for public or third-party inspection throughout the first half of this century and beyond. This inaccessibility influenced not only actual negotiations but also the literature on concessions. Articles purporting to analyze concession agreements in the forties, fifties, and sixties often began with laments concerning the lack of access to the very phenomenon under study.[17] Such contracts were considered secret by both the country and the company. Unable to compare terms of agreements, and hence unable to undertake functional analyses of the agreements as they were implemented, those writing about concessions concentrated on arbitral decisions, general theory, and issues normally confronted in the litigation stage of a concessions relationship. This perspective doubtless played some role in diverting attention away from issues relating to the avoidance of conflict and litigation.[18] For both governments and analysts, the inaccessibility of concession contracts persists today.

In defining other information needed by the host country, we begin with data on the quality and quantity of the resource to be extracted. Often, of course, this information will be inaccessible at the outset to both the host country and the foreign company, although the company is likely to have preliminary data that may not be made fully available to the government. If the host country has neither conducted its own investigation nor had a third party do so, the contract is likely to incorporate a theory of high risk and major uncertainties. This theory will be reflected in favorable terms for the investor, such as a low tax rate or major tax incentives to develop the concession. Where the facts later disprove the theory, a lag period will typically intervene between the time when the company begins to profit from the arrangement and the time when the government perceives the imbalance in the relationship. When developing countries have been able to benefit from exploratory work by third parties, such as the United Nations Development Programme,[19] more realistic assessments of resources have been made by both parties before negotiations began.

Information on the industry, marketing and trade patterns, and the particular firm's role in the industry is critical for assessing the host country's bargaining power. The host country needs to know whether the resource is widely available, how badly the particular firm needs the supply, whether other firms might be interested in this source, and whether a bidding procedure is feasible. For these questions, many developing countries have not only not had answers, but have not even systematically sought answers.

The second stage at which the government needs information is in the general administration of the arrangement—to assure that the government receives its fair share of profits and to determine whether the factual basis on which the agreement was premised has changed to the extent that its terms should be modified. Typically, both tasks require the deciphering of complex financial transactions engaged in by the company. The ability of multinational enterprises, through transactions with affiliated entities, to understate profits and overstate expenses to the detriment of host countries is well known.[20] The government must know, to begin with, what entities are affiliated with the company. Relationships among companies, where ownership and control may extend vertically and laterally through a number of companies, can form a complex maze.

Finally, to determine through an "arm's length" test what price the resource would have brought on the open market, the government must have a reliable free market standard against which to measure the transaction. Comparable transactions between unaffiliated companies are usually employed as such a yardstick. But in industries where all production and marketing is controlled by a few companies through vertically integrated operations, there may be no readily ascertainable free market price for the raw material or for materials processed in the host country. In some cases, the free market may be so thin as to be meaningless. Since the critical data are controlled by the company, the central question is: How can a host country gain access to this and other information essential for rational decision making?

Mechanisms for Securing Critical Bargaining Information

Many developing countries have weak rules concerning the disclosure of corporate information. Even in the United States, where disclosure rules are among the most advanced in the world, companies may in fact disclose very little.[21] Typically, developing countries negotiate with foreign firms contractual arrangements that simply provide that the companies will disclose such information as the government finds useful. However, the host country officials are often given little direction concerning what information to seek. Moreover, the actual giving of information is often left to the discretion and initiative of the company.

Nor has the experience of LDCs in obtaining information from the foreign firm's home country been encouraging. Although most tax treaties between developed and developing countries contain provisions for the exchange of tax information, the exchange-of-information provisions—potentially a powerful weapon in policing the financial transactions of foreign firms—have in fact been little utilized. In any event, many tax treaties are silent on the exchange of information most critical to policing the activities and transactions of foreign investors. The Model Convention for the Avoidance of Double Taxation with Respect to Taxes on Income and Capital, prepared by the Organization for Economic Cooperation and Development, does not expressly provide for the exchange of information relating to non-arm's length transactions, including the underpricing or overpricing of invoices, royalties, and interest.[22] Moreover, bilateral tax conventions—to the extent they are effective at all—are useful primarily in dealing with bilateral tax evasion. Where more than one country is involved in the enterprise's operations, information may be needed from several countries. Hence, multilateral tax conventions and the establishment of one or more international tax agencies for joint investigation of tax evasion have been suggested.[23]

It must also be recognized that the home countries of multinational enterprises are often themselves consumers of the resource developed by the foreign firm. In this respect, the home country is itself in an adversary relationship to the producing country—although the argument has been made that consuming countries may find it more advantageous in the long run to cooperate with producing countries in order to ensure an uninterrupted supply of commodities at acceptable prices. The cost of obtaining uninterrupted supplies may be a package of benefits for the producing country, including liberalized tariffs, debt rescheduling, and information on companies based in the consuming country.[24]

The international commodity organizations represent a growing source of industry information. World attention in 1973-75 focused on the ability of OPEC to increase the profits shared by the producing countries with the private companies. But as noted above, the information-sharing function of the organization was generally overlooked. It is significant that in 1975 the newly formed association of eleven countries exporting iron ore specifically renounced price setting in favor of exchange of information as the group's goal.[25]

For years prior to 1973, OPEC was providing model agreements and industry information to nonmember countries—for example, Liberia in the late 1960s—which were just entering the industry.[26] Such information meant not only better contractual arrangements for these countries but also that the terms being negotiated by the OPEC countries would not be undercut by new entrants. While CIPEC, the organization of the copper-producing countries, has proved unable to sustain high copper prices, it has played a similar information-sharing role, although apparently somewhat more reluctantly than OPEC.[27] There is evidence that more information may be shared among mineral-producing and timber-producing countries in the future,[28] provided that sufficient incentives to encourage this sharing are forthcoming.

The effectiveness of the newly formed commodity groups will be tested when individual countries face the problem of determining what information they want to release to potential competitors.[29] The same problem will face other countries in which the firm may be operating but which do not belong to the commodity group. It has been reported, for example, that the Commission of the European Community has had to compile inadequate data on corporate mergers because of the reluctance of some member countries to share information in their possession.[30] When, in 1971, the government of Malaysia began negotiations for a copper development project with a Japanese firm, it did not enjoy access to any copper agreements negotiated with other copper-producing countries—despite the fact that CIPEC had been in existence for some years.

As noted, it has been difficult for all but the most intrepid to gain access to concession agreements. And while the situation has been improving, many developing countries must still rely on consultants who bring copies of agreements collected from other countries. Outside of the oil industry, there is no central clearing house for information of this sort, although some commodity groups may now be sharing contract information.

There have been recommendations to establish a comprehensive global economic intelligence system to make world markets and multinational enterprises more "transparent."[31] In 1974, the report of the United Nations Group of Eminent Persons, brought together to study the impact of multinational corporations on development and international relations, recommended an information and research center within the U.N. Secretariat.[32] The center, established in late 1974, is mandated to collect, analyze, and disseminate information on such matters as restrictive business practices, transfer pricing, taxation, legislation and policies of host and home countries, and the geographical and industrial distribution of activities of multinational corporations. Given the variety of multinational corporate activity, as well as the fact that the center will deal not only with the resource industries but also with the manufacturing sector, one cannot be optimistic that the center will have an immediate impact in individual cases. It may be necessary to limit the goals of an international information center to serving as an intermediary, advising individual countries on various sources of critical data dealing with a single commodity or one critical subject, such as taxation.

The problem of framing acceptable guidelines for estimating "free market" prices against which to test prices the company receives from affiliated buyers will be among the thorniest to deal with. In 1974, France introduced a draft U.N. resolution calling for the establishment of a central economic observatory to collect information on the prices actually quoted in major raw materials transactions; to analyze the conditions that determine the prices of raw materials (supply and demand, reserves and stocks, operating costs, feasibility and cost of replacement, marketing channels); to determine short-term and long-term outlooks for market development; to establish weighted average prices as reference bases; and to provide objective basic data for the negotiation of international agreements on raw materials.[33] These goals can be achieved, perhaps, only by specific commodity groups.

It is likely that any individual country will have to rely on a mixture of information sources in order to develop the type of data base needed to negotiate natural resource contracts and to police resource development arrangements with foreign firms. The company's home country, other countries which produce the same resource, other countries in which the firm operates, and international agencies may be able to provide, cumulatively, the information needed. But whether this information will be accessible to an individual host country will depend on the inclination of these third parties to cooperate with the LDC in question. It will also depend on the ability of the individual country to identify the type of information which may be critical to rational decision making and then to assimilate and use the data effectively once it is obtained.

Obstacles to the Identification, Assimilation, and Use of Data

To appreciate the institutional and bureaucratic hurdles developing countries face in collecting, assimilating, and using information relating to natural resource development, one must understand the starting point from which many of them have proceeded.

As recently as 1962, rights in minerals and timber in Ghana vested not in the state but in individuals or kinship groups.[34] Concessions were negotiated not through government officials, but through private landholders. Until the early 1970s, Jamaica, for twenty years the world's leading producer of bauxite, and Guyana and Surinam, both bauxite producers for fifty years, had no Ministries of Mines.[35] Liberia did not, in the late 1960s, have a single individual with full-time responsibility for the administration of concession arrangements, despite the fact that the government was, at the time, a party to over one hundred concession agreements, including arrangements with such major companies as Firestone and Bethlehem Steel. Indonesia negotiated major concessions with such firms as Freeport Minerals and Kennecott Copper in the late 1960s *before* it took steps to improve the capacity of its Ministry of Mines. Both agreements were signed by the government in virtually the forms initially presented by the companies.

Many countries have either been unwilling to make the necessary investment to establish a capacity for knowing an industry and supervising those charged with developing its natural resources or else have proved unable to retain skilled personnel long enough to develop competence. Some governments have simply not appreciated the need—or have not wanted—to police concession arrangements. Corruption may be a factor retarding the establishment of a secretariat capable of bringing skill to bear on concessions analysis.

Pertamina, the Indonesian state oil company, had, in 1966, a highly skilled staff capable of dealing with foreign firms on close to equal terms. Yet none of this know-how was transferred to those departments which were concerned with drafting hard mineral and timber contracts at that time—a lack which, indeed, is reflected in the terms of the hard mineral and timber contracts of the second half of the 1960s.

The problem of bureaucratic inertia was dramatically illustrated in the case of transfer of another resource—food. It has been reported that during the Sahelian food disaster of the late 1960s and early 1970s,

The most conspicuous failure to the relief efforts [in the Sahel] . . . was the failure to gather, retrieve and use information. At every stage of the disaster, every piece of information missing added up to yet a larger void. The absence of information paralyzed planning. But it was not only the lack of data. There was data, as the AID October study complained, "lying in the files," [and] knowledge and time [were] wasted because a bureaucracy ostensibly living by facts and figures could not organize its institutional memory.[36]

Some problems of information seem particularly intractable. With regard to transfer pricing[37]—an area of critical importance in maximizing government income from natural resource development—a leading expert on problems of international taxation thus describes the situation:

It seems not too much to say that in many developing countries transfer prices are now virtually at the discretion of the multinational corporation. Prices for petroleum exports are an exception, as also are prices for certain other exports where concession agreements have embodied formulae or procedures for setting the transfer price. Otherwise, both for imports from and exports to the parent company . . . the tax officials of the developing country often have so little time or expertise available for contesting the transfer prices adopted that they leave them undisturbed.[38]

Where improvements have occurred in the LDCs' capacity to assimilate information and administer concessions, the impetus often comes not from inside the government, but from international agencies such as the International Monetary Fund and the World Bank, which have made improved capacity a condition for financial assistance.[39] But even where such demands are made and institutional improvements are recommended, institutional change may take five or six years to implement. Low-paid bureaucrats in developing countries often only reluctantly hire high-priced advisers to provide interim assistance. Given these circumstances, it is not surprising that even the best intentioned investor may end up with a highly favorable—but imbalanced—concession arrangement.

Implementing the Dynamic Bargaining Model:
The Role of Third Parties

What can be done? There have been demands from both consuming and producing countries for institutional restructuring of the relations between multinational companies and the producing countries. Members of the U.S. Congress have called for increased government control over any contractual arrangements between American companies and producing countries.[40] Recent proposals for creating a "new economic order" imply a need for institutional reform.[41] Such proposals may provide an opening wedge for rethinking the relationships between company and country. They may also facilitate acceptance of an institutional role for third parties, including some form of international organization, to provide critical information at the bargaining stage.

It has been observed that the literature relating to contracts between developing countries and foreign investors has focused on the contract in the context of litigation or potential litigation. Because little attention has been paid to the processes through which concession agreements *come into being* or are renegotiated, analysts have tended to take for granted the interactional relationships that characterize the negotiation of concession contracts.

The concessions relationship is similar in a number of respects to that between an employer and a labor union. The latter relationship has been described as follows: The parties concerned

(1) being two in number, find themselves (2) in a relationship of heavy interdependence exerting a strong pressure to reach an agreement, an agreement that will (3) combine elements of an economic trade with (4) elements of a written charter or constitution for the governance of their future relations; this agreement is (5) negotiated by agents, not principals, and (6) the employer occupies throughout a dual role, being, on the one hand, director of the enterprise and, on the other, a co-equal with the union in the negotiation and administration of the collective bargaining agreement.[42]

Given these similarities, one may ask whether the successful use of third parties—mediators—in employer-union negotiations can be replicated in concessions negotiations. In collective bargaining, the mediator often conveys insights that the parties themselves may lack. The mediator's assistance

can speed the negotiations, reduce the likelihood of miscalculation, and generally help the parties to reach a sounder agreement, an adjustment of their divergent valuations that will produce something like an optimum yield of the gains of reciprocity.[43]

The mediator also brings information that either or both of the parties may lack: information on the general economic setting in which the negotiations take place, on contracts negotiated between other labor unions and other companies, or on the potential viability of alternative sets of terms.

In the concessions context, a mediator may be able to suggest areas of mutual interest to the parties and to help them achieve a new perception of a developing relationship. He or she may be able to help parties identify areas in which the data base from which critical judgments are to be made is inadequate and recast their attitudes toward each other by recognizing implicit assumptions that may be incorrect. The use of concession agreements from other developing countries as part of the data base for negotiations provides one example of the role that the "information broker" might play.[44]

The mediator might be an employee of an international agency charged with collecting and disseminating information on natural resources. Indeed, given the range of information needed in concessions negotiation, the mediator might, in certain circumstances, see the necessity of bringing in other information brokers from his or her agency or elsewhere to educate the parties.

The availability of such mediators and brokers would put less of a premium on the skill and resources of individual countries. Shifts in staff and discovery of new resources would not imply the degree of retrenchment that is now required when circumstances change. The use of third parties might also lead to a greater degree of consistency in the concession terms negotiated in different countries, thus helping to dissipate some of the atmosphere of competition which now prevails among developing countries.

The proposed international agency for developing seabed resources may furnish the catalyst for introducing third parties into the concessions process. Proposals to mine resources in a restricted area seaward of existing limits of national jurisdictions call for the sharing of the right to mine between the coastal state and a regional or international authority, while mining of the rest of the high seas would require the vesting of mining jurisdiction in an international agency.[45] This international (or regional) agency would serve as a third party in the first case, bringing information which may not be available to the individual country. In the latter case, the international agency would be likely to develop an expertise in specific resource areas, as well as in the general area of taxation. It could eventually transfer much of such expertise to countries concerned with developing land-based resources.

The more traditional role for third parties in concession arrangements is that of dispute settlers. Agreements commonly call for the submission of disputes to such agencies as the International Center for the Settlement of Investment Disputes or the International Chamber of Commerce. It may be possible to combine this traditional role with the information-sharing role for some subject areas. The problem of transfer pricing may be one such subject. Thus, one authority on international taxation has suggested the establishment of "some non-national board, or panel of industry and economics experts" to which the foreign firm or the host country could submit disputes involving transfer pricing. Under an appropriately drawn arbitration agreement, the board (or subboards with expertise in particular commodities and industries) might be empowered to examine the tax returns filed by the particular subsidiary company in the host country, the returns of the parent company in the home country, and the returns of affiliated companies in third countries.[46]

It should also be noted in connection with the problem of transfer pricing that proposals have been put forth for adopting an approach that would facilitate access to critical information by altering the required data base. Under the factor-formula technique used in some U.S. states, a taxing authority allocates to itself a proportion of the firm's worldwide profits. Each factor— worldwide payroll, worldwide sales, worldwide property, for example—is apportioned and given a stated weight. The weighted factors are then averaged. This average is the proportion applied to the firm's worldwide profits to determine the amount of profit taxable in the host country.[47] The information needed to establish the factor formula is more accessible than is the information needed under approaches currently used in international taxation. There are, however, a number of shortcomings in the factor-formula approach which must be contended with before it receives general acceptance.[48]

Summary and Conclusions

It is difficult to be optimistic that improved data sources and information sharing of the quality and varieties suggested here will develop quickly. Needed, as initial steps over the next decade, are (1) improved information on the costs to a developing country of negotiating and administering natural resource agreements from a basis of relative ignorance; (2) pilot attempts to assemble complete information packages for several countries and several resources; and (3) efforts to create an atmosphere in which both parties to a concessions relationship would consider information mediators to be a desirable addition to the negotiating process.

Few analyses have been made of the costs—and benefits—to particular developing countries of various terms and forms of agreements with foreign firms.[49] More is known about the financial implications of an inability to police the agreement effectively. But overall, reliable studies are few. Liberia, for which some of the best analyses have been made, appears to have suffered significantly in financial terms from opting for equity sharing in one agreement[50] and for failing to police affiliate transactions in another.[51]

Developing countries, in opting to move from one form of agreement to another—typically, from a straight concession to equity sharing through a "partial nationalization" of the industry—often make the move for political rather than economic reasons.[52] Economic analyses of the financial implications of such moves are seldom adequate. It is reported that Zambia was, at best, no better off financially when it took over majority control of two copper-mining operations in 1969.[53] In the early 1970s, Sierra Leone, apparently following Zambia's lead, took steps toward nationalizing a foreign company but backed off after the financial implications became clear.[54] Once analytical tools for the analysis of outcomes under alternative assumptions are available, the importance of improved access to data is likely to become more apparent.

This chapter has suggested that a particular country in the process of developing a natural resource with the assistance of a foreign firm is likely to need a variety of information from a variety of sources; that the type and source of information is likely to vary according to industry; and that the assimilation and effective use of this information is likely to place heavy demands on the host country's bureaucracy. Given these facts, the information-sharing problem is not apt to be easily solved. The most appropriate first step for an international organization (perhaps the research and information center associated with the U.N. Commission on Transnational Corporations) would be to put together information "packages" in two or three countries. These packages would include information on the quantity and quality of the resource, the structure of the industry, the particular firm's corporate structure and worldwide activities, trade and marketing patterns in the industry, and agreements for the same resource in other countries. As the international organization itself seeks to draw upon various sources of information, it could identify those subjects for which data are unavailable or difficult to acquire.

Whether such an organization could eventually serve as an "information mediator" would depend on the multinational companies' acceding to such a third-party role. The force of international public opinion can be powerful in improving the behavior of governments. It is not inconceivable that this same force can be brought to bear on multinational firms to alter their traditional mode of doing business.

Notes

1. On the issue of host country consciousness, see for example, the Action Programme proposed by the Conference of Developing Countries on Raw Materials, February 1975 (U.N. Conference on Trade and Development, doc. no. TD/B/C.1/L.45), reproduced in *International Legal Materials* 14, no. 2 (March 1975): 520 ff; Agreement Establishing the International Bauxite Association, March 1974, reproduced in *International Legal Materials* 13, no. 5 (September 1974): 1245 ff. For a summary of information problems as they relate to foreign investment generally, see United Nations, Economic and Social Council, *The Impact of Multinational Corporations on Development and on International Relations* (Report of the Group of Eminent Persons, U.N. doc. E/5500/Rev. 1/ST/ESA/6), 1974. For thoughtful analyses of information problems relating to natural resources, see Zuhayr Mikdashi, "Influencing the Environment for Primary Commodities," *Journal of World Trade Law* 8, no. 2 (March-April 1974); Zuhayr Mikdashi, "Policy Issues in Primary Industries," *Vanderbilt Journal of Transnational Law* 7, no. 2 (Spring 1974), especially Part I, dealing with " 'freeing' the supply of key information not normally accessible to less developed countries." See also Robert O. Keohane and Van Doorn Ooms, "The Multinational Firm and International Regulation," *International Organization* 29, no. 1 (Winter 1975): 201 ff.

2. See, e.g., C. Fred Bergsten, "The Response to the Third World," *Foreign Policy*, no. 17 (Winter 1974-75); and James D. Theberge, "A Minerals Raw Material Action Program," *Foreign Policy*, no. 17 (Winter 1974-75).

3. C. Fred Bergsten, "Coming Investment Wars?" *Foreign Affairs* 53, no. 1 (October 1974): 138.

4. On the ability—or inability—of commodity groups to emulate the actions of OPEC in affecting prices and supplies, see "One, Two, Many

OPEC's . . .?" a symposium of three articles, in *Foreign Policy*, no. 14 (Spring 1974).

5. For a discussion of the benefits derived by OPEC members from the organization's information sharing and collective bargaining activities, see Zuhayr Mikdashi, "Cooperation Among Oil Exporting Countries with Special Reference to Arab Countries," *International Organization* 28, no. 1 (Winter 1974): 24-25:

The [OPEC] Secretariat has . . . attempted to induce member governments to seek terms and adopt policies and practices vis-à-vis concessionary companies in line with the best economic terms prevailing in various member countries. One study commissioned by OPEC analyzed, on a comparative basis, members' posted prices, royalties, taxes, transit and port dues, guarantees and timing of payments, and other economic benefits offered to host countries. The best terms were to be used as guidelines by host governments in their negotiations with concessionaires. Information, studies, and advice have produced far-reaching economic benefits, essentially in the form of improved fiscal terms claimed, and eventually obtained, from oil operators.

The contribution of OPEC to its member countries, especially those with limited oil experience, is notable in the areas of analyzing conditions in the international petroleum industry, offering advice, and training nationals in the technical and economic aspects of the industry. The OPEC Secretariat has performed a useful function in acting as a clearinghouse and in filling gaps of information on oil markets. Detailed, accurate, and increasingly comprehensive information, supplied on a regular basis, assists top officials of OPEC governments in formulating appropriate policies and regulations, whether dealing with the oil sector or with other related sectors of the economy—especially in view of the general unwillingness of their concessionaires to supply them with certain data on technical and economic matters (e.g., prices realized on oil exports). International companies classify such information as trade secrets, bearing in mind that national companies of host countries are their active competitors. [Reprinted by permission of *International Organization*]

See also Zuhayr Mikdashi, "The Community of Oil Exporting Countries: A Study in Governmental Cooperation" (American Univ. of Beirut, 1970, private draft), pp. 83 ff.

6. This does not mean that there have not been improvements in contracts from the host country point of view. There have, for example, been increasing movements toward the hiring of local labor and the linking of foreign operations to local sources of supply and other businesses in the host country. But these improvements often result from the foreign firm's desire to create good will or from the fact that, having invested substantial capital in the country, the firm becomes something of a "hostage."

7. Although the texts of agreements are seldom published, there are a number of sources that report the signing of contracts. One of the most useful sources is the U.S. Department of the Interior, Bureau of Mines, Mineral Trade

Notes. For a list of contractual arrangements between twenty-six developing countries and foreign companies (with a brief description of terms), see United Nations, General Assembly, *The Exercise of Permanent Sovereignty over Natural Resources and the Use of Foreign Capital and Technology for Their Exploitation* (Report of the Secretary-General, U.N. doc. A/8058), 14 September 1970, pp. 62 ff. Agreements in the oil industry are much more accessible. Many have been published by the Organization of Oil Producing Countries. See *Selected Documents of the International Petroleum Industry* (OPEC, Vienna, various volumes covering years since 1966).

8. Although arrangements between developing countries and foreign firms are now known by a number of names (production sharing agreements, service contracts, work contracts, etc.), the term "concession contract" has become something of a generic description for such arrangements, and that term will be used here. The resources referred to include timber as well as minerals.

9. A number of training courses, sponsored by the United Nations and others in the first half of the 1970s, seem to have this emphasis.

10. See, for example, R.L. Curry and D. Rothchild, "On Economic Bargaining Between African Governments and Multi-National Companies," *The Journal of Modern African Studies* 12, no. 2 (1974): 173.

11. The concept of static and dynamic bargaining models in host country-investor relationships is developed in a forthcoming book by the author and Professor Louis T. Wells, Jr. on the mineral concessions process.

12. United Nations, General Assembly, *Declaration and Action Programme on the Establishment of a New Economic Order*, Sixth Special Session (U.N. doc. A/RES/3201 [S-VI]), 9 May 1974. "The gap between the developed and developing countries continues to widen in a system which was established at a time when most of the developing countries did not even exist as independent states and which perpetuates inequality." (Preamble)

13. "The central position of [the concept of good faith] in Indonesia has led to a lesser concern with protective clauses spelled out for specific contingencies than is the case in the American tradition. . . . The tendency of some American lawyers to try to impose on us American legal concepts . . . seems to us sometimes rather excessively one sided." Soedjatmoko, "Foreign Private Investment in a Developing Nation: An Indonesian Perspective," in Virginia Cameron, ed., *Private Investors Abroad—Problems and Solutions in International Business in 1969* (1969), pp. 322-23.

14. It has been common in the past for the investor to present the "negotiating draft." A comparison of these drafts with the final documents in a number of countries shows minimal host country input. The Indonesian hard mineral and timber contracts of the late 1960s are one example.

15. See, for example, G. Adams, "The Small Claims Court and the Adversary Process: More Problems in Function and Form," *Canadian Bar Review* 51 (1973): 583.

16. See William H. Speck, "The Use of Discovery in United States District Courts," 60 *Yale Law Journal* 60 (1951): 1132, 1155. For an examination of the practical effects of the Federal Rules of Civil Procedure relating to discovery, see generally "Field Survey of Federal Pretrial Discovery," Report to the Advisory Committee on Rules of Civil Procedure (Confidential Draft for Discussion) (Columbia University, Project for Effective Justice, 1965).

17. "A comprehensive list and functional analysis of development agreements . . . would be a useful research tool. A sampling of available sources convinced the writer that within these pages such an analysis and listing would not be possible because of practical difficulties of assembling primary source material." James Hyde, "Economic Development Agreements," *Recueil des Cours* 105 (1962, Vol. I): 272, 283; "It will be noticed that most of the concession agreements which are reproduced here are of older concessions. This is due to the fact that concession agreements are nearly never published. They are jealously hidden in the archives of state departments, company lawyers, international experts or arbitrators. . . ." Guldberg, "International Concessions, A Problem of International Economic Law," *Nordisk Tidsskrift for International Ret* 15 (1944): 47, 50; "Information as to the details of existing concessions is sparse, and that as to the actual tax results of operating under these concessions is elusive." Brudno, "Review of Considerations Arising in Foreign Oil Operations," Ninth Annual Institute on Oil and Gas Law and Taxation 397 (1958). The lack of source material is reflected in the limited nature of the concession section of the United Nations study *The Status of Permanent Sovereignty over Natural Wealth and Resources* (U.N. doc. A/AC. 97/5/Rev. 2), 1962. See comment at page 241 of the study.

18. The fact that concession agreements were considered secret documents may, of course, have suited the needs of both the foreign firm, which was not anxious to have the terms of a "one-sided" contract revealed, and the host government, which may have felt sensitive about the "bargain" it struck.

19. See United Nations, General Assembly, *The Exercise of Permanent Sovereignty over Natural Resources and the Use of Foreign Capital and Technology for Their Exploitation*, (Report of the Secretary-General, U.N. doc. A/8058), 14 September 1970, pp. 133 ff. See also United Nations, Department of Economic and Social Affairs, *Mineral Resources Development with Particular Reference to the Developing Countries* (U.N. doc. ST/ECA/123), 1970, Annex: "International Cooperation in Mineral Development." The United States Geological Survey, in cooperation with USAID, has provided assistance to a number of developing countries in assessing mineral resources and in developing a capacity to appraise such resources. See the various U.S. cooperative programs listed in the Appendix to Herman Pollack and Michael B. Congdon, "International Cooperation in Energy Research and Development," *Law and Policy in International Business* 6 (1974): 677.

20. "Transfer pricing," as these intracorporate transactions are known, may influence not only the price received for the sale of a commodity but also the

cost of transferring services, loans, and technology within the corporate family. The general problem of transfer pricing and the information problem raised by it were the subjects of attention by the U.N. Group of Eminent Persons. See note 1. See also Carl S. Shoup, "Taxation of Multinational Corporations," in United Nations, Department of Economic and Social Affairs, *The Impact of Multinational Corporations on Development and on International Relations*, Technical Papers: Taxation (U.N. doc. ST/ESA/11), 1974; and "Summary of the February 27-28, 1975 Meeting on Economic Criteria for Policy Formulation on Taxing Foreign Income," Round Table IV: *The Problem of Disclosure of Pertinent Data by USMNC's and Specifically the Issue of Transfer Pricing*, pp. 13 ff. (Harvard Law School, International Tax Program, 1975). For a forceful statement on the inequities created by transfer pricing, see Richard Barnet and Ronald Muller, *Global Reach* (1974), pp. 157-58.

21. See U.S. Senate, Hearings before the Subcommittee on Monopoly of the Select Committee on Small Business, *The Role of Giant Corporations in the American and World Economies*, Part 2, Corporate Secrecy: Overviews (November 1971).

22. See United Nations, *Tax Treaties Between Developed and Developing Countries*, Fourth Report (1973), Part II.

23. Ibid., p. 110.

24. Theberge, "A Minerals Raw Material Action Program," p. 75; and Bergsten, "The Response to the Third World," p. 6.

25. "Agreement Signed for an Association of Iron-Ore Nations," *New York Times*, 4 April 1975, p. 50.

26. The formal responsibilities of certain working units of OPEC include the study of resources, productive capacities, and marketing in nonmember countries; the organization's Legal Section is specifically charged with "the duty of studying the legal aspects of the oil business in various countries with a view to ... giving guidance to member countries *and to any other countries having interests in common with the Organization.*" (Emphasis added.) Res. II.9.1, *Resolutions of the Second Conference* (OPEC, 1961). In addition, new patterns of government-company relations set by OPEC have served as models for nonmember oil exporting countries. See Mikdashi, "The Community of Oil Exporting Countries," p. 131; and Henri Bazin, *Cooperation Among Developing Countries with Regard to Commodity Exports*, U.N. Conference on Trade and Development, Trade and Development Board (U.N. doc. TD/B/293), 1969.

27. CIPEC's Copper Information Bureau, like OPEC's Secretariat, provides analyses of the industry with which it is concerned, and its formal information-sharing responsibilities are directed to its member countries. See Wolf Radmann, "CIPEC—The Copper Exporting Countries," *Intereconomics* (August 1973): 245-49; and Mikdashi, "The Community of Oil Exporting Countries,"

pp. 182-83. CIPEC's Annual Reports focus primarily on the state of the copper market as it relates to Zaire, Zambia, Peru, and Chile—the four member nations. See *CIPEC Annual Reports* (Paris: 1970).

CIPEC did not come to the assistance of Malaysia in 1971 when that country negotiated a copper contract with a Japanese company. In 1974 Peru, apparently acting individually, assisted the Papua-New Guinea government in its negotiations with Kennecott. A CIPEC economist was sent to assist Papua-New Guinea in the same year with renegotiations of the Bougainville agreement.

28. The organizational meeting of the International Bauxite Association, which took place in November of 1974, ended with an announcement that a study of joint pricing policies for bauxite was underway. "Jamaica Seeks Cure for Its Myriad Social Ills in Higher Profits from Sought-After Bauxite," *Wall Street Journal*, 11 November 1974, p. 28. The International Tin Agreement of 1970 calls for the furnishing of relevant data by participating countries and the study of industry-wide problems. See United Nations Tin Conference, 1970, *Summary of Proceedings* (U.N. doc. TD/TIN. 4/7/Rev.1). With regard to the sharing of information among iron-producing countries, see note 25.

29. Although Australia joined the new Association of Iron Exporting Countries in 1975, it warned that it would not be able to provide information on iron ore contracts supplied "in confidence" by companies. "Agreement signed for an Association of Iron-Ore Nations," *New York Times*, 4 April 1975.

30. Joseph S. Nye, Jr., "Multinational Corporations in World Politics," *Foreign Affairs* 53, no. 1 (October 1974): 174.

31. Oscar Schachter, "Just Prices in World Markets: Proposals De Lege Ferende," *American Journal of International Law* 69, no. 1 (1975): 101, 109; Mikdashi, "Policy Issues in Primary Industries".

32. The report is cited in note 1. The establishment of a Commission and Information and Research Center to deal with problems of transnational corporations is discussed in "Commission Will Serve as U.N. Forum for Considering Questions on Transnational Corporations," *U.N. Monthly Chronicle* 12, no. 3 (March 1975). For an earlier recommendation for the creation of such an agency, see Dudley Seers, "Big Companies and Small Countries: A Practical Proposal," *Kyklos*, 16 (Basel 1963). Various agencies of the United Nations have, for some time, been active in providing information relating to natural resource production to developing countries. See "The Use and Development of Natural (Non-Agricultural) Resources," in *United Nations Yearbook* 1965 ff. (Office of Public Information, United Nations).

33. "United Nations Economic Observatory," (U.N. doc. A/AC.166/L.35/Rev.1), 29 April 1974, reported in *International Legal Materials* 13, no. 3 (May 1974): 737.

34. *Report of the Commission of Enquiry into Concessions* (Accra, Ghana: Government Printer, 1961), p. 6.

35. Norman Girvan, "Making the Rules of the Game: Company-Country Agreements in the Bauxite Industry," *Social and Economic Studies* 20, no. 4 (1971): 383.

36. Hal Sheets, *Disaster in the Desert* (1974), p. 60.

37. See note 20.

38. Shoup, "Taxation of Multinational Corporations," para. 81, pp. 29-30.

39. The Harvard Development Advisory Service has, for a number of years, provided a number of countries—including Liberia and Indonesia—with assistance in improving the terms of their contractual agreements with multinational corporations. See Joseph S. Nye, Jr., "Multinational Corporations in World Politics," *Foreign Affairs* 53, no. 1 (October 1974): 174.

40. In 1974 the U.S. Foreign Relations Subcommittee on Multinational Corporations held hearings on the feasibility of greater government participation in oil negotiations. "Government Role in Oil Questioned," *New York Times*, 7 June 1974, p. 47. See also "Washington's Role in Oil Industry Stirs Controversy," *New York Times*, 5 February 1975, p. 43.

41. See United Nations, General Assembly, *Declaration and Action Programme on the Establishment of a New Economic Order*, Sixth Special Session (April 9 to May 2, 1974) (U.N. doc. A/RES/3201) 9 May 1974, reproduced in *International Legal Materials* 13, no. 3 (1974): 715 ff.

42. Lon Fuller, "Mediation—Its Forms and Functions," *Southern California Law Review* 44, no. 2 (1971): 312.

43. Ibid., p. 318.

44. An experienced labor arbitrator has told this writer that he has long felt that an "information broker" is needed in negotiations between local governments and such negotiating units as police and fire associations. The misuse of statistics and data from other communities creates situations where the two parties are negotiating from either unsound or differing data bases.

45. See A.O. Adede, "The System for Exploitation of the 'Common Heritage of Mankind' at the Caracas Conference," *American Journal of International Law* 69, no. 1 (January 1975): 31.

46. Shoup, "Taxation of Multinational Corporations," para. 82, p. 30.

47. Ibid., paras. 98-99, p. 34.

48. Ibid., paras. 100-101, pp. 34-35.

49. This has been done in some unpublished materials. See Eldon G. Warner, "Mixed International Joint Ventures in the Exploration, Development, and Production of Petroleum" (Unpublished M.S. thesis, Sloan School of M.I.T., June, 1972); and Thomas R. Stauffer, "Economics of Petroleum Taxation in the Eastern Hemisphere" (Paper delivered at an OPEC seminar on International Oil and Energy Policies of the Producing and Consuming Countries, Vienna, June 30 to July 5, 1969).

50. For an analysis of the Liberian National Iron Ore Company Agreement and the financial implications of the government's equity-sharing arrangement, see Robert W. Clower et al., *Growth Without Development* (1966), pp. 203 ff.

51. Ibid., pp. 210 ff. (LAMCO Joint Venture).

52. See Raymond Vernon, "What Strategy for the Third World?" *Saturday Review*, 22 November 1969, p. 45.

53. Mark Bostock and Charles Harvey, eds., *Economic Independence and Zambian Copper* (1972), pp. 131 ff.

54. "Opting Out of Iron Ore," *West Africa*, 5 March 1973, p. 303; and *West Africa*, 30 April 1973, p. 577.

6

Managing the World's Ocean Resources: Problems of Equity and Efficiency

Lennart J. Lundquist

For more than three hundred years, from Hugo Grotius to Harry Truman, "freedom of the seas" was the dominating principle of the regime of the ocean. This principle implied the right of all states to use oceanic resources outside the tiny fringe of national territorial seas. Two premises underlay this right. The resources in question, as *res communis*, were not liable to appropriation or exclusive use by any single state. Furthermore, the resources were regarded as virtually inexhaustible. Since it never occurred to anyone that they needed to be conserved, there existed no justification for any restrictions on their free use. The principle was sometimes modified by bilateral agreements concerning certain fisheries and the limitations of navigation. But the general principle remained: States could extract and keep the ocean's natural resources as long as they did not claim permanent sovereignty or exclusive rights outside their territorial seas.

In 1945, President Truman set in motion the forces that have eroded this historic principle. The United States, Truman proclaimed, had inherent rights to jurisdiction over the continental shelf, i.e., the submerged land mass extending seaward from its coast. His purpose was to reserve exclusive rights to the minerals and hydrocarbon deposits believed to exist under the shelf. Truman did not claim "ownership" but only asserted that the United States had the right to resources on and under the continental shelf.

The Truman Proclamation—which was not intended to restrict other international uses of the ocean—led to even more extensive ocean claims among other states. In some instances, the territorial sea was unilaterally widened. Some countries, especially in Latin America, extended their claims of "exclusive rights" to exploitation - of oceanic resources as far as 200 nautical miles offshore.[1] The U.N. Convention on the Outer Limits of the Continental Shelf of 1958 codified as a rule that coastal nations have the exclusive right to oceanic resources on and under the continental shelf out to a depth of 200 meters, or as far as their technological capabilities permit effective exploitation. In the years since, scientific discoveries of new oceanic resources, rapid technological developments that have enhanced nations' capabilities for effective exploitation, and a dawning recognition that ocean resources are limited have given rise to an

I am grateful to several people who shared their "common pool" of knowledge and intellectual resources by commenting on earlier drafts of this chapter: Gerald Garvey, Leon Gordenker, Sverker Gustavsson, Jeffrey Hart, Jan Kolasa, Lars Nyberg, and Nicholas Onuf. However, they do not share in "common" any responsibility for lingering inconsistencies or deficiencies of the chapter; that I consider my private "enclosure."

107

accelerating trend toward national "enclosure" of oceanic areas. In the ongoing U.N. Law of the Sea Conference, the concepts of large "economic zones" and "fisheries zones" spanning 200 nautical miles offshore have gained majority acceptance.

Parallel to the enclosure trend has been another, also within the U.N., toward establishing the ocean outside of national jurisdictions as a "common heritage of mankind," and thus to be exploited exclusively for the benefit of mankind as a whole. In 1970, a resolution to this effect was passed by the U.N. General Assembly. Since the "common heritage" concept was made contingent on the width of the space claimed by the enclosure-minded coastal nations, much emphasis in the Law of the Sea Conference has been put on the assignment of property rights and on the demarcation of boundaries.

The clash between the concepts of commons and enclosures can also be seen in the light of the theory of collective goods and common property resources. A collective good has low appropriability, suggesting a serious "imperfection in property title." But unlike some of the other characteristics of collective goods, appropriability can be imposed. Whether it will occur in fact has less to do with the intrinsic "nature" of the good than with the willingness of some authority, e.g., a coastal state government, to pay the costs of enforcing national claims to title or ownership. That there is such a willingness on the part of coastal nations is no surprise, even with a most cursory look at the resources at stake.

At Stake: The Amount and Future Importance of Oceanic Resources

The world ocean, covering 73 percent of the earth's surface, holds vast resources of vital importance to the future of mankind. The annual catch of commercially valued species of fish increased from 20 to 70 million tons between 1950 and 1970. According to some recent projections, the present catch provides twice the necessary protein intake of 4 billion people. Still, it represents only a fraction of the conservatively estimated maximum sustainable yield of between 120 and 200 million tons annually.[2] If conservation measures were successfully undertaken, the annual catch could increase by as much as 30 million tons in 1980, with the bulk of the increase expected to come from the presently underexploited southern world oceans, especially the Indian Ocean. Given the needed capital and technology, and a favorable outcome of issues concerning international versus national access to fisheries, the developing countries could double their fish supplies by 1985.[3]

At present, the hydrocarbon resources of the ocean are prime targets for national enclosure. After only twenty-six years of oil drilling beyond the sight of land, offshore oil and gas in 1974 accounted for 19 percent and 12 percent respectively, of total Free World production. Offshore production soared 38 percent in 1970-74, as compared to a 26 percent increase in total production. Offshore oil and gas reserves, which constitute as much as 50 percent of future hydrocarbon resources, may account for 45 percent of total oil production by 1990. Some 90 percent of this important oceanic resource is located on the continental margin at depths "where techniques of drilling and production are already available" or will soon be developed.[4] The greater costs of offshore production seem—at least for the time being—sustainable, given the surging demand for energy in the industrialized countries. Moreover, recovery of offshore hydrocarbons could lessen some countries' dependence on "uncontrollable" foreign oil. Present offshore oil production—at postembargo prices—represents an annual wellhead value of $40 billion.[5]

The mineral riches of the manganese nodules on the deep ocean floor are subjects of competitive interest by several potential exploiters. Ventures already underway evidence that any remaining technical problems of mining the nodules are soon to be solved. However, extraction of minerals from the recovered nodules is more complicated, and successful operations are not expected until the late 1970s. Given the concentrations of minerals in these nodules, a few successful mining operations could disrupt the current markets for cobalt and manganese, with important consequences for the economies of certain mineral-exporting developing countries.[6] Estimates of the potential of seabed production vary. Depending on the particular mineral, output could range from less than half of a percent up to 79 percent of total Free World production by the early 1980s.[7]

With such prospects, the drive toward national enclosure of ocean space becomes understandable. Some two-thirds of the nations attending the Law of the Sea Conference in the mid-1970s enjoyed the potential of gaining large enclosures for exclusive national resource exploitation—a fact that helps explain the acceptance of the "economic zone" concept—promising coastal nations exclusive rights to resources as far out as 200 nautical miles offshore. The strongest opposition comes from landlocked and shelf-locked countries.

If accepted as part of the new world order for the oceans, these economic zones would partition up to 90 percent of the known living and nonliving resources of the world seas from the commons of the oceans.[8] Thus, the perceptions of immediate windfalls to enclosing nations could create on a global scale new forms of such economic and social stratifications as have been the historical results of earlier enclosure movements.

But—possible as it may be in principle to nationalize benefits and revenues through more restrictive patterns of access to ocean resources—the enclosure concept nevertheless falls short of dealing effectively with the biological and ecological properties of the oceanic environment. The characteristics of water, the dominant part of ocean space, offer little hope of unilateral escape by any nation from such universal costs as marine pollution and resource depletion.

The staggering problem of future ocean resources management is to establish patterns of access and revenue allocation that are (1) accommodated to scientific knowledge about the character and capacity of the oceanic environment and its resources; (2) acceptable in terms of both economic efficiency and widely held notions of global equity and justice; and (3) compatible to the bewildering flora of "national interests" of sovereign states. What follows is a discussion in economic, political, and to some extent legal terms of the concepts of "enclosure" and "commons," measured against these criteria.

Access, Property Rights, and the Efficiency of Exploitation of Ocean Resources

The idea of ocean resources as common property, with access open to everybody on an equal and competitive basis, developed at a time when neither the number of users nor the state of the art of resource exploitation created any externalities or implied any necessary restrictions on access. Newcomers using the resources of the oceanic commons could do so without in any measurable way interfering with already established uses. Today, this situation has changed. As the number of users increases, and as technological innovation permits accelerated exploitation, individual utilization of oceanic resources increasingly restricts others' possibilities of using the same resources. Increasingly, individual exploitation also causes externalities, i.e., divergencies between private and social costs and benefits.

In economic theory this is called a "common-pool" problem caused by an "imperfection in property title," i.e., by the difficulty of identifying, keeping track of, and asserting property rights over some part of a common-pool resource. Each actor with access to the resource has an incentive to exploit today as much as possible in a profitable way. If the actor saves some of the resource by taking less now, other actors will come into the common pool to harvest the resources and capture its profits. This situation leads both to superoptimal rates of exploitation and to superoptimal allocation of capital and labor resources.[9]

Thus, the competitive private activity allowed by open access results in inefficient resource usage. In the face of market failure and externalities, some collective agreement among resource users is called for to achieve a more efficient and optimal economic outcome. But the characteristics of such agreements are not immediately obvious. Evident differences in the characteristics and location of oceanic resources, differences in the modes of resource use and production, as well as different legal and political developments create a complex web of future management issues.

Nowhere is the problem more complex than in ocean fisheries. Access to the resource is difficult to restrict on the grounds of "ownership" because fish cannot be contained within man-made boundaries. However, there are substantial biological and ecological differences among migratory, anadromous, and sedentary species. These differences point to the possibility—and perhaps to the necessity—of access agreements differentiated according to resource characteristics. Furthermore, the possibility of overfishing would seem to be a strong argument in favor of restricting access. But such restrictions would be very complicated, since one characteristic of species is that they are interdependent members of very complex ecosystems.[10]

With respect to economic efficiency, under the "open access" system of ocean fisheries, all fishermen have been able to enter the fisheries that seemed profitable. Technologically sophisticated distant-water fishing fleets from developed countries have moved across the ocean, swiftly fishing out promising grounds. Entry continues until the catches are far above the maximum sustainable yield, and the high sea fisheries are operating at a point where they produce little or no economic rent. Clearly, optimal utilization of the resource could be reached with considerably fewer fishermen entering the operations.[11]

From a strictly economic point of view, it would thus seem defensible to restrict access according to a combination of criteria (e.g., maximum economic yield, full utilization so as to reach an optimal number of operations for each fisher). In view of the enforcement costs of economically preferable alternatives, enclosure of a 200-mile fisheries zone would be acceptable. Ninety percent of the fisheries occur within that boundary. Highly migratory fish stocks, such as tuna and salmon, could be subject to separate regimes. A coastal state unable to fully utilize its enclosure could sell, grant, or lease to other nations rights to take optimal amounts of each fish stock. This would ensure proper conservation as well as exploitation by the most efficient fishermen (who could make the highest bids and thus win the rights). Where the common-pool problem extends over two or more enclosures, supranational agreements would be needed. To promote economic efficiency, however, such agreements should be bilateral or regional rather than global, since the latter alternative presumably involves higher decision-making costs.

The location of offshore hydrocarbon resources in the subsoil adjacent to coastal states makes them more amenable to exclusive national access and control. Indeed, as already noted, international law gives coastal states such exclusive rights out to a depth of 200 meters or else as far as technology allows efficient exploitation. This 200-meter limit "encloses" two-thirds of known offshore reserves. The proposed 200-mile enclosure would reserve about 90 percent of the offshore oil and natural gas for exclusive coastal state use, in some places by extending exclusive national access out onto the abyssal plain.[12]

Yet, like fisheries, offshore hydrocarbons present a common-pool problem since an oil reservoir can be emptied from any point on its perimeter. Two or more drillers can race to pump from the same pool, creating an externality by lowering the reservoir pressure and increasing pumping costs. Economic inefficiencies would also result as several exploiters tie up more capital and human resources than are necessary for an optimum rate of recovery. Since each producer in the pool knows that others may pump "his" oil if he moderates his take-rate, the inevitable outcome is that all pump too rapidly. However, it must be remembered that—apart from environmental quality problems—the relevant externalities extend only over a given pool. Producers may therefore have sufficient incentives to reach common agreements to internalize spill-overs, provided transaction costs are sufficiently low.

For the purpose of efficient offshore oil drilling, it would appear desirable to correct "imperfections in property title" through large coastal state enclosures that would allow the leasing of large tracts, thus eliminating much of the risk of a common-pool problem. Furthermore, should such problems occur, enclosures would allow for the adoption and enforcement of national municipal legislation and regulations. In the case of oil pools that cross the boundaries of two or more national enclosures, any economic inefficiencies could, as with fisheries, be reduced through bilateral and regional agreements.[13]

The characteristics of manganese nodules show some important differences from those of fish and offshore hydrocarbons. Nodules do not move around. Their reproduction rates are independent of the total existing stock of nodules. Nodules also differ from oil in that they do not flow from one site to another—i.e., they are divisible—and as a consequence, separate dredging operations do not interfere with one another. In effect, then, the externalities inherent in common-pool fisheries and oil reserves do not apply to manganese nodules. Finally, most nodules are located in the commons beyond the enclosable ocean. This situation calls for a somewhat different analysis of the relationship between international regulation and economic efficiency, especially since the other closer-in resources are already subject to different degrees of international regulation.

To the poor nations, the nodules would provide the backbone of the international seabed regime, i.e., the implementation of the "common heritage" concept. However, to miners and major powers, regulation of nodule exploitation through allotments of exclusive rights would minimize potential conflict, contribute to the avoidance of discrimination from land-based production, and promote easier financing of dredging operations. To some economists, too, regulation through the granting of exclusive rights to large tracts would help avoid suboptimization by preventing any common-pool problem.

But according to other economists, there should be as little regulation as possible.[14] No common-pool problem is possible in any case with nodules. And the free rider problem is exaggerated, since different nodule locations call for different mining technologies. Moreover, the discrepancy between the number of miners and the possible mining sites is large enough to make the opportunity costs of foregoing internally funded—and possibly successful—exploratory searches very high. These economists argue that inefficiency would be higher *with* than without international regulation. Not only would an international license clearinghouse give positive incentives to free riding, but revenue sharing between an international organization and the miner's home country would create several disincentives: higher taxes, possibly arbitrary site selection, high decision costs through cumbersome political decision-making processes, and the like. Furthermore, an international operating authority might create a regulatory situation conducive to inefficiency through politically determined protection of land-based mining and—as envisaged at present—involving high decision-making costs. Exponents of this view conclude that the costs of international regulation are positive and possibly large, while the costs of nonregulation—i.e., of retaining open access to the commons—are trivial and in some cases nonexistent. No regulatory activity is necessary as long as (1) there are enough first generation, prime mining sites; (2) the prospect of high capital outlays—$250-400 million per site—keeps the number of countries with the necessary technological capacity down; and (3) no existing nodule recovery technology monopolizes the mining market.

Thus, efficiency criteria, when applied to the different concepts of a desirable oceanic order—commons versus enclosures—suggest that aside from certain necessary international regulations for conservation and pollution control, national enclosures are indeed economically desirable for fisheries and hydrocarbon exploitation. With respect to manganese nodules, efficiency criteria seem to be better met by "masterly inaction" and preservation of free access than by international regulation through a global seabed regime that embodies the principle of "common heritage." Overall, where international regulation does seem needed, the efficiency criterion suggests bilateral or regional, rather than global, agreements.

But would a regime based on what is economically desirable also be politically feasible? In the cases of fisheries and offshore oil, enclosure is indeed acceptable to most nations, since they happen to be coastal states. But their arguments—especially those of developing coastal nations—are cast in terms of political self-interest and norms of equity rather than efficiency. To the landlocked countries, the concept of enclosures without transit and revenue-sharing guarantees is abhorrent.[15] And the proposal to let the technology-controlling nations play exclusive games with the manganese nodules—considered the backbone of the "common heritage of mankind"—is politically unacceptable to all developing nations, coastal and landlocked alike.[16] We now turn to the clash between the economic notion of efficiency and the political-legal concept of equity, and to the implications of the latter for a future ocean regime.

Revenue Sharing and the Equity of Distribution of Oceanic Resources

It is clear that the main factor underlying the endeavor of nations to establish favorable—or at least acceptable—patterns of access allocation is the desire to appropriate as much as possible of the potential revenues from ocean resource exploitation. An *ideal* system of "ocean revenue sharing" would be based on globally accepted criteria of equity and justice. Furthermore, it would be totally inclusive instead of making the receipt of benefits dependent on geographical location or on a nation's exercise of "exclusive" or "historic" rights to a resource. The establishment of such a system seems both difficult and improbable, and no attempt will be made here to outline one. Instead, we will look at present patterns of wealth distribution and their implications for the future, at the relations between different resources that may influence these patterns, and at different interpretations of "national interest" in light of the concepts of commons and enclosures.

A proper indication of the size of the expected net returns from oceanic resources would require detailed knowledge of the economics of production for each resource as well as for each region of the ocean. For simplicity's sake, the distributable wealth will be taken here as the 10 percent tax on the before-processing values of extracted resources, i.e., the landing value for fish, the wellhead value of oil and gas, and the onboard value of nodules. In 1974, the value of ocean fish landings was around $14 billion. Offshore oil represented a wellhead value of $40 billion, and natural gas just about $1 billion. Minerals extracted offshore accounted for just under $1 billion.[17] If 10 percent of $56 billion were equally distributed, every person in the world would get $1.40. But actually, the revenue would be much less, since many of the resources covered are exploited within already established national enclosures. It is notable that the early estimates of the expected wealth from exploitation of manganese nodules seem somewhat inaccurate.[18] Even in the unlikely event that deep ocean mining would replace all land-based production of copper, nickel, manganese, and cobalt, the revenue at a 10 percent rate would be no more than $1.5 billion, or seventy-five cents per capita to people in the developing world.[19] In actual fact, the estimated *total* value of annual nodule mineral production may just reach $425 million by 1981.[20] Thus, an international regime implementing the notion of the "common heritage" outside national enclosures would have very little to pass on to the needy of the world. Especially is this the case if such a regime were to regulate exploitation, and thus revenues, according to a principle that precluded the disturbing of the economies in those developing countries which already have large land-based production of nodule minerals. So barring any dramatic technological breakthroughs that would bring swift changes in the demand patterns for these metals, it is the resources of the continental margin that constitute the main source of revenue for the foreseeable future.

As already pointed out, a 200-mile enclosure of the oceans would grant the coastal nations exclusive rights to the revenues from as much as 90 percent of known living and nonliving resources of the world seas. However, efforts to change the legal regimes of the ocean according to the concept of enclosure have created several lines of conflict. Nations favored by the intricacies of the existing regime find it difficult to accept changes that would leave them with less revenue than they now get. The conflict between coastal nations and the land-locked countries turns on the proper boundaries between enclosures and the "common heritage": the larger the enclosure, the less revenue remains in the commons for noncoastal nations. Even among coastal nations, differences in levels of economic and technological development lead to conflicts over the proper regulation of ocean fisheries, especially between developing coastal nations and distant-water fishing countries such as Japan and the Soviet Union.

The 200-mile fisheries zones presently favored by coastal nations—sometimes "creamed" with preferential easements to states with "historic" rights and to developing countries—would drastically change patterns of access, and thus also revenues, where 120-mile zones have been the rule.[21] Arguing that enclosure would lead to underutilization of resources and lower productivity in the world's fishing industry, since so many of the developing coastal nations lack economic and technological "capacity of full utilization," distant-water fishing nations seek to retain as much as possible of the prevailing system of access and revenue allocation.[22]

Such arguments are understandable in light of the historic development of international fisheries regulations. Rapid technological innovations after 1950 led to overfishing, diminishing returns, and efforts to restrict entry to promising fisheries. Technologically advanced fishing nations have resorted to national quotas, systems of preferential rights, and various forms of regional agreements to keep new entrants out. Coastal nations which are heavily dependent on their fisheries, and developing coastal nations which want to preserve their fisheries for the future, have extended their exclusive fisheries zones.[23] Many of these restrictions have created severe political conflicts.[24]

The political complexity of fisheries regulation is compounded by regional differences: resource abundance and underutilization in the Indian Ocean; stock depletion and scarcity in the North Sea; basic cleavages between coastal and distant-water fishing nations in the East Central Atlantic.[25] These differences in capacities and utilization among different oceanic regions are important influences on the behavior of nations toward proposed changes in access and revenue patterns. The same is true for differences among species.

With respect to highly migratory species, countries such as Japan, the Soviet Union, and the United States, having invested large sums in distant-water fishing fleets, want decent returns on their investments. Since only 50 percent of the catch in Pacific and Atlantic areas bordering on North America is presently taken by North Americans, it is only natural that the United States asks for more exclusive patterns in these areas in return for any internationalization of revenues from the tuna fisheries.[26] Between 1966 and 1972, the fraction of the total marine fish catch coming from the "northern" and "central" areas of the Atlantic and Pacific increased from 69 to 70 percent, although these areas have only 61 percent of the estimated potential ocean catch.[27] The possibility of increasing revenues from the southern part of the ocean adds impetus to the developing coastal nations' drive for enclosure—the more so, in view of the fact that some of the underexploited areas are also the ones where the coastal nations' share of the catch, and hence of the revenue, is the least. Thus, African coastal nations take only half of catches in the profitable grounds outside West Africa. And the coastal state catch in the Indian Ocean is under 90 percent. It is not to be wondered, then, that coastal nations in such areas invoke equity concepts to get enclosure when they see that the 200-mile-claiming South American coastal nations already cover practically all of the catch in ocean areas adjacent to them.[28]

By denouncing on equitable grounds a system of revenue allocation based on the efficiency of technologically advanced distant-water fishing fleets, the developing coastal nations are on a collision course with the distant-water fishing nations. In fact, Japan and the Soviet Union alone accounted for 68 percent of the total increase in fish landings between 1966 and 1972. A substantial amount of this increase was acquired through distant-water fishing operations.[29] In view of strong consumer demands in many developed nations—demands that resulted in a doubling of their deficits in international trade of fish products between 1966 and 1972—it is likely that these countries will make efforts to retain as much as possible of their "historic" rights to oceanic fisheries. Conversely, since the developing countries doubled their net revenue from international trade in fisheries during the same period, they are likely to implement enclosure concepts as soon as possible.[30] It is indeed ironic that arguments for the prevailing system of access and revenue allocation are so heavily based on inapplicable concepts of free competition and efficiency, while the developing countries argue for enclosure on grounds of equity when they could use arguments of economic efficiency to support their position.[31]

In terms of revenue allocation, a global 200-mile enclosure would not change much of the prevailing pattern for oceanic hydrocarbon resources. It would serve mostly to reaffirm the existing system under which coastal nations have exclusive rights to offshore oil and gas out to the 200-meter limit or as far as is technologically practicable and economically feasible to drill. Even if hydrocarbon deposits were found outside the 200-mile enclosure,[32] the chances of economically recovering such deposits in the next few decades seem slim. The increasing costs of production from deeper wells would simply leave less revenue to distribute as a "common heritage."[33] To yield any substantial benefits for the international community, oil production outside a 200-mile enclosure would have to operate under even more favorable market conditions than those prevailing in the postembargo era.

In this era, who would benefit from enclosure? Although the embargo intensified exploratory activities throughout the coastal world, it is still true that the OPEC countries hold three-fourths of known offshore oil reserves. But they accounted for only two-thirds of offshore production in 1974. Thus, their share of revenues may increase in the future.

The situation is not entirely comforting to the major energy-importing nations. The United States has 6.5 percent of known resources, but 16.6 percent of actual production,[34] indicating that the exploration of the Atlantic will probably not await constitutional judgments or environmental decisions. The North Sea oil fields will not make Europe self-sufficient. However, Norway is reportedly having trouble absorbing the offshore revenues with its small economy.[35]

The postembargo market situation seems more favorable to developing coastal nations. The surging demand has led to stiffened competition among exploring companies, enabling developing coastal nations to obtain increasingly favorable conditions in concession agreements. The risks increasingly fall on the explorers, while more of the revenues go to the coastal nation which lets the concession.[36] No wonder, then, that coastal nations, developed and developing alike, are inclined to reject any internationally inclusive revenue allocation arrangements which would impinge on their present rights and future prospects.

But is enclosure the answer to developing nations' quest for rapid economic development and for a more equitable distribution of global wealth and oceanic revenues? And what about the prospects of the land-locked developing nations?

The answer to these questions is, as one observer put it, "doubly ironic" in view of the fact that the United States has been promoting "internationally acceptable" solutions, while the developing countries have pressed hardest for recognition of the 200-mile enclosure. Under a 200-mile zone, thirty-five countries will acquire half of the total ocean space to be enclosed. Among these thirty-five are ten developed nations, including the United States, the Soviet Union, Canada, Australia, New Zealand, and Norway. Among themselves, these ten would share 30 percent of the 200-mile enclosure. The United States stands out as the most benefited single nation from an international acceptance of enclosure. Only a small number of developing countries will benefit—those with both long coastlines and abundant offshore resources. "The big losers," A. Hollick has observed, "will be the land-locked and shelf-locked nations, countries with short coastlines, and countries with comparatively few resources off their coasts—a group of nations which includes among its numbers the poorest countries in the world."[37]

The problems of revenue sharing and equity inherent in the notions of enclosure and commons thus produce some paradoxes. The concept of "common heritage," implying an international regime for the oceanic resources outside national jurisdiction, is most emphatically supported by the developing nations. At the same time, a majority of these nations fervently support the notion of a 200-mile enclosure, would drastically reduce both the economic viability of an international seabed regime and the revenues potentially distributable from the "common heritage." And although enclosure is frequently supported in terms of global equity, it would actually compound global inequities by benefiting the already rich—who, furthermore, have the technologies in hand with which to utilize their economic zones—much more than the poor and needy nations, which even lack the exchange with which to buy the necessary technology.

Still, the coastal nations of the world—which are in the majority—will most likely implement the concept of enclosure. However defensible from the viewpoint of economic efficiency, this enclosure would have severe political ramifications. In addition to accentuating the gap between rich and poor nations, it would create new divisions among the developing countries by splitting the coastal and landlocked nations. Furthermore, the establishment of direct boundaries in the ocean would lead to increased interdependence and potential conflict, as one nation's appropriation of oceanic wealth would influence how its neighbors develop their own enclosures.

That outright national enclosure would thus compound already existing global, regional, and local problems makes it necessary to seek new approaches to ocean resources management. To promote efficiency, these alternatives should be on a level less inclusive than a global commons, which has been shown to create certain inefficiencies. To promote equity and satisfy national interests, the approaches should be on a level more inclusive than that of national enclosure. Finally, the alternatives should be compatible with the ecological wholeness and the resource characteristics and configurations of different parts of the world ocean.

Partial Reconciliation Through Regional Management of Oceanic Resources

A major consequence of national enclosure would be the internationalization of new tensions and strains within existing regional blocks and alliances. This regionalization of critical management problems is especially salient in geographically enclosed or semienclosed areas of the world ocean—areas that are not large enough to allow the full extension of the coastal nations' claim for 200-mile enclosures.[38] In most cases, the ocean regions subject to overlapping claims correspond to the oceanographic concept of marginal seas or small ocean basins. More or less surrounded by land, such basins form distinct physical, biological, and ecological entities. Often rich in sediments, they hold prospects of large hydrocarbon findings. They also frequently display high rates of biological productivity.[39]

The physical "closedness" of a basin usually indicates a high degree of human utilization not only for resource extraction but also for transportation, recreation, and waste disposal. Thus, the highly resourceful marginal seas and small sea basins are also the ocean regions most exposed to economic and social activities that are potentially detrimental to their resource productivity. The same is true also for other ocean regions on the continental margin, such as bays and areas off concave coastlines. In the following discussion of regional ocean management, the basin concept will be used to cover all these ocean regions, without in any way discriminating against regional arrangements that might be devised or develop along open coastlines.

It can also be shown that individual enclosures may lead to superoptimization, externalities, and market failures. Coastal nations eager to realize revenues from their enclosures could very well allow such a number of licensees—fishermen and oil producers—into their individual parts of the basin as to make resource exploitation superoptimal and inefficient for the sea basin as a whole. These international externalities are such that benefits and costs alike generally taper off from a given point of origin rather than being spread equally among the members of the global community. Therefore, one should not jump to the conclusion that these externalities should be dealt with at the highest possible level of international agreement. Instead, one might look to the trade-off models developed in the economic theory of fiscal federalism. These models address the question of the optimal level of governmental intervention and regulation. In general, theories of fiscal federalism stress the importance of less than all-inclusive regulation, unless it can be shown that such regulation has substantial inherent cost savings. More specifically, the trade-off model of "governmental interdependence" deals with externalities occurring across national boundaries and suggests the internationalization of externalities at a somewhat more centralized level than the purely national.[40] Efforts to solve problems of externalities and inefficiency at the regional or basin level will probably meet many of the criteria for rationality and efficiency set forth in these theories of fiscal federalism.

But enclosure could also lead to suboptimization, since there will be mismatch between the scale and cost of certain technologies and the individual size of basin-state economies and enclosures. The costly technology of offshore hydrocarbon exploitation is in most cases not indigenously available to small coastal states. The capital costs in the North Sea fields run as high as $4,000 per barrel, and the plateau output must be at least 150,000 barrels per day to make exploitation profitable.[41] Not only may these costs be prohibitive to many developing nations, but it is possible that the size of individual enclosures in small sea basins will be too tiny to host deposits capable of justifying the needed production investments. Such nations would find themselves in an unfavorable position vis-à-vis technology-controlling nations and corporations. On the other hand, it could be argued that production costs depend mainly on water depth and distance offshore. Hence the narrow, shallow sea basins may be relatively cheap to exploit.[42] In any event, it would seem that basin-wide cooperation could avoid many of the inefficiency problems just mentioned.

In the case of sea basins surrounded by developing nations, some fascinating possibilities open up. These littoral states might be able to create basin-wide cooperative arrangements, clearing "property title" issues on a level beyond the national enclosure and joining in revenue-sharing agreements, as well as pooling skills and capital and creating common policies toward the technology-controlling exploiters. Such actions would represent an important step toward regional cooperation for economic development.[43]

But would economically desirable basin cooperation also prove politically feasible, especially when strong nationalist feelings are already coupled to the idea of enclosure?

In the last century and a half, international regionalism has primarily been conceived of in terms of land masses, not as cooperation among opposite coastal states in sea basins. And the historical experience of earlier basin integration, associated with strong empires extending their dominance—often by force—into the coastal areas and hinterlands of whole sea basins, has little appeal today. In terms of equity, several factors affect the political feasibility of basin-wide cooperation schemes. First, such schemes may create further differences between developed and developing countries. Second, developing coastal nations which under a truly global system of ocean management would qualify for significant shares of the revenues would, in effect, be donors under regional arrangements. Third, basin-wide arrangements are not necessarily inclusive of neighboring landlocked states.

Yet in some areas, political action toward basin cooperation is under way. Despite their political, economic, and ideological differences, the states around the Baltic Sea have embarked on a course of cooperation for basin resource management and environmental protection.[44] In the Mediterranean and the Caribbean, extensive studies of regional cooperation alternatives are under way.[45] Many law-of-the-sea proposals from developing nations reflect a far-reaching acceptance of regional cooperation among coastal and landlocked states and especially stress the need for states in a given region to control fully the oceanic enterprises operating within that region.[46] But there are also areas marked by political conflict over basin resources. In the Yellow and East China Seas, conflicting claims to the continental shelf by China, Japan, and Korea—plus joint development agreements between the latter two, but covering areas claimed by China—seemingly block basin-wide agreements for the near future.[47]

There exist no "natural" political units or "independent" functional contexts which easily lead to supranational arrangements, regardless of the will of sovereign nations. Multilateral regional cooperation occurs only when states recognize that national objectives cannot be achieved without such arrangements. Regional regimes to deal with resources displaying "collective good" or common-pool characteristics—such as fish, oil, and environmental quality—thus depend on national recognition that the exploitation lends a collective dimension to national behavior. The activities of one state are affected by, and have consequences for, other states. As this is recognized, collective arrangements may be seen as "cheaper" than unilateral action, i.e., the trade-off between the gains of regional cooperation and the costs of transferring national authority to a multilateral unit is seen as positive.[48]

The arguments over whether and when such recognitions will occur in the real world are well known. Some say it will come about only if a situation takes on crisis proportions. Others are more optimistic about the rationality of nations. My own view is that the multinational establishment of enclosures in small and narrow ocean regions will make the collective dimension of national behavior much more directly and easily recognizable. Boundaries in the sea will make the mutual interdependencies in dealing with common-pool resources so obvious that cooperative arrangements will evolve before crises occur.

No true precedent in international law and organization yet exists for comprehensive basin-wide management of resources with such diverse collective properties as fisheries, hydrocarbons, environmental quality, and "resources of use" such as transportation and research.[49] Legal and administrative problems must thus be approached by way of analogies and through such precedents as exist in more limited international agreements concerning supranational management of natural resources.

In essence, the implementation of national enclosures would bring littoral states around sea basins as closely together as is the case with opposite riparian states in international river basins. This analogy of a river or drainage basin comes close to reconciliating the concepts of commons and enclosures, since in river basins the riparian states enter into agreements regulating individual uses of a single common resource—water. Several concepts of river basin law could be transferred to sea basin agreements. The "community of cobasin states" concept introduces the possibility that some community members could act as trustees of other basin states in an effort to achieve an optimal utilization of basin-wide resources. The idea of "limited sovereignty" implies that cobasin states must limit their utilization of common-pool resources in such a way that other cobasin states will be also secured of their reasonable beneficial use. Although not identical to equitable division of resources, the concept of "equitable utilization" suggests a principle for the establishment of an acceptable division of access and revenues, based on "objective economic and social needs," "relative dependence on common resources," and "historic patterns" of access and revenue allocation.[50]

The river basin analogy provides no solution, however, to the problems of landlocked-state participation. Perhaps the more inclusive drainage basin concept could be used to assess the rights of up-river states to take part in the management of basin resources on a basis resembling that which governs such states' shares in the resources of rivers which flow into the basin.[51] To provide for economic efficiency of utilization and for equity in the sharing of revenues from common-pool resources such as oil and fisheries, cobasin states could use precedents in municipal oil law[52] and in international fisheries agreements.[53] Especially in the case of fish conservation, equity problems are crucial.

Since the utilization of different basin resources with different "collective" dimensions would be involved in a multiple-use basin regime, several critical administrative problems are raised. It will be necessary to coordinate activities with existing international ocean resource management agencies. Furthermore, the implementation of a plan for comprehensive sea basin management necessitates a rethinking of the "common heritage" concept, so as to divert it from the current focus on a single-use international seabed regime toward a more flexible multiple-use "ocean space" regime that would lock in with the different sea basin authorities.[54]

Sea basin regimes, then, present a way of reconciling the conflicting concepts of commons and enclosures. Such regimes would be consistent with efficiency criteria, in that they would present solutions to the problems of "imperfections in property title" and of market failures at a level likely to create the least costs in terms of information and decision making. They would also provide a vehicle for equitable sharing of common-pool resource revenues among cobasin states. But although they could provide possibilities for "cooperation for independence" among developing countries, they would *not* tend to create equity on a global level. Here arises a crucial question: Are the problems of the political economy of resource flows so different among different sea basins as to make the sea basin concept void of meaning as a common denominator for international cooperation? The answer seems to be that there are indeed collective goods and common-pool problems that are similar, if not identical, among basins around the world, thus implying a general validity of the concept for organizational arrangements.

This does not, however, mean that sea basin regimes cannot be coupled to different overarching purposes, depending on the international interdependencies that are seen as most crucial in different parts of the world. Thus, it may well be that sea basin regimes in the technologically advanced parts of the world will be closely linked to purposes of improving the quality of life by controlling those dimensions of science and technology which jeopardize it, while sea basin regimes in the developing world may be most intimately linked to purposes of rapid economic development and increased production of goods and services.[55]

Notes

1. A valuable description and analysis of the historical development of different ocean resource management concepts from the Truman Proclamation onward is found in L. Juda, *Ocean Space Rights: Developing U.S. Policy* (New York: Praeger, 1975).

2. FAO, *The Prospects for World Fishery Development in 1975 and 1985* (Fisheries Circular No. 118, Rome, June 1969). Cf. the discussion of different estimates in M.B. Schaefer, "The Resource Base: Present and Future," in E.M. Borgese, ed., *Pacem in Maribus* (New York: Dodd, Mead, 1972), pp. 113 ff.

3. United Nations, World Food Conference, Rome 5-16 November 1974,

Assessment of the World Food Situation: Present and Future (E/CONF/65/3), pp. 83 f., 93, 116; idem, *The World Food Problem: Proposals for National and International Action* (E/CONF/65/4), p. 77 f.

4. J. Birks, "Proven Resources of Offshore Oil Are Produced at Different Rates," *Offshore* 34 (June 1974): 66 ff.; see also "How Much Oil Under the Sea?" *The Petroleum Press Service* 40 (September 1973): 328 ff., and the different calculations summarized in Schaefer, "The Resource Base," pp. 103 ff.

5. The value is calculated from the 1973 production of 10.4 million barrels per day at a price of $10 per barrel. Cf. *Offshore* 34 (June 1974): 85, and *The Petroleum Economist* 41 (August 1974): 303. For an example of discussions of offshore oil and its implications for interdependencies in world economics, see, e.g., "Nordsee Öl: Rettung vor den Arabern?" *Der Spiegel* 28 (23 Dec. 1974): 28 ff.

6. Cf. A.L. Hammond, "Manganese Nodules (I): Mineral Resources on the Deep Sea-Bed," *Science* 183 (4124, 8 February 1974): 502 ff., and "Manganese Nodules (II): Prospects for Deep Sea Mining," ibid. (4125, 15 February 1974): 644 ff. See also J.N. Barkenbus, "International Implications of Manganese Nodule Mining," *World Affairs* 136 (Spring 1974): 306 ff., and R. Branco, "Rational Development of Sea-Bed Resources: Issues and Conflicts," *Ocean Management* 1 (1973): 49 ff.

7. U.S., Congress, Senate, Committee on Interior and Insular Affairs, *Mineral Resources of the Deep Seabed: Hearing before the Subcommittee on Minerals, Materials, and Fuels*, 93rd Cong., 2d sess., March 1974, p. 1013.

8. United Nations, General Assembly, *Economic Significance, In Terms of Sea-Bed Mineral Resources, of the Various Limits Proposed for National Jurisdiction* (Report of the Secretary-General, U.N. doc. A/AC.138/87), 4 June 1973.

9. Cf. the discussion in R.J. Sweeney, R.D. Tollison, and T.D. Willett, "Market Failure, The Common-Pool Problem, and Ocean Resource Exploitation," *Journal of Law and Economics* 17 (April 1974): 179 ff.

10. Cf. Schaefer, "The Resource Base," pp. 110 ff.

11. F.T. Christy, Jr., "Fisheries: Common Property, Open Access, and the Common Heritage," in Borgese, ed., *Pacem in Maribus*, pp. 194 ff.

12. Cf. T.M. Franck et al., "The New Poor: Land-Locked, Shelf-Locked and Geographically Disadvantaged States," *New York University Journal of International Law and Politics* 7 (Spring 1974): 45 ff.

13. Cf. the arguments put forth in L.B. Terr, "The 'Distance Plus Joint Development Zone' Formula: A Proposal for the Speedy and Practical Solution of the East China and Yellow Seas Continental Shelf Oil Controversy," *Cornell International Law Journal* 7 (December 1973): 59 ff.

14. The following discussion is based on R.D. Eckert, "Exploitation of

Deep Ocean Minerals: Regulatory Mechanisms and United States Policy,"
Journal of Law and Economics 17 (April 1974): 143 ff.; and Sweeney, Tollison,
and Willett, "Market Failure."

15. Cf. Franck et al., "The New Poor"; and E.D. Brown, "The 1973
Conference on the Law of the Sea: The Consequences of Failure to Agree," in
L.M. Alexander, ed., *The Law of the Sea: A New Geneva Conference* (Kingston,
Rhode Island: University of Rhode Island, 1972), p. 37.

16. See resolutions of the Council of Ministers of the OAU of 1971
(concerning fisheries and permanent sovereignty over natural resources) and the
1971 Resolution of the Ministerial Meeting of the "Group of 77," printed in S.
Oda, *The International Law of the Ocean Development: Basic Documents*
(Leiden: Sijthoff, 1972), pp. 361 ff. See further the *Santo Domingo Declaration*
concerning a "patrimonial sea" (U.N. doc. A/AC.138/80), 26 July 1972; and the
OAU *Declaration on the Issues of the Law of the Sea* (U.N. doc. A/CONF.
62/33), 19 July 1974.

17. For fisheries, see FAO, *Yearbook of Fisheries Statistics*, vol. 34 (Rome:
FAO, 1972), p. 4 f.; and ibid., vol. 35, pp. 26 ff. For crude oil, cf. note 5. For
natural gas, see U.S. Bureau of Mines, *Minerals Yearbook of 1972*, vol. 1
(Washington, D.C.: Government Printing Office, 1974), pp. 817 ff. For minerals,
see J.B. Rigg, "Minerals from the Sea," *Ocean Industry* 9 (April 1974): 213.

18. Cf. the introductory remarks in J.J. Logue, ed., *The Fate of the Oceans*
(Villanova: Villanova University Press for the World Order Research Institute,
1971), pp. xvi ff.

19. The calculation is based on 1973 average prices and production figures
for manganese, nickel, copper, and cobalt. It should be compared to a similar
calculation, based on 1967 prices and production figures, in F.L. Laque, "Deep
Ocean Mining: Prospects and Anticipated Short-Term Benefits," in Borgese, ed.,
Pacem in Maribus, pp. 143 ff.

20. U.S., Congress, Senate, Committee on Interior and Insular Affairs,
Mineral Resources of the Deep Seabed, p. 1013.

21. See proposals by Australia and New Zealand (U.N. doc. A/AC.138/
SC.II.L.11), 11 August, 1972, and by Canada et al. (U.N. doc. A/AC.138/
SC.II.L.38), 16 July 1973.

22. See proposals by the USSR (U.N. doc. A/AC.138/SC.II.L.6), 18 July
1972, and Japan (U.N. doc. A/AC.138/SC.II.L.12), 14 August 1972. See also
the discussion in A.W. Koers, *International Regulation of Marine Fisheries. A
Study of Regional Fisheries Organizations* (West Byfleet: Fishing News, 1973),
pp. 233 ff.

23. See FAO, *Limits and Status of the Territorial Sea, Exclusive Fishing
Zones, Fishery Conservation Zones, and the Continental Shelf* (Rome: Fisheries
Circular no. 127, 1971). For texts of bilateral and regional agreements, see S.H.
Lay et al., *New Directions in the Law of the Sea: Documents*, vol. 1 (Dobbs
Ferry: Oceana Publications, 1973), pp. 41 ff.

24. See, e.g., E.D. Brown, "Iceland's Fishery Limits: The Legal Aspect," *The World Today* 29 (February 1973): 68 ff.; P. Frydenberg, "Fiske-resursser—Kontrol og Konflikt i Nord-Atlanten," *Internasjonal Politikk*, no. 2 (April-June 1973): 375 ff.; D.C. Loring, "The United States-Peruvian 'Fisheries' Dispute," *Stanford Law Review* 23 (February 1971): 391 ff.; and different contributions to G. Pontecorvo, ed., *Fisheries Conflict in the North Atlantic: Problems of Jurisdiction and Enforcement* (Cambridge, Mass.: Ballinger, 1974).

25. D. Krieger, "The Oceans: A Common Heritage?" *Peace Research Reviews* 5, no. 6 (May 1974): 22 f.

26. FAO, *Yearbook of Fisheries Statistics*, vol. 34, pp. 522, 535, 549.

27. Cf. ibid., p. 522. See also J.A. Gulland, *The Fish Resources of the Ocean* (West Byfleet: Fishing News, 1971), p. 248.

28. FAO, *Yearbook of Fisheries Statistics*, vol. 34, pp. 522, 538, 540 f., 544 f., 552 f.

29. Ibid., pp. 4 f., 12 ff., 522 ff.

30. Ibid., vol. 35, pp. 32 ff.

31. Cf. Koers, *International Regulation of Marine Fisheries*, pp. 233 ff., 238 ff.

32. P.A. Rona, "New Evidence for Sea Bed Resources from Global Tectonics," *Ocean Management* 1 (1973): 153 ff.

33. Cf. Schaefer, "The Resource Base," p. 109 f.

34. According to *Offshore* 35 (January 1975): pp. 107 ff., offshore exploration drilling rigs were to 55 percent operating offshore developed countries by the end of 1974. For the U.S. figures, see ibid. 34 (20 June 1974): 85 ff.

35. See "Norway's Embarrassing Riches," *The Petroleum Economist* XLI (October 1974), pp. 367 ff. However embarrassed, Norway has nevertheless been a most ardent supporter of extended coastal state rights to offshore resources. Cf. U.N. doc. A/AC.138/SC.II.L.36 (July 16, 1973).

36. Cf. "From Concessions to Contracts I," *The Petroleum Economist* 41 (December 1974): 459 ff.; and "II: End of an Era," ibid. 42 (January 1975): 21 ff. Cf., however, D.N. Smith's contribution to this volume.

37. A. Hollick, "What to Expect from a Sea Treaty," *Foreign Policy*, no. 18 (Spring 1975): 71 ff. See esp. p. 71n and 76n.

38. For definitions of such geographically enclosed and semienclosed seas, see L.M. Alexander, "Regionalism and the Law of the Sea: The Case of Semi-enclosed Seas," *Ocean Development and International Law Journal* 2 (Summer 1974): 151 ff. See also U.N. doc. A/CONF.62/C.2/WP.1 (October 1974), p. 114.

39. K. Lomniewski, *Physical Oceanography* (Warsaw: Polish Scientific Publishers, 1973), p. 43 f.

40. For definitions and a general discussion, see W.E. Oates, *Fiscal Federal-*

ism (New York: Harcourt, Brace Jovanovich, Inc., 1972), pp. 33 ff.; and R.A. Musgrave, *Fiscal Systems* (New Haven: Yale University Press, 1969), pp. 296 ff. For special discussions of costs of collective decision making and "governmental interdependence," see G. Tullock, "Federalism: Problems of Scale," *Public Choice* 6 (Spring 1969): 19 ff.; and M.V. Pauly, "Optimality, 'Public' Goods, and Local Governments: A General Theoretical Analysis," *Journal of Political Economy* 78 (May-June 1970): 572 ff.

41. According to Birks, "Proven Resources of Offshore Oil," capital costs of North Sea oil were eight times higher than those of Middle East onshore oil in 1974. Cf. "Economics of North Sea Ventures," *The Petroleum Economist* 41 (December 1974): 446 ff., which gives a 10:1 ratio for the same capital costs.

42. Cf. "Economics of North Sea Ventures," p. 446 f., and the arguments in Terr, "The 'Distance Plus Joint Development Zone' Formula," p. 59.

43. This argument is made in D. Krieger, "A Caribbean Community for Ocean Development," *International Studies Quarterly* 18 (March 1974): 76. Whether such regional arrangements will also present solutions to problems of the stability of foreign investments in "enclosure" areas is highly uncertain. Cf. T. Stevens, "The Future and Our Continental Shelf and Seabeds," *Natural Resources Lawyer* 4 (1971): 647 ff. for statements of what "investment stability" means to energy corporations.

44. Bo Johnson, "The Baltic Conventions" (Lecture delivered before the Colloquium on International Law and the Environment arranged by the British Institute of International and Comparative Law, London, July 11, 1974 (mimeo).

45. D. Krieger, "The Oceans: A Common Heritage," pp. 31 ff. and 37 ff.; idem, "A Caribbean Community for Ocean Development," pp. 75-103. On Mediterranean cooperation, see also U.N. doc. A/CONF. 48/IWGMP.I/5, Annex VII (June 21, 1971).

46. See proposals by Kenya (U.N. doc. A/AC.138/SC.II.L.10), 7 August 1972; Uganda and Zambia (U.N. doc. A/AC.138/SC.II.L.41), 16 July 1973; the OAU *Declaration on the Issues of the Law of the Sea* (U.N. doc. A/CONF. 62/33), 19 July 1974; Jamaica (U.N. doc. A/AC.138/SC.II.L.55), 13 August 1973; Uruguay (U.N. doc. A/AC.138/SC.II.L.24), 3 July 1973; China (U.N. doc. A/AC.138/SC.II.L.34), 16 July 1973.

47. Cf. Terr, "The 'Distance Plus Joint Development Zone' Formula"; Choon-Ho Park, "The Sino-Japanese-Korean Sea Resources Controversy and the Hypothesis of a 200-Mile Zone," *Harvard International Law Journal* 16 (Winter 1975): 27-46. But cf. China's commitment to regional cooperation and solutions (U.N. doc. A/AC.138/SC.II.L.34), 16 July 1973.

48. For a discussion of the relationships between "collective" dimensions of state behavior and forms of international organization, see J.G. Ruggie,

"Collective Goods and Future International Collaboration," *American Political Science Review* 66 (September 1972): 886 ff.

49. The Baltic Conventions involve only management of fisheries and pollution abatement; cf. Johnson, "The Baltic Conventions." No agreements exist concerning joint development of seabed resources. In fact, the possibilities of oil deposits east of the Gotland island have stalemated the Swedish-Russian negotiations on continental shelf boundaries. Cf. *Oil & Gas Journal* 73 (January 27, 1975): 75.

50. The foregoing discussion is based on J. Lipper, "Equitable Utilization," Chap. 2 in A.H. Garretson et al., eds., *The Law of International Drainage Basins* (Dobbs Ferry, N.Y.: Oceana Publications, Inc., 1967).

51. Cf. M.I. Glassner's discussion of different means of securing access for land-locked states (international law, political and economic integration, and regional cooperation and development) and his assertion that international law can lay the groundwork, but not alone assure access; ". . . a solution to the question of access . . . must be sought in regional economic cooperation and regional development programs." M.I. Glassner, *Access to the Sea for Developing Land-Locked Countries* (The Hague: M. Nijhoff, 1970), Chap. VII, quotation p. 246.

52. Cf. Terr, "The 'Distance Plus Joint Development Zone' Formula," p. 67.

53. Cf. the arguments in C.T. Christy, Jr., "Fisheries Management and the Law of the Sea," in *Economic Aspects of Fish Production. International Symposium on Fisheries Economics, Paris, 1971* (Paris: OECD, 1972), pp. 21 ff.

54. E.M. Borgese, "Boom, Doom, and Gloom over the Oceans: The Economic Zone, the Developing Nations, and the Conference of the Law of the Sea," *The San Diego Law Review* 11 (May 1971): 549 f.

55. A very provocative analysis of "what should be coupled" and "what should not" in future international regimes is found in J.G. Ruggie and E.B. Haas, "Science and Technology: Reorganizing for the Evolution of International Regimes" (University of California at Berkeley: Institute of International Studies, 1975, mimeo).

Part IV
The Solutions to Scarcity II:
Applications of Science
and Technology

7

Global Resource Transfers: A Scientific Perspective

Lynton Keith Caldwell

Science, which historically has served as handmaiden to technological, political, and economic interests in global natural resources transactions, is now, almost for the first time, also being independently applied to prognosis of the future. It continues to be applied to the discovery and exploitation of minerals and to the harvesting of living resources, animal and vegetable. It has revolutionized traditional agriculture and greatly increased the availability of energy for all human purposes. But science is now being applied analytically to relationships between human societies, their environments, and their natural resources.[1] Such analysis is implicitly predictive, and in the modern world, science-based prediction has been a force for change. Scientific assessment of future prospects for resources in relation to needs and demands has already profoundly affected international relationships. And it seems probable that the impact of science on global resources transactions will be even greater in the future.

There is an obvious risk in generalizations regarding the behavioral consequences of new knowledge with predictive implications. Scientific findings that imply a chain of consequences may speed the actualization of those consequences. But they may also stimulate efforts to avoid or reverse them. Thus, scientific knowledge regarding the available supply, the distribution and consumption, and the probable demand for various natural resources has influenced the behavior of supplier and consumer nations. The advent of price-controlling cartels among the less developed nations appears to correlate with their "discovery" of estimated depletion rates of various materials in relation to the apparently indefinitely escalating materials demands of the developed nations.

Science-based information on international resources reserves initially worked almost wholly to the advantage of the developed nations or their corporate infrastructures. Private companies with scientific exploratory capabilities developed information regarding the location, quantities, qualities, accessibility, and demand for the natural resources of nations. But until recently, few national governments had this information. The user nations were thus advantaged until scientific information generated by international experts and organizations, revealed the extent of their dependence on foreign suppliers. The effect of this awareness on political behavior was illustrated dramatically by the Arab oil embargo of 1973. Much of the force of David Smith's proposal for the institutionalization of this process of scientific information exchanges lies in the contribution it would make to a more equitable balancing of power and responsibility in the pricing and allocation of natural resources.

131

Demonstration of the developed nations' vulnerability has fired ambitions and latent resentments among the less developed countries, reinforcing demands for redistribution of the world's wealth and resources and leading to the Special Session of the General Assembly of the United Nations in the summer of 1974 that declared the advent of a new world economic order.[2] But the declaration may have been premature. The circumstances and assumptions upon which it was based were hardly less vulnerable than previous conditions had been to radical changes in international relationships following from changes in scientific information. In brief, Third World euphoria over newly found political and economic advantage might stimulate a countervailing reaction. The discomfiture of the developed nations has already spurred science-based efforts to reduce their dependence on external sources of essential fuels and materials.

Propositions regarding the political and economic consequences of the uneven distribution of supply and demand for resources should therefore be framed with caution. Crystalized assumptions concerning the character, substance, and the extent of global interdependence may be flawed or even shattered by science-based innovations that theretofore have been unforeseen because no one troubled to look for them. The present state of scientific capability in the world *does not indicate that the distribution and demand for natural resources will inevitably compel a greater international interdependence.* In the short run, and for some nations, it may. But as Gerald Feinberg's chapter makes clear, the opposite effect is also possible, and in the long run, at least in the United States, dependence on external materials resources might dramatically be reduced.

The Earth and the World: Contrasting Global Realities

It is axiomatic that attitudes, behaviors, and institutional arrangements are influenced by how matters are perceived and evaluated. Confusion among perceptions, and inferences drawn from those perceptions, may contribute to error in human judgment. Theories of human and international relations have been especially susceptible to perceptual confusion and misapplied knowledge. Humans find objective appraisal to be most difficult when applied to humanity itself. It has therefore followed that accurate descriptions of the evolved earth have been misconstrued and often misapplied in propositions regarding human relations and international policies. This generalization especially applies to policies on the possession, distribution, and use of natural resources.

A common error in global perception has been the extrapolation of the interrelatedness and ultimate unity of the evolved earth and the world of man. The natural systems of the earth aggregate to form a biophysical planetary unity, whereas the nations of man aggregate to a discordant diversity. The concept of "one world" is thus a moralizing misapplication of the demonstrable unity of nature's earth to the obvious disunity of man's world.

Propositions regarding international relations are characteristically weighted with assumptions and assertions derived from moral philosophy. Allegations regarding just and equitable distribution of natural resources—allegations concerning who owes what to whom—are commonplace in the literature of international economic relations. But they are statements of moral conviction rather than of empirical necessity.

Although alien to the scientific perspective, the concepts of *justice-injustice* and *equity-equality* must be included in a holistic view of the politics of global resources transfers. These concepts may confuse tragedy with injustice and equity with equality and may postulate goals that will not be realized in the real world. Nevertheless, they may in the short run influence global resource transfers more powerfully than the aggregate of scientific understanding. One need not accede to those moral claims or accept them as valid. But they are facts that a scientific perspective must take into account. In order to discover what rational alternatives there may be in coping with the problems of international resource flows, it is necessary first to have an accurate picture of the physical systems through which these resources move and second to understand realistically the human systems, including their irrational aspects that influence the course of this action.

Let us then first examine the earth as described by science. The planet and its natural systems have evolved over millions of years through mutually interactive, self-organizing processes. The atmosphere, oceans, and continents have evolved to a present condition which is neither immutable nor eternal.

In the inorganic phase of this evolution, geologic processes involving pressure and heat concentrated various mineral substances in the upper crust. Liquified metallic ores were squeezed into pressure cracks, forming veins which human ingenuity would one day discover and mine. But these deposits were unevenly distributed, occurring only where the conditions of geophysical stress were condusive to the formation. Similarly, deposits of coal, limestone, and petroleum were formed only where conditions permitted. Although the perception of these substances as "resources," and hence as potential wealth, is a cultural phenomenon, their distribution is explained by geophysical events that have nothing whatsoever to do with the industry, merit, or deservedness of the people who subsequently have asserted "ownership" over them.

The so-called living resources of the earth comprise the organic biosphere. In organic evolution, natural systems developed in numbers and complexity until human interposition altered and accelerated natural selection, multiplied the rate of extinctions, and began a radical simplification of ecosystems in the processes of agriculture and urbanization. Organisms and ecosystems have the capacity for self-renewal within certain limits of tolerance. But extinction follows when these limits are transgressed.

Ecological systems, however, have homeostatic capacities to adapt to change and restrain uncontrolled growth. Cancerous growth destroys individual organisms, but ecosystems have generally evolved in ways that prevent or correct such destructive tendencies at the level of the ecological community.

But the human species emerged as an apparent exception. During the most recent geologic epoch, which we call the Pleistocene, this species invented culture and, through it, escaped the ecological controls that kept other animal populations in check. This is not to say that humanity has irrevocably escaped ecological controls. Rather, it has used technology to enlarge its niche in the biosphere. Man has discovered elasticities in the so-called laws of nature, but the ultimate parameters that set the conditions for life and survival have not changed. Transgression of these parameters carries penalties for which there is neither suspended sentence nor pardon. Christians, Jews, and Marxists may rail at the injustice of nature, but none of them have yet succeeded in imposing their moral judgments upon the execution of natural laws.

Science is progressively revealing ways in which the earth of nature differs from the world of man. But so-called primitive or precivilized peoples, whose world primarily *was* the earth, often sensed intuitively processes and relationships that modern man has "discovered" more precisely through science. Some of these properties of the earth are fundamental to man's environmental relationships and to his management of natural resources. Ancient and primitive folkways often acknowledged these properties of nature. But modern political theory is curiously innocent of any substantial influence from the findings of modern science. Excepting possibly Engel's dialectics of nature,[3] almost nothing in the political thought of the nineteenth and twentieth centuries would not have made sense to Plato.

Our scientific knowledge of the natural world has been enlarged and refined with respect to the dimensions and periodicities of time and space. For example, since Planck and Einstein, the relativity of time and space has become common information if not common understanding. Scientific concepts such as critical mass, threshold effects, lead times, lag times, and critical paths have been adapted to industrial and military uses, but rarely to civil government, policy, or law. And in a human world in which social disorder appears to be expanding exponentially, the unsophisticated sense of time prevailing among decision makers in national capitals should be viewed as frightening. A nation today incurs enormous risks when its governors believe that clocks and calendars tell them the time in all of the ways in which they need to understand it. That governments and nations have fallen because their rulers did not know how to tell the time is hardly news. But future historians may puzzle over the apparent failure of modern political leaders to apply what science could teach them about the relationships of time, space, and change in the world of human affairs.

Equally astonishing is the apparent failure of modern economic or political thought to have learned anything from science regarding the processes of growth. The ultimate absurdity of contemporary political-economic debate is the growth-no-growth controversy. The *growth* in English covers too many meanings and invariably requires a modifier if its meaning is to be clear. In their report to the Club of Rome, Mesarovic and Pestel distinguished organic from cancerous growth.[4] Other studies have distinguished selective from undifferentiated growth and have identified various forms of controlled growth as cyclical, renewal, guided, or ecological.[5]

In the biosphere, growth in the ecological sense is a concomitant of life (and also, of course, of death). The economy of nature can never for long assume a no-growth status, because the laws under which life has evolved require "renewal growth" to offset the inexorable forces of decay, the most basic of which is described in the second law of thermodynamics.[6] But growth can never for long be exponential. Expansive growth is eventually curbed by natural countervailing forces which, in drastic instances, may entail the extinction of overgrowing organisms. Utopian and optimistic opinion to the contrary notwithstanding, science gives us no reason to believe that modern society, or indeed mankind generally, has secured a perpetual dispensation from nature exempting it from these constraining forces.

In summary, scientific perspectives on the properties of the earth that set the terms for the survival of man's world suggest the following:

The continuing drama of the biosphere is the struggle between the forces of organization and disorganization—between life and order, and death and disorder. At the physical base of this "conflict" is the thrust of the order-seeking or negentropic tendencies of nature, counteracting the randomizing or order-destroying entropic tendencies of energized matter.[7]

The biosphere may not be unique in the universe, but it represents a highly improbable state of being. The fitness of the earth for life is unique as far as humanity is concerned. This terrestrial environment has two contrasting characteristics: *the vulnerability of its evolved temporal conditions and ecosystems, and the immutability of its basic elements and parameters.* Mankind can, in some measure, influence the biosphere and guide its continuing evolution. But the geophysical earth is governed by laws beyond human control—which may, however, be employed to serve human purposes, provided that man conforms to their exactions. Thus, the energies of the sun and the atom may be utilized, provided that mankind learns how to obtain and deploy their power safely.

Although it may be conceded that man's view of the earth is determined by his perceptual capabilities, there is nevertheless a discrete earth and ecosphere with a reality independent of human volition. The world of man, on the other hand, is a human invention and has no existence apart from man and his institutions. This dualistic concept of earth and world is not a mere play upon words, but is built into many aspects of man-environment relationships. There is a metaphysical aspect to the earth-world dualism that is explained by the presence of man's world on the earth. Earth and world share a partial common identity. Mountains, rivers, and iron ore deposits belong to both. Sovereignty, natural boundaries, and political ideologies are of the world, but not the earth.

The earth and its ecosystems are objects of investigation by the "natural" sciences. The world and its attributes are studied by social and behavioral scientists, by humanists, legalists, and historians. The object of their concern is the sociosphere—the realm of human societies and culture. Their concern with the earth is its relationship to the world. The geochemist studies the material substance of the lithosphere, but the economist views the same material as productive soils and minerals. From the earth's forests comes timber; from marine ecosystems, seafood; from rivers, water power, transportation, and water supply for industrial, domestic, and agricultural uses. Thus, in a man-centered structure of relationships and values, certain elements of the natural world are redefined as resources.

In the world of politics and economic affairs, this utilitarian perspective on resources assumes a greater relevance and reality than does the natural world itself. Man's beliefs, values, and commitments have greater worldly significance than do natural materials and forces. Yet the natural factors act upon, and interact with, these cultural factors, and some of the errors of man's economic and environmental policies may have occurred for lack of an integrated or holistic perception of the interrelationships involved.

The time has now arrived when humanity can no longer safely continue to act upon a split view of reality. If the economic and ecological problems of modern society are to be faced effectively, man's world must be made consistent with the realities of the earth, including its limits and requirements for renewal.

Difficulties of Dual Perspectives

To look through binoculars, each lens of which was set at a different calibration, would surely be to see a distorted image. The viewer's tendency might be to look through one eyepiece or the other, selecting whichever ocular gave him the more satisfactory view. This circumstance may be analogous to the two principal alternatives for viewing the human environment—*the scientific view of the earth and the humanistic view of the world.* Some people see the world from both viewpoints but cannot obtain a clear or congruent image as long as the calibrations of the lenses differ. To obtain an undistorted view, both oculars must be brought into a common focus.

Oversimplified as this analogy is, it nevertheless illustrates the difficulty of obtaining a reliable perspective from viewpoints that are inconsistent. To see the situation of mankind clearly, the scientific and humanistic viewpoints must be brought together to form a unified perspective on the earth and the world. In short, the separate images must be as consistent as possible with each other as well as with the reality that is perceived. The perspective of political economy should be consistent with that of science, and the science perspective should be holistic—should provide a synthesized view of the biophysical reality in which the world exists.

Unfortunately, the viewpoints afforded by nearly all of the distinct sciences are partial. The sciences are specialized and reductionist. The reductionist methods of the physical sciences help us to learn more and more about less and less. But it is not their function to assist us in seeing the earth as a whole. Comprehensive, inclusive views of the earth are provided by only two sciences—geography and ecology.

All of our sciences, including the social and behavioral, show deficiences in systematization and synthesis. Our image of man in relation to his social environment is singularly inadequate; we have no adequate organizing concept for uniting the findings of the several sciences in an integrative science of mankind. And there are major gaps in our knowledge. For example, our image of man fails to reveal either the parameters of his capabilities for cooperation or the limits of his tolerance for interdependence. It does not define the possible limits to human organizational and administrative skills. How far can man be counted on to control and guide the expanding, increasingly complex tendencies of human society? Are there, as Arthur Koestler (among others) has suggested, congenital limitations in the capability of the human brain to handle either the information or the psychic stress needed to cope with the problems that modern man has created for himself?[8]

Our purpose does not require a comprehensive listing of the ways in which past applications of science to resource policies have been inadequate or misleading. Several illustrations of major difficulties will suffice.

Misleading consequences of efforts to apply science to resource policy have resulted paradoxically from efforts to obtain precise measurements—to quantify information. Statistical data, when adequately descriptive of what they represent, are essential to rational decision making. But statistics are highly abstract and simplified descriptions of selected aspects of reality. As with remotely sensed orbital satellite data on resource distribution, statistics must be tested against "ground truth." The graphs, charts, and tables on resource availabilities and flows must be checked periodically against actual physical reality. Yet sophisticated economists, business executives, and public officials often reveal a naive reverence for statistics inadequately checked against the reality that they are purported to represent. This tendency toward an uncritical faith in statistical information may account for some of the failures of expectation and prediction in studies of resource economics. International development planning has been especially vulnerable to misleading inferences drawn from statistical data that were inadequate to support the decisions based upon them.[9] Misuse of statistics may, of course, occur when data valid for one purpose are applied inappropriately to another. The most notorious illustration from the American experience is the popular interpretation of gross national product as an indicator of national economic "health."

A second illustration of the failure of the scientific perspective to serve policy needs has already been suggested—the reductionist and specialized character of science, which often causes its truths to be of limited applicability. For example, reliable information on the availability of particular resources may fail to inform decision makers of the costs of obtaining them. Thus, assurances that the world is not about to "run out" of minerals may be based on the assumption that energy and technology will be available to extract them from seawater or granite and that the consequences—ecological, economic, and aesthetic—will be tolerable.

Gerald Feinberg's chapter makes a case for early development of technologies that may avoid future materials shortages and suggests that equity in resource use may extend to future generations, not merely to the contemporary inhabitants of the earth. Yet, to obtain minerals through massive applications of energy to pulverizing rock may truly be doing things the hard way. A broader view of the materials needs of the future would consider the levels of population that the present generation will bequeath the future. From the broader perspective of science, the technology most likely to ensure that mankind's materials needs can be met in the year 2100 is one that would reduce the population of the globe to somewhere around one billion per capita by that date.

A third problem in applying science to resource policy is that the state of scientific knowledge has been, to a large extent, determined by the particularized purposes of the people who paid for its advancement. We have noted the tendency of science to be used as a servant rather than a teacher—a tendency implicit in Western society and Marxist ideology. This is not to suggest that the diversion of science to commercial, industrial, and military purposes is intrinsically a misapplication of knowledge. Such diversions are not necessarily perversions. But to the extent that they represent the justifications for scientific research and development, they may account for the adequacy of science to answer some questions rather than others. Yet, even if the scientific research were brought into a balance more congruent with human needs, it does not follow that science could compensate for all human improvidence. There may well be limits to man's ability to extend, organize, and apply scientific knowledge. An important question to ask of science as a teacher is *how far science can (or should) be relied upon as a servant.*

An obvious difficulty in applying scientific perspectives to reality is the vulnerability of science (along with other forms of knowledge) to distortion by values, especially by political values. The argument (which is valid in principle) that reality can never be free from bias has been used to excuse the politicization of science. Marxism is notably, but not uniquely, guilty of this fraudulent use of knowledge. There is also a tendency in some less developed countries to view science as a peculiarly Western form of knowledge, prejudicial (as indeed it has often been) to the communal and ethnic values of non-Western people.

Insofar as scientific perspectives contribute to a more valid understanding of global resource needs and uses, four problems require attention.

First is the need for a conceptualization across disciplines of man's relationships with the earth. This implies a better balancing of the reductionist or analytic capabilities of science by an enlarged capacity for synthesis. Expressions of skepticism that multidisciplinary synthesis is feasible may be countered by the proposition that, unless this occurs, the prospect that modern society can cope with its difficulties is not encouraging.

The second problem is that of objectification. Imputation to Thomas Kuhn's *The Structure of Scientific Revolutions*[10] notwithstanding, the general direction of scientific thought has been toward obtaining the closest approximation to a valid understanding of objective reality. Wholly instrumental interpretations of science reduce the possibility that science-based information will either be objective or be used objectively. Persons who look to science to serve their predetermined purposes cannot be expected to welcome knowledge that indicates that their intentions may be infeasible or unwise. When science is viewed primarily as a servant of social purposes, it is not likely to be employed as a critic or teacher. The servant is not expected to volunteer unwanted information or unwelcome findings—or to talk back to its political or economic sponsors.

A third problem, soluble only to the extent that the two preceding problems are manageable, is the identification of critical variables. This identification is necessary to establish priorities and foci of attention for resources and environmental policies. Knowledge of interdependencies and interactive relationships among and within natural systems is a precondition to any planning for desired results without undesirable concomitants. Too often the question "What requires attention and when?" is answered through competition among exigencies for official attention. The issues that command attention may not be those of greatest social importance or even urgency, but rather those that possess the greatest personal significance for the official decision makers.[11] No one, but perhaps least of all a political figure, enjoys embarrassment. It would be unrealistic to assume that officials will put public interest above self-interest in their selection of priorities. But self-serving inclinations are most easily indulged when no demonstrable ordering of public priorities provides a yardstick against which to compare the actions of public officials. Science should not be expected to indicate priorities to which everyone would agree. But the development of more reliable criteria for identifying and defining critical problems and estimating their significance would be highly beneficial in a deeply troubled world. In brief, science could be used more effectively than heretofore in developing public priorities.

The fourth problem is perhaps the oldest and yet the most urgent for effective policy: development of reliable mechanisms to bring the right scientific knowledge to bear on policy issues at the right time and place. An essential property of a delivery system for scientific knowledge is that it makes useful information available in a form that decision makers can use. But the short-comings of scientific knowledge as applied to the policy process do not lie wholly with the delivery system. A major problem lies in the receptors, in the personalities of the decision makers. Many political leaders are indifferent to science as an intellectual enterprise and are unfriendly to science as a potential source of contradictions or embarrassments to their political principles. How can societies be taught to select political leaders who have respect for validated knowledge and receptivity to scientific evidence? For this question, no ready answer is apparent. But emergent developments in the organization and projection of knowledge may improve the prospects of finding an answer.

The credibility of science in public affairs would be increased to the extent that scientific knowledge or capability conferred a clearly demonstrated political advantage upon its possessor. Although it seems evident that possession of scientific information has worked to the advantage of the developed nations—in relation to natural resources, for example—extrapolation from specific benefits to more generalized policy guidance has not followed. Perhaps this is because, until very recently, the input of science to public decisions largely took the form of discrete facts, and only rarely the form of operational propositions that might be applied to the solution of major public problems. In brief, *science, being largely reductionist, has often been unable to assist the political decision maker, whose task is largely one of synthesis.* Knowledge may be power—but only when the contextual circumstances are favorable.

Two relatively recent developments in the technology of science—the growth of systems analysis and the computer—may change this situation. These developments represent new ways of dealing with reality. They result from and facilitate conceptual breakthroughs in conventional thinking. Their importance depends more upon their effects in the future than upon their contemporary impact because, as their detractors point out, they are operational techniques and in themselves represent no new knowledge beyond that incorporated in their own technology. It may be true that the output of these technologies can be no better than the information fed into them—a truism not unique to these instruments. But plausible as this proposition appears to be, it is oversimplified in relation to actual circumstances.

Systems and computer techniques have two great advantages over other technologies of inquiry: they can more easily manipulate complex variables, and they can do so within a narrow time dimension. These are precisely the capabilities most obviously missing from most conventional political analyses. They are, too, the capabilities most needed for anticipating and planning for the future. Until now, the information processed through these techniques was generated by other methodologies. *But the logic of research in systems dynamics is ultimately to force multidisciplinary inputs, followed by synthesis within a progressive time dimension.* The computer is capable of manipulating a vastly greater number of variables than the human mind—or even a team of unaided minds—can simultaneously process. It can simulate changes among variables at differing rates among other changes in time. Thus, it can use existing information in ways that may make it more meaningful. But it can also induce new knowledge, better adapted in form and content to the processes of decision making.

This inducive property of systems and computer techniques could be their most significant advantage, if they caused people to begin to see the world more realistically. To the extent that believable new perspectives were opened to society generally, one effect of these inducing techniques could be a fundamental change in the relationship between scientific knowledge and political decision making. As long as one man's conjectures regarding the future are considered to be as good as another's, scientific information is no more credible than are other forms of knowledge. Moreover, to the extent that the early results of computerized systems studies "bring bad news to the king," they are likely to be rejected by the political establishments that have replaced monarchs. Rejection has been the apparent fate of the "First and Second Reports to the Club of Rome on the Predicament of Mankind."[1][2] But the complacency of skeptics may be ill founded. If systems analyses prove to be prophetic and offer verifiable alternatives to disaster, receptivity might be greatly increased.

The computer, combined with systems analysis, thus affords a means by which scientific knowledge can be organized in ways that are meaningful for public decisions. But this capability is as yet potential rather than actual. The predictive value of systems techniques remains to be demonstrated under circumstances that are politically convincing. Disasters that have been scientifically forecast may yet give credence to scientific evidence and prognosis. Many such disasters could be environmental; others might arise out of the uneven distribution and impending exhaustion of natural resources.

Science versus Political Economy: Limitations and Prospects

Economists should long ago have conceded their reputation for professing the dismal to ecologists and earth scientists. Actually, conventional economists and Marxist ideologists seem to be inherently optimistic, or largely unconcerned, about future prospects for resource availability and the practical difficulties of allocation. Capitalist and socialist dogmas alike assert a faith in the ability of technological ingenuity and science to solve such genuine problems of shortages as may arise. Many resource economists, and all orthodox Marxists, see the problem of shortages as political rather than physical. In Marxists' eyes, the faulty allocation of actual or potential abundance, a consequence of the exploitive practices of capitalism, causes scarcity. Technologists are more ready to concede the eventual exhaustion of natural resources than they are to agree that materials shortages will occur: "Technology will find ways to substitute one substance for another." "Technology will find ways to do more with less." But these are testaments of faith, not of science. Unfortunately, no evidence supports the belief that technology can or will provide solutions to all problems of resource depletion.

Of course science, like economics, has its speculative aspects, and moreover, the perspective of scientists may be ideologically biased. Thus, Marxist scientists generally deny that physical resource scarcity per se (as distinguished from artificial monopoly-created scarcity) limits economic growth. And they have almost uniformly rejected the proposition that natural resources are becoming scarce. A common viewpoint is that expressed by Soviet biologist Nikolai Timofeyev-Ressovsky: "The biosphere is ten times richer than we think."[13]

The perspective of Soviet scientists was stated in characteristic language by academician E.K. Fedorov in the Plenary Session of the 1963 United Nations Conference on the Application of Science and Technology for the Benefit of the Less Developed Areas:

As it is known, some economists state that "the bomb of over-population" is a tremendous threat and may be the main one for the development of the whole of mankind at present. However we are not interested in oil, coal, certain kinds of animals or other natural resources by themselves—their amount may be larger or smaller and the moment may come when there will be no resources at all.

They don't count, but what is important is to what extent the vital needs of human society in power, food, materials, etc., are satisfied now and how they will be met in the future.

Here again we see a rapid growth of *per caput* potential resources on the earth.

An example of this kind is a swift increase of the possibilities of energy production—connected with growing efficiency of energy transformers as well as due to the uninterrupted discovery of new resources.

The potential energy resources *per caput* on the earth are now some dozen times greater than 100 years ago.

The same applies to the productive potentialities of food and various materials and products.

And finally the striking progress in space research provides possibilities for an unlimited expansion of the sphere of human inhabitancy much faster than a critical situation may arise connected with the dimensions of the earth itself.

There is no danger of a scantiness of natural resources, but there does exist another danger—that is their spontaneous unorganized utilization.

This point of view is clearly instrumental and illustrates the perspective of controlled socialist planning. "It is high time for all of us," declared academician Fedorov, "to pass from the primitive 'hunting' economy to a regulated cultivation of the natural resources on the earth as a whole."

The human society becomes such a mighty factor in the life of our planet, that already it cannot permit unorganized actions anywhere on the earth or outside it.[14]

The perspective of the British "Blueprint for Survival"[15] scientists, and of many North American ecologists and environmental scientists, is radically different. These scientists do not see the reduction of all nature to human regulation as a historical imperative. They assume the existence of limits to the growth and manageability of human society, even though those limits may not be delineated with precision.

And so, although the theoretical concern of science is to understand the forces governing nature (including human nature), it is evident that not all science perspectives are the same. This fact suggests that no single perspective is likely to be wholly right. A comprehensive unified science would thus be a tremendous asset in seeking a conceptually sound set of policies relating to man-environment relationships and to the utilization of natural resources.

Without a more comprehensive, synthesizing, self-critical science to provide a factual base, there seems little prospect that students of political economy can with justifiable confidence prescribe answers to the problems of international resource flows. The assumptions and propositions of political economy have been grounded in moral philosophy, with science no less a handmaiden than it has been to technologists and industrializers. The humanitarian precepts of one-world political economists are as likely to lead to a universally impoverished earth and a degraded world as are the alleged monopolistic, neoimperialistic practices that liberals and socialists decry. Many ways exist to filter perceptions of reality. But no amount of high-minded cleverness or sincerity will validate a false image. Yet, acceptance of this truism carries no guarantee that conventional interpretations of reality will be critically examined. It has been the custom of modern man first to define his view of reality and then to employ science to explain (i.e., rationalize) it.

If the basic sources of wealth today are knowledge and energy, then transfers of natural resources among nations will not, in themselves, decisively influence the distribution or intensity of political power. Should some of the less probable, but more powerful and sustainable, sources of energy be developed (e.g., controlled thermonuclear fusion), international resource interdependencies might be sharply altered or reduced.

With unchecked population growth in many of the poorer nations, the international science or knowledge gap is probably widening.[16] The greatest resource of the developed nations—their reserves of knowledge and of technical competence (even though inadequately developed)—cannot be "redistributed" except through arrangements which must be unacceptable to one or both of the groups of nations concerned, quite apart from the preferences of individuals.

One major step toward a more even (but not necessarily a more equitable) distribution of world resources would be to halt further growth in scientific or technical knowledge within the developed countries until all countries were at approximately the same level of advancement. Such national self-denial might satisfy a moral commitment to formal international equality, but—except in a dogmatic or ideological sense—probably at a high cost in environmental and intellectual deterioration everywhere. Moreover, to seek international economic equality by transfers of wealth from richer to poorer nations might seem unfair to the better informed, more efficient, and more purposeful of the developed nations, or at least to those who do possess these qualities.

The perspectives of contemporary science therefore give little specific guidance to national and international policies for natural resource transactions. There are, however, implications to be drawn from existing science perspectives, and although inconclusive, they are worth examining as the best information obtainable within existing political systems.

Problem-oriented synthesis of information through systems dynamics and the computer is beginning to intimate what a unified comprehensive science might offer. Scientists today can at least make educated guesses regarding the state of the earth and its significance for the peoples of the world. Assuming continued population growth for the world as a whole, shortages of critical materials across a broad spectrum of uses seem highly probable. Traditional methods to compensate for resource losses (e.g., colonial conquest or substitutions) may have diminishing applicability in the world of the future.

One almost universal effect of the shortages that have already appeared has been initially to increase the vulnerability and instability of the more developed countries—an effect that follows from discovery in the less developed materials-supplying countries that they can use their supply capabilities for political purposes. The more developed countries' economies are characterized by complex internal interdependencies, so the effects of any constrictions in the flow of materials quickly ramify throughout the system. These economies are highly organized, and their governments are susceptible to pressure by unions, trade associations, corporations, and political action groups—or resource cartels.

But real shortages affect *all* nations. Less developed countries—in which public opinion is poorly articulated, poverty is endemic, and agricultural subsistence is the normal way of life—could formerly adjust to resource deprivations more easily than could the more finely tuned economies of the developed countries. However, the threat of food shortages in those less developed countries with rapidly expanding populations makes them dependent on a flow of critical materials to and from the developed world or more favored developing countries. Exchange with which to pay for these inputs has largely derived from sales of raw materials. Hence, inability or unwillingness within the developed world to buy these materials restricts the options of the less developed suppliers.

The resource policies and declarations of less developed nations thus show a paradoxical ambivalence. On the one hand they are highly critical of the developed nations for depleting their resources. Urged on by the Soviet Union and China, they have nationalized natural resources and have applied both legal and extralegal forms of pressure in order to obtain concessions from foreign corporations wishing to develop these resources. The American consumption is widely criticized as an inordinate drain on the world's resources. But conversely, the fear is expressed, and was embodied in several resolutions at the United Nations Conference on the Human Environment in 1972,[17] that developed countries might cease to buy the natural products of the less developed countries. Objections were also raised to the substitution of synthetic substances for natural materials and to the possible barring of natural-products development in less developed countries because of environmental protection or ecological reasons. The issue of compensation was raised by spokesmen for the developing countries in Conference Resolution Number 103 (b):

That where environmental concerns lead to restrictions on trade, or to stricter environmental standards with negative effects on exports, particularly from developing countries, appropriate measures for compensation should be worked out within the framework of existing contractual and institutional arrangements and any new such arrangements that can be worked out in the future.

The developing nations generally rejected the compensation argument. Moreover, their unwillingness to become dependent on external supplies of natural resources has led directly to the involvement of science and technology in national materials policies aimed toward independence from unreliable sellers. This involvement includes the use of science to locate new domestic sources of supply, to make more efficient use of existing materials, to recover and recycle resources used in manufacturing, to find substitutes for scarce materials, and perhaps most importantly, to develop new methods and new systems for meeting human needs on an indefinite self-sustaining basis.

Allowing for time-lag effects, the ultimate consequence of resource supply uncertainties in the more developed nations will probably be a strongly augmented emphasis on the use of science. But because all but the last of the aforestated alternatives will encounter the limits of finite resources supplies, fundamental systems change may prove to be the science-based alternative with the highest security and potential. Yet, one cannot foresee where, when, how, or even *if* such response may be forthcoming—partly because *no nation today appears to have a belief system able to support a massive deployment of science and technology toward development of an ecologically responsible, self-renewing economic system.*

These observations end, therefore, on a tentative note. It is not clear that humanity will be able to use science in such a manner as to secure a selective advantage on an indefinitely sustainable basis. All modern societies have given intellectual hostages to fortune. All have reinforced these commitments through institutional arrangements which their governments, as presently constituted, cannot easily change. The instrumental uses of science are as likely to be damaging as beneficial as long as no valid, comprehensive, long-term view of man-environment relationships provides criteria for choice. The advancement of science itself may slow or even halt if human ability to organize, process, and manage information reaches its limits.

The best—but still very uncertain—hope for a more rational world would seem to lie in the union of a scientific perspective, made plausible by systems dynamics and the computer, with a reality-oriented political movement. The logical consequence of such a movement would be to reduce or minimize international resource flows as we see them today. This diminishing interdependence should not imply autarchy. It should suggest a more even balance of advantage among trading nations and a reduction of vulnerabilities resulting from resources dependencies. The search for reduced dependency may stimulate international federations or the formation of new multinational states. Indeed, the disappearance of a large number of autonomous nations might be one consequence of such a development, so that many flows which might continue would be intranational in nature. The regrouping of nations, and especially of former colonial states, on regional bases seems probable. And new forms of suzerainty and trusteeship may emerge in the wake of severe ecological and socioeconomic distress in the less developed world. Improbable as it now seems, relationships that would today be decried as "imperialist" may reemerge if inducing conditions reappear. The possibility of benign imperialism based on symbiotic relationships between technologically advanced nations and materials—producing dependencies should not be discounted. A continuing widening differential in technoscientific capabilities among nations would constitute an inducing factor.

On the other hand, the undercutting of traditional moral authority is a negative inducing factor. The greater part of the world today is at least formally committed in belief to the ethical assumptions of the Judeo-Christian tradition or of its Islamic or Marxist devolutions. But these ideologies are based primarily upon metaphysical revelation; their doctrines do not fully square with demonstrable human experience. They emerged under historical conditions that no longer exist, and they rest on assumptions that cannot be demonstrated to be true. In the past, these ideologies have sustained some societies, while contributing to the dissolution of others. They represent powerful and historically persuasive concepts of justice and morality, infusing the political and economic systems of today's world. But unless their assumptions can be brought into greater congruity with the realities revealed by science, their survival value to societies in the future seems questionable.

Whether the perspectives of a unified science will afford a foundation for a new concept of relations among men and between their world and the earth remains to be seen. But how societies cope with their resource problems, and how they relate to one another in this process, will be influenced, possibly decisively, by this essentially philosophical development. In the long run, the survival of humanity would seem to require the reestablishment of congruity between the exactions of man's world and the necessities of nature's earth.

Notes

1. Among such analyses are the following, prepared for the National Commission on Materials Policy: *Man, Materials, and Environment: A Report by the Study Committee on Environmental Aspects of a National Materials Policy . . . Environmental Studies Board, National Academy of Sciences/ National Academy of Engineering* (Cambridge, Mass.: M.I.T. Press, 1973); *Materials Requirements Abroad in the Year 2000: A Report Prepared . . . in the Wharton School, University of Pennsylvania, 1973* (Malenbaum Report); Jacob J. Kaplan, *International Aspects of a National Materials Policy* (Washington, D.C.: International Finance and Economics, 1973); *United States Materials Policy: The International Legal-Political Factor* (Washington, D.C.: Interfax Research, 1972). Note, in addition, Earl Cook, "The Depletion of Geologic Resources," *Technology Review* 77 (June 1975): 14-27.

2. GA res 3201 (S-VI) 1 May 1974.

3. Friedrich Engels, *Dialectics of Nature*, trans. and ed. by Clemens Dutt, with a Preface and Notes by J.B.S. Haldane (New York: International Publishers, 1940).

4. Mihajlo E. Mesarovic and Eduard Pestel, *Mankind at the Turning Point: Organic or Cancerous Growth?* (New York: E.P. Dutton, 1974).

5. Note, for example, Kan Chen, Karl F. Lagler, et al., *Growth Policy: Population, Environment, and Beyond* (Ann Arbor: University of Michigan Press, 1974).

6. See generally, Harold Blum, *Time's Arrow and Evolution* (Princeton: Princeton University Press, 1972).

7. See generally, Erwin Schroedinger, *What Is Life?* (Cambridge, England: Cambridge University Press, 1972).

8. See *The Ghost in the Machine* (New York: Macmillan, 1968).

9. It is easier to defend the almost axiomatic proposition that development planning is vulnerable to inadequate statistical analysis than to show specifically how and where particular projects or plans have been led astray by uncritical acceptance of statistical data. Examples of misapplied information, some of it statistical, may be found in John P. Milton and M. Taghi Farvar, eds., *The Careless Technology: Ecology and International Development* (New York:

Natural History Press, 1972). A comparison of W.W. Rostow, *Stages of Economic Growth: A Non-Communist Manifesto* (Cambridge, England: Cambridge University Press, 1960) with the ensuing history of most developing countries suggests that the conventional statistical methods of economists may have poor predictive value for human behavior. Cf. Nancy Baster, ed., *Measuring Development: The Role and Adequacy of Development Indicators*, reviewed by C. Arnold Anderson in *Economic Development and Cultural Change* 23 (July 1975): 771; Simon Kuznets, "Problems in Comparing Recent Growth Rates for Developed and Less-Developed Countries," *Economic Development and Cultural Change* 20 (January 1972): 185-209; Ralph E. Strauch, " 'Squishy' Problems and Quantitative Methods," *Policy Science* 6 (June 1975): 175.

10. Thomas Kuhn, *The Structure of Scientific Revolutions* (Chicago: University of Chicago Press, 1962).

11. Cf. Delbert C. Miller, James L. Barfoot, Jr., and Paul Planchon, *Power and Decision Making in Megalopolis, with Special Reference to Environmental Quality Programs* (Washington, D.C.: Resources for the Future, 1970).

12. Donnella H. and Dennis L. Meadows et al., *The Limits to Growth* (New York: Universe Books, 1972); and Mesarovic and Pestel, *Mankind at the Turning Point.*

13. *The UNESCO Courier*, January 1973, pp. 29-31.

14. *Science and Technology for Development: Report on the United Nations Conference on the Application of Science and Technology for the Benefit of the Less Developed Areas.* VIII: *Plenary Proceedings . . .* (New York: United Nations, 1963), pp. 69-70.

15. See *The Ecologist* 2 (January 1972), whole issue.

16. See P.M.S. Blackett, "The Ever Widening Gap," *Science* 155 (February 24, 1967): 959-64.

17. *Report of the United Nations Conference on the Human Environment: Stockholm, 5-16 June 1972.* (New York: United Nations, 1972).

8

Material Needs and Technological Innovation: Some Hopes—and Some Doubts

Gerald Feinberg

The history of mankind has been described by writers as different as Hesiod[1] and the founders of modern archeology[2] in terms of the materials used in successive periods. Thus, civilization is said to have passed through the Stone Ages, old and new, followed by the Golden, Bronze, and Iron Ages. Such an unsophisticated classification is no longer considered an accurate description of any period and must instead be taken merely to indicate the kinds of artifacts that remain available for later study. Yet without doubt, there has been a long process of change in man's uses of materials in terms of both diversity and the increased amounts used. While this growth is only one factor in the development of the present way of life in industrialized countries, the materials that we can and do use clearly play an important role in what we accomplish and what we aspire to.

The concerns of recent years have focused on whether and how the present pattern of materials use in the industrialized countries can continue. Little attention has been given to the possibility of major changes in materials usage in the industrialized countries as a result of changing needs and technology in these societies, rather as a consequence of shortages that imperil the present system. Yet, since the former factor will surely help in determining the future of the materials economy, some efforts to explore the technological frontier should be included in any survey of the global resource problem.

The entries on the supply side of the materials ledger are determined by complex interactions among several factors—including the relatively constant structure of the earth, improving technological capabilities to extract and transform materials from their natural state into the forms we use, and those variables of social organization that determine whether people are willing or able to devote the effort necessary to obtain particular materials. This last factor is probably least well understood, but it may be decisive of the eventual pattern of materials usage.

These considerations suggest the following question, which I believe should be at the center of a discussion of future materials usage: Are the main constraints on our use of materials in the future going to arise from what we *desire* to do? from what it is *possible* for us to do? from what we are *willing* to do?

Technological optimists such as Alvin Weinberg[3] imply that the first of these is the answer. Resource pessimists such as Dennis Meadows et al.[4] would stress the second, while Jay Forrester,[5] in some recent discussions, has suggested

149

that the main constraint will come from man's willingness. My own position tends in the direction of the technological optimists. However, given the vagaries of the social order, I must share the doubts of those who question man's willingness to plan with sufficient rigor and foresight for future materials needs and then carry these plans through on a global scale. It nevertheless seems essential to investigate the possibilities for future sources and uses of materials, lest any failures be traceable to a want of forethought on those subjects where forethought is feasible.

The emphasis in the following discussion will be on fundamental factors such as the prospects allowed by scientific laws as applied to the earthly environment, rather than the historical or accidental circumstances that so largely determine the use of materials in industrial societies today. In addition, I will discuss some connections between materials and other aspects of social life, considering some of the problems likely to occur as we attempt a transition from present to prospective patterns of materials use.

Current Patterns in the Use of Materials

It will be useful to review the ways in which materials are used at present, taking the United States as an example.[6] The whole process of transformation of materials—from their acquisition in raw form, through the various changes we make in them for our own purposes, to their ultimate disposition—is relevant. For most materials, each stage influences estimates of the need for, and supply of, the material. Moreover, each stage can be influenced by technological and social changes.

At present, almost all of the eighty-eight naturally occurring chemical elements are used to some extent, either in elemental form, in mixtures such as alloys, or in chemical compounds. The amount used yearly varies from a fraction of a ton for osmium to more than 10^9 tons for carbon and for silicon. Table 8-1 lists the amounts used of some representative elements. The term "used" is somewhat ambiguous, since some common materials, such as water, have many relatively transient uses—for example, cooling or irrigation—which involve only minor changes in the properties of the resource during its period of utilization. Some constraints do apply to such short-term uses, but they are qualitatively different from those I wish to consider.

Another sort of materials usage that I shall not discuss, even though it is obviously both very important and relevant to the problem of global resource flows, applies to minerals of high specific energy content, such as carbon in coal or petroleum. It is mainly—though not completely—the energy in such minerals that is of interest, rather than the particular material which carries it. For example, if alternative energy sources such as fusion reactors became readily available, the carbon required because of its chemical and physical properties

Table 8-1

Amounts of Selected New Materials Used in 1972 in the United States and the World[a]

(In Metric Tons)

Element	Yearly Use in U.S.	Yearly Use in World
Iron	$.86 \times 10^8$	4.5×10^8
Aluminum	3.7×10^6	1.1×10^7
Copper	1.5×10^6	6.6×10^6
Lead	0.6×10^6	3.4×10^6
Zinc	0.6×10^6	5×10^6
Phosphate (P_2O_5)	1.1×10^7	3×10^7
Molybdenum	5×10^4	8×10^4
Vanadium	4×10^3	1.8×10^4
Titanium	0.48×10^6	1.4×10^6
Sulfur	0.85×10^7	2.3×10^7

[a]These figures are derived from *The Minerals Yearbook, 1971* and Bureau of the Census, *Historical Statistics of the U.S.*

would be less than 10 percent of that currently demanded as an energy source. I shall not discuss materials used principally for their energy content, except where energy uses are directly pertinent to the availability of materials for other purposes.

Sources and Transformations of Materials

The twentieth century has seen a gradual shift in the materials base of our society. The shift has been from organic or naturally—occurring inorganic materials which require little processing to materials that do not occur in the form in which we use them and therefore must undergo substantial processing. This processing may involve chemical or physical separations and recombinations or changes in physical form.

Technological man's growing capability to perform such processing has made available a much greater proportion of the earth's matter. It has also enabled us to do things with available raw materials that were simply impossible in previous periods. One effect of technological progress has been to extend greatly the scope of the very concept of a "resource"—that is, a source of useful materials—at the same time it has required more effort to transform the material from its original state into a usable form. The required additional effort can show up in several ways: as a greater difficulty in extracting elements from low-grade ores; in the form of higher energy requirements to separate elements from their chemically combined natural forms; or in the need for greater purification of material in order to use it. These complications, in turn, translate into greater energy requirements to complete the total processing of a unit weight of material. By the same token, each bit of material must go through more processing steps before reaching its final useful form. Even materials such as wood, which are obtained from organic sources, may be substantially transformed into such forms as plywood before use. This is less true for materials such as gravel and stone. But these materials, while used in large quantities, seem to be available in any necessary amount and do not therefore restrict the availability of materials. Hence, I shall not consider such materials here, but instead focus on those that must be transformed from their native form.

The original source of most such materials is ore which contains a compound of the element in a concentration that is much higher than the average crustal concentration. The actual concentration in a usable ore will differ substantially from material to material. The economically recoverable concentration also changes with time for each material, gradually declining as the higher grade deposits are used up. (Some representative figures are given in Table 8-2.) For example, between 1951 and 1971, the total amount of materials handled in the mining of nonfuel minerals increased by 48 percent, while the crude ore produced increased by only 32 percent and the useful product of metals by 22 percent. This trend indicates the greater effort required per unit of useful material.[7]

It follows that estimates of reserves that are based on the availability of ores of fixed concentration are misleading. There is no principle—at least, no *physical* principle—that restricts us from moving to ores of lower concentration as the higher grades are exhausted. On the other hand, as we exploit ores with even lower concentrations, the effort needed to obtain a fixed amount of the

Table 8-2
Ratio of Useful Material to Ore Mined for Various Elements

Element	Useful Material/Ore Mined
Copper (1931)	0.015
Copper (1941)	0.012
Copper (1951)	0.009
Copper (1961)	0.008
Copper (1971)	0.006
Iron (1972)	0.15
Lead (1972)	0.06
Gold (1972)	6×10^{-6}
Phosphate (1972)	0.11

demanded element must increase—generally with an increase in the cost of the end material as well.

Several elements—oxygen and nitrogen in the air, helium in natural gas, and hydrogen, chlorine, and magnesium in ocean water—are found in usable concentrations in forms other than ores. Extraction of these elements from their source mixtures is often much easier than it would be from ores, even if the latter did exist. However, for most of the elements presently in use, the oceans are not a practical source because of the very low concentrations there, unless and until we can develop much more effective methods than are currently available for increasing the concentration.

Transformations of materials do not end with the extraction of elements or compounds from their natural form. An extensive chemical processing industry has emerged as a result of the need to manipulate elements into various inorganic and organic compounds for distinct uses. The total energy used in such chemical processing is approximately equal to that used in the extraction of primary elements. Comparable numbers of workers are also involved in the two stages.

Uses of Materials

The total material use in the United States each year, excluding food, fuels, and water, runs to approximately 2.5 billion tons. However, about 90 percent of this figure is accounted for by (1) unprocessed construction material such as sand, gravel, dry and cracked rock, where availability is not in question, or (2) agricultural and timber products, whose availability involves rather different considerations than does that of minerals. The remaining 2.5×10^8 tons of nonfuel mineral products consist, in the main, of newly extracted material rather than reused quantities of previously extracted material. The time that a typical bit of material remains in use varies with the use, but an average value is about twenty years,[8] perhaps slightly higher for "permanent" structures, such as buildings. Thus, most of the material we use remains in artifactual form for much less than a century before it reenters the general stock of the earth's materials, albeit in a rather different form than that in which it initially appeared to man. Coupled with the increase in the yearly use of materials that has occurred in this century, this fact means that the standing stock of materials in present use is not many times greater than the yearly additives to that stock.[9]

We are, then, at least in most industrialized countries, largely living on (and in) materials that the present generation has extracted and transformed. Of course, this is only possible because of the scientific and technological basis provided by past generations.

Some 1.5×10^8 tons of metals are used each year, either in almost pure elemental form or in mixtures known as alloys. The properties of metals relevant to most of their uses include their superior weight-supporting abilities, their ability to resist stresses, and their relatively high melting temperatures. These properties are important in the major uses of metals—to enclose or support nonmetallic objects, as in construction and in transportation. A major secondary use of certain metals, principally copper and aluminum, stems from their high electrical conductivity. Still smaller amounts of metal go into chemical compounds. The latter two types of metals use are probably more specific than the first, in that many more metals have similar properties for construction purposes than have high electrical conductivity. Ultimately, the main uses of many metals seem likely to change in the direction of uses that are presently considered secondary, continuing a trend that has already occurred to some extent for metals such as lead and copper.

The substitution of some nonmetals for metals, such as plastics and fiberglass in construction, has accelerated and will probably continue to do so, relieving some of the burden on the use of metals. Nonmetals, whose total use compares with that of metals, are used mainly in chemical compounds. However, relatively small amounts of some nonmetals are used as elements in needs which tend to be very specific. In some of these cases, the elements are unsubstitutable. For example, only helium remains liquid at low enough temperatures for use as a coolant in certain cryogenic applications. With the exception of helium, the availability of the useful nonmetals seems to raise no substantial problems for the future, since most can be extracted from water, air, or widely distributed rocks.

Disposition of Materials

Two forms of disposition of human artifacts and the materials they contain are possible. After their useful lives are over, products may be recycled with some of the material being remade into other artifacts, or else they may be discarded, eventually to reenter the environmental stock of materials. The latter is certainly the fact of many materials in our culture.

When materials are recycled, a certain rate of loss occurs with each cycle of use. Unless this loss rate is extremely small, after a number of cycles all of the original material will have returned to the environment. Even when artifacts Even when artifacts remain in use, corrosion, weathering, vandalism, and the like act to decrease the amount of contained material. Ultimately, all of these processes return the material to a state in which it is neither readily distinguishable from the general distribution of materials on earth nor readily usable as a source of new materials. Some changes, such as a transfer of materials from land to water, may have important environmental effects but exert a negligible effect on the availability of materials because of the still small scale of human activity.

Thus, the present pattern of materials use begins with relatively high-grade ores, subjects them to substantial amounts of processing, maintains the resulting products in use for relatively short periods of time, and eventually returns the material to a more dispersed state than existed at the beginning, leaving the process to be repeated by succeeding generations. Partly because of the growth in the use of materials, especially in the last century, but also because our patterns of social and economic behavior do not stimulate the long-term use of materials, there is little passing down of materials from generation to generation, although the information on how to process materials is passed along.

Future Technological Prospects

Future developments in technology may influence our use of materials through changes at each of the stages along the chain of processing operations outlined above.

As a first approximation, we may imagine that we will want to accomplish the same things through the use of materials in the future as we do at present. In this section I shall indicate a number of points along this chain at which technology seems to promise new options for aspects of our materials processing and use. We cannot know which options are viable, but we can consider how any one of them fits in with other human purposes, directing our efforts toward those which appear most desirable from that standpoint.

Beyond this, there may also occur changes in the goals we wish to realize through the use of materials. We may, for example, want to achieve new levels of transformation of the environment, requiring huge amounts of material. The long-term increase in per capita utilization of most materials seems likely to continue in the world as a whole, if not in the developed countries. At least the colloquy at the U.N. Stockholm Environmental Conference[10] in 1972 showed quite clearly that spokesmen for many LDCs remain unpersuaded that they cannot reach present consumption levels of the developed countries. Nor is there valid reason for them to believe it. Therefore, future materials supply systems may have to supply both greater amounts and (perhaps) different types of materials than are required at present.

Availability of Elements on Earth

What stock of materials, then, is actually present on earth? Fairly accurate figures are available for the average elemental compositions of the crust and the oceans.[11] It thus becomes simple to estimate the total stock of various elements available in the upper one hundred meters of the land area of earth. Table 8-3 presents these figures for a representative sample of elements. Comparison of these figures with the present yearly usage of the elements indicates that human beings in every case are presently using an inappreciable fraction of the amount

Table 8-3
Amounts of Various Elements in the Earth's Crust Compared to Present Yearly World Use of Similar Elements

Element	Amount in Upper 100 Meters of Earth's Crust (Metric tons)	Ratio of Amount in Crust to Present Yearly World Use
Magnesium	5.5×10^{13}	2.3×10^8
Aluminum	2.7×10^{15}	2.5×10^8
Phosphorus	2.7×10^{13}	2.2×10^6
Sulfur	9×10^{12}	4×10^6
Titanium	9×10^{13}	6×10^7
Vanadium	3.6×10^{12}	2×10^8
Chromium	5.5×10^{12}	
Manganese	2.7×10^{12}	
Iron	1.8×10^{15}	4×10^6
Nickel	1.8×10^{12}	2.8×10^6
Copper	1.8×10^{12}	2.7×10^5
Zinc	2.7×10^{12}	5.4×10^5
Molybdenum	2.7×10^{10}	3.3×10^5
Tin	9×10^{11}	4×10^6
Lanthanide Rare Earths	2.7×10^{12}	2.7×10^8
Tungsten	3.6×10^{10}	9×10^5
Gold	9×10^7	6.6×10^4
Mercury	1.8×10^9	1.9×10^5
Lead	3.6×10^{11}	10^5
Uranium	9×10^{10}	4×10^6

Sources: Concentrations taken from *Handbook of Chemistry and Physics*, 54th ed., P F - 184 (Cleveland: CRC Press, 1973). Data on world mineral use obtained from *The Minerals Yearbook, 1971*, Vol. 1, Table 3.

of the element that is physically near at hand. At present rates, because of the limited span of time in which virtually all human artifacts remain in use, the integrated use-time of elements is such that men will never deplete any significant fraction of the earth's upper crust by mobilizing it for human purposes.

This conclusion remains valid even if the use of materials increases substantially. Even if the whole world were to use materials at several times the present per capita rate in the United States, and the world population is several times greater than at present, the yearly use of materials could for almost all elements be drawn from a negligible fraction of the total amounts in the upper crust. If the extension of a high consumption to the whole world proves to be impossible, as some writers contend, it will not be for a physical lack of raw materials.[12]

Some authors[13] too, perhaps as a rhetorical device, have pointed out that total use of many materials has been increasing exponentially over several doubling periods. They have concluded that such an increase, if continued for several centuries, would eventually require our using all of the earth's crust each year. While this conclusion is arithmetically correct, its pertinence to serious discussion of the resource problem may be questioned for several reasons. The required extrapolation of growth exceeds a factor of 10^9, whereas the actual growth thus far has yet to reach a factor of one hundred. Already in the United States, there are clear indications that the use of nonfuel materials is growing more slowly than exponentially.[14] Furthermore, in order to approach the doomsday situation, we would literally have to transform the earth's surface into a human creation, in which all rocks, clays, and sands were remade into human artifacts. Even if one could imagine the one-time completion of such a project, say in carrying out some grand design, it is hard to imagine the purpose or the method of repeating the exercise year after year to maintain the hypothesized rate of materials use. Realistically, many obvious factors—not least among them the availability of time and energy to carry out the transformations—will limit materials use to levels far short of the amounts physically present in the upper crust.

New Sources for Old Materials

In view of the actual availability of potentially useful elements in the earth's crust, it would seem an obvious idea to develop techniques for extracting and using them. Economically feasible plans could gradually be introduced as higher-grade ores are depleted.

Furthermore, in many countries, there are no high-grade ores for some materials. For example, almost all of the chromium used in the United States is imported. Development of an indigenous source in each country for each material, based on techniques to extract elements from common rocks, would be prudent in a period when export cartels are of general concern. Materials independence for each country, together with a corresponding energy independence, would also go far to eliminate the increasingly strident complaints of exploitation that trade in raw materials has stimulated from both sellers and consumers. Finally, this source of materials is applicable to a steady state economy, at present or even much higher levels of use of materials, whereas continued reliance on high-grade ores could support a steady rate of consumption only with attainment of the unattainable—that is, perfect recycling of materials.

What, then, are the technological possibilities for using common rocks in the earth's crust as the major source of most chemical elements? While there are some complex technical matters involved in answering this question, the following points would seem to be among the most relevant. For many important elements—e.g., iron, aluminum, and titanium—the concentrations in average crustal rocks is much higher than are the concentrations of other materials in what metallurgists now consider high-grade ores of the elements in question. The differences between reliance on high-grade ores and use of common rocks as a source of any materials are mainly quantitative differences rather than differences of principle. In either case, with present technology, there is involved a physical separation of the compound containing the desired elements from the matrix in which they are found, followed by a series of chemical transformations leading to the commercial production of pure elements or their alloys or compounds.

The concentration in the original source is most relevant to the first step involved in the chain (separation of relatively pure compounds of the element), although the chemical compounds actually present in the matrix can also affect the second step (chemical extraction of the element). Generally, the expenditure of energy and human effort needed to extract the compound from the source increases inversely with the concentration of the material being separated. The significance of this increasing amount of input energy depends on the relative difficulties of the first and second steps. For some materials, including aluminum and iron, the chemical separation is substantially more difficult. Thus, even the use of sources with lower concentrations than characterize present ores would require relatively modest increases in energy and labor.[15] But for other materials, such as copper, chemical separation is relatively easy; so the total energy and effort required to produce a fixed amount would scale inversely with the concentration in the source. Some detailed estimates are given in Table 8-4.

Despite the existence of a wide range of variation dependency on which elements are emphasized, an overall increase in the total energy devoted to metal processing will be required to obtain the same amount of various metals from common rock as we now do from high-grade ores. Clearly, this approach is possible only if the energy available to us increases significantly by the time this method is used. In view of the limited reserves of fossil fuels, such energy must come from alternative sources—breeder reactors, fusion reactors, or solar convertors. It is interesting to note that a ton of common rock contains some fifteen grams of fissionable uranium and thorium. The energy content of this material, if converted in a breeder reactor, would equal that in forty tons of coal. This exceeds by a considerable margin the energy needed to extract most elements, including the uranium and thorium themselves, from the rock. So in principle, common rock can be simultaneously a source of materials and a source of the energy to extract those materials. Whether this is possible in practice remains to be seen. And whether it is desirable requires more thought.

If a sufficient supply of elements can be obtained from common rock, it is

Table 8-4
Estimated Amount and Cost of Energy Required to Obtain Various Elements from the Earth's Crust and High Grade Ores[a]

Element	Present Energy Required per Ton	Energy Required to Obtain from Crust per Ton	Cost of Energy from Crust per Ton[b]	Total Energy Required from Crust for U.S. Consumption[c]
Iron	5×10^3 Kwht	2×10^4 Kwht	$ 20	1.7×10^{12} Kwht
Copper	2×10^4 Kwht	9×10^5 Kwht	$900	1.4×10^{12} Kwht
Aluminum	5×10^4 Kwht	1.3×10^5 Kwht	$130	4.8×10^{11} Kwht
Titanium	1.3×10^5 Kwht	1.6×10^5 Kwht	$160	7.7×10^9 Kwht

[a]Energies have been obtained from the formula $E = A + B/C$, where A and B are constants for each element and C is the concentration of the element. Data to obtain A and B are taken from J.C. Bravard and C. Portal (ORNL-MIT-132).
[b]The cost of the amount of energy estimated in column 3—assuming an energy cost of 10^{-3} dollars/Kwht, which is approximately the present cost of coal in the United States.
[c]Total energy needed to obtain the 1972 U.S. consumption levels of these elements from crustal materials.

possible, through a suitable use of energy where necessary, to synthesize whatever chemical compounds of these elements may be desired. It would be possible, for example, to synthesize plastics and other substances which at present require hydrocarbons, from carbon dioxide and water. Of course, a hydrocarbon molecule already has a large energy content, and this would have to be supplied if elemental or oxidized forms of carbon were used in the synthesis of needed materials.

Another potential limit to the use of common rock as a source of materials hinges on the amount of rock that would have to be processed and the consequent amount of waste generated. As a reference figure, we may take the 1.5×10^9 tons of metallic minerals handled in 1971 to produce some 1.5×10^8 tons of usable metal. What amount of rock of average crustal composition would be required to produce a corresponding amount of metal, assuming an average recoverability of 50 percent of the metal content? Table 8-5 shows that for many useful elements—excluding copper and some of the heavy metals—we could obtain equal or greater amounts by processing about 10^{10} tons of common rock as we now extract from the high-grade ores in use. This tenfold increase corresponds to the change expected in any case over a period of about fifty years at the present rate of acceleration in materials use. Hence, we are not speaking about anything unimaginable here. The ratio of usable metal to waste would then be about 1.5 percent, or less by a big factor than is the average at present. However, even this ratio exceeds that presently acceptable in the mining of many metals, such as copper, gold, or uranium. Also, the ratio might be improved if the waste rock could be used to supply some or all of the yearly

Table 8-5

Amount of Average Crustal Material Needed to Obtain 1972 U.S. Yearly Use of Various Elements[a]

Element	Amount of Crustal Material Needed to Obtain One Year's U.S. Consumption (Metric Tons)
Iron	3×10^9
Aluminum	9×10^7
Copper	6×10^{10}
Lead	8×10^{10}
Zinc	10^{10}
Phosphorus	8×10^9
Molybdenum	10^{11}
Vanadium	6×10^7
Titanium	10^8
Sulfur	3×10^{10}

[a]A 50 percent extraction efficiency is assumed.

consumption of gravel and stone, which comes to 2×10^9 tons at present. Furthermore it would be possible to raise the ratio of usable metal by increasing the use of metals such as aluminum and titanium, which are relatively plentiful in common rock, as opposed to copper and the heavy metals, which are uncommon. Still, it seems likely that the amount of waste material connected with metal processing would increase by a factor of two or three, aggravating the problems of finding available land for mining rock and dumping wastes. The environmental effects of this type of processing might also become much more severe.

We cannot continue to deal with such problems on an ad hoc basis. Already, severe conflicts have arisen over such questions of land use.[16] An integrated land use policy in which some sections are permanently set aside for mining and kindred uses might represent the most satisfactory national solution to the problem. But whether such a policy would be a politically viable solution is another matter.

If common rock mining were to be accomplished without inadmissably high expenditures of energy and effort, we would have to develop techniques for parallel extraction of many elements. Some existing techniques may be adaptable for this purpose. However, it would be wise to initiate a study of suitable techniques for large-scale parallel extraction. Perhaps an experimental program to do this could be set up in order to gain a more accurate picture of costs and of possible bottlenecks. While such an effort might be undertaken by a forward-looking metal processing company, my guess is that so far ahead of an actual need for the process, this is unlikely. However, a government-funded effort seems more possible, perhaps financed through a technological development bank of the sort proposed in other contexts.[17]

New Replacements for Old Materials

At present, we use many materials for rather inessential reasons, partly for historical reasons and partly as a result of the materials' past easy availability. A discussion of substitutions of materials should begin by considering inessential uses that call for increased use of other materials that will be more readily available in the future. Such changes have occurred already in the past. We would not think of eating from silver plates, as some people did in the past, yet we do continue to use lead in paints, chromium in auto trim, and platinum in razor blades. Substitution for such uses tends to be relatively simple and hence happens fairly naturally as shortages develop. In some cases, intelligent substitutions could reduce the amount of particular elements used by substantial fractions of current use.

However, substitution as a simple matter of course will be insufficient in other cases to decrease the use of elements in short supply. For example, copper is used in large amounts for its high electrical conductivity: small quantities of platinum are used to catalyze chemical reactions. Such uses depend on specific properties of the elements involved, so the substitution possibilities are more subtle. Of course, one possibility would be to reduce or even eliminate the functions served by use of these elements. If we were to decrease substantially the use of electricity, we would need less copper. This type of curtailment has been proposed by some of the resource pessimists. Since this approach has received detailed, if not persuasive, treatment by its proponents,[18] of whom I am not one, I shall not discuss it further, except to remark that one should not confuse the possible desirability of life styles alternate to our own with their possible necessity for lack of viable alternatives.

To find substitutes for the major uses of elements which may be in short supply, two approaches can be followed. One is to find more plentiful elements, or alloys or compounds of such elements, which have properties similar to those of the element in short supply. For example, aluminum is almost as good an electrical conductor as copper and can be used instead of copper for many electrical purposes. It also has the advantage of being 1,500 times more plentiful on earth. At present, aluminum requires about twice the energy per ton to produce from ore that copper does. But eventually, if both were produced from common rock, this situation would reverse. Aluminum is not perfectly substitutable for copper because its other properties are somewhat different. This does not mean that a complete all-aluminum electrical system could not be designed. It does, however, mean that aluminum cannot just be substituted for copper in all existing uses without some problems arising.

There is another approach to substitutes, one that is more fundamental and hence involves a deeper understanding of the physical and chemical properties of the materials themselves. Almost all materials in use are somewhat impure, either because they are chemical mixtures or because their physical structures contain microscopic imperfections. Both kinds of impurity can have tremendous effects on the useful properties of the material, as can be seen, for example, by a comparison of cast iron and stainless steel. To a certain extent, we have learned to manipulate the structures of materials semiempirically, through such metallurgical techniques as alloying and heat treatment. We may even have exhausted the possibilities of those techniques for the metals in common use. But we are far from doing so for many others, including some like titanium, whose crustal abundances are quite high. Substitutes for several of our scarcer metals can probably be produced by improved metallurgical techniques applied to these lesser-known elements.

Recent advances in solid-state physics and chemistry have made it possible in some cases to tailor-make materials with certain desirable properties not present in "natural" materials.[19] My impression is that we are just beginning to explore the applications of the latter approach. Metal samples with reduced amounts of the microscopic imperfections known as dislocations[20] are expected to have much greater strength than do the familiar bulk samples, and they would probably enjoy much longer useful lives as well. If produced in significant quantities, they could reduce the overall use of the metal considerably or at least allow the substitution of improved versions of one material for another material. Much more effort would probably have to go into preparing each sample than goes into a corresponding sample of ordinary metal, implying a trade-off between more effort in mining and more in preparation. The development of "perfect" metal samples is not yet practical, and so we cannot tell whether this type of substitution in form rather than in kind will work out. However, it seems plausible that improvements in materials properties through systematic application of basic science can reduce the need to rely on any specific material for a particular function.

We can also imagine new materials with properties sufficiently different from "natural" materials to permit completely new approaches and functions. One example involves the property of certain elements at low temperatures known as "superconductivity"—a loss of the electrical resistance of the material, permitting an indefinite and unimpeded flow of currents. Superconductors at present exist only at temperatures below $-251°$ Centigrade, but the trend of discovery suggests that superconductivity may exist at substantially higher temperatures.[21] It is tempting to imagine superconductors replacing ordinary metallic conductors for the transmission of electricity at great materials savings. While superconducting materials tend to be relatively uncommon metals, such as niobium, the amounts necessary are so small that the problem of scarcity would hardly arise. For example, all the electricity used in New York City could be transmitted along a superconducting strip with a diameter of 10^{-2} inches instead of the copper wires now in use, which are many square inches in diameter. But superconducting transmission lines will pose problems in refrigeration and safety quite different from those of ordinary transmission lines.[22] The price paid for better performance is more care in development and design of the new technology, in the original construction, and in maintenance of the system. This is, indeed, the general trend as we advance from simple to sophisticated technologies.

There seem to be few specific uses of materials for which one cannot imagine replacements involving new technologies. But the new technologies themselves would probably require materials of other kinds, so we must expect that one constraint on technological innovation would be the relative availability of the required materials. Clearly, this cannot be the only criterion. It may well be, as I shall argue below, that innovation is more severely constrained by social and human inertia than by physical shortages. However, it is perhaps of some comfort to realize that the ways in which we presently use materials are far from unique. Human ingenuity and the laws of nature allow for alternative ways of accomplishing similar objectives.

New Patterns of Materials Use

Given the rather short life in use of most materials, perhaps the most effective way to decrease the use rates of new materials would be through an extension of the period over which our artifacts remain in use. In a steady-state situation, the amount of new materials required each year varies inversely with the effective life of artifacts. So, for example, if automobiles could be made to last twice as long as they do at present, the quantities of steel and other materials needed for their construction would be halved. While some technological factors—such as better forms of corrosion resistance and reduction of metal fatigue—could extend the life of artifacts, it is my impression that it is mainly social factors which determine how long products remain in use.

A significant social factor is the desire of each generation to distinguish itself from past generations by using different products, even when the "differences" are only minor variations in form. Perhaps this factor alone would make it difficult, at least in the United States, to extend the lifetime of consumer goods beyond the "generation" time, whatever that may be.

There also exist other factors, not necessarily so irrational as the desire for generational uniqueness. To the extent that objects are continuously being improved in function, short product lifetimes may serve a useful goal, since artifacts are then most readily replaced by new objects which function better. A trade-off between conflicting aims—conservation and improvement—is involved here. One might expect, over time, a shift in the direction of conservation and longer product lifetimes, as any given class of artifacts, such as the automobile, approaches the limit of its perfectibility. However, there seems to be little evidence that this is happening in the case of consumer goods.

A general move toward conservation would involve significant changes in the American economy. If the lifetime of a given product is increased while its use remains fixed, output will drop correspondingly, leading, as a first approximation, to a loss of jobs and of profit in the affected industry. Such effects could perhaps be compensated for by additional work needed to produce the longer-lasting product. However, since such compensations do not come about easily, at the least we might expect temporary dislocations. Ideally, if longer-lasting artifacts could be produced with equal effort, society would benefit. In addition to the savings gained in conserved materials and energy, the workers no longer needed to produce the products in question could be employed in other capacities, or even be allowed to pursue idle pastimes at the public expense.

Similar prospects were raised some time ago by the expected wholesale automation of production processes, but the evidence suggests that such transitions do not occur spontaneously in our society. Movement in the direction of longer-lasting products implies a need for systematic planning to control the social dislocations that will ensue.

New Requirements for Materials

Future materials requirements need not simply involve replacements or substitutes for materials that are now used. We can expect that qualitatively new uses for various materials will also emerge, including both new uses for familiar materials and uses for materials that are not much used at present. Past examples of such developments abound. They include, for example, the emergence of copper as an electrical conductor in the nineteenth century and the emergence of titanium and aluminum as important structural materials in the twentieth century. The kinds of similar changes that may occur in the future will depend partly on scientific discoveries yet to be made. However, some speculative examples may be given.

If solar energy should come to be used on a large scale to generate electricity, an effective solar cell that can be produced in large quantities will probably be necessary. None is presently available, although appropriate experiments are being carried out.[23] One approach involves a "sandwich" made of two materials that will produce a current when exposed to light. Various materials are being tried, including germanium and indium compounds. Hence, such an approach could lead to a major demand for such presently exotic materials.

Another example of a novel materials requirement would arise if we should transition to a "hydrogen economy" in which hydrogen gas were regularly used as a portable fuel and as a reducing agent in place of hydrocarbons and coal.[24]

As much as a billion tons of hydrogen might be used annually, representing over a thousandfold increase in our present use of elemental hydrogen. Free hydrogen gas is not available on the earth in large quantities. Hence, it would be necessary to produce the hydrogen, say by the electrolysis of water, using an energy source such as solar energy or thermonuclear fusion.

Since we will probably eventually find substantial uses for all of the stable chemical elements, rational policy for future materials sources should allow for this possibility of requirements for materials not widely used at present.[25]

This brief survey indicates the range of possibilities for technological innovations at various stages of the process of materials use. These possibilities suggest that future patterns of materials acquisition and use may differ radically from past and present patterns. Hence, on the one hand, extrapolations to disaster from present patterns are not necessarily valid because of the various technological options that exist for changing these patterns. On the other hand, if we wish to use any of these options, it is necessary to examine the problem of a transition from present to desired future patterns. Serious difficulties can arise in getting "from here to there." Many of these difficulties arise from various social and economic factors which I shall now consider.

Social Factors in Changing Uses of Materials

Technology—which is, in the first place, *knowledge of how to do things*—may be based either on theory or on empirical procedures. There has been a gradual shift from the latter to the former as the hegemony of theoretical science has spread. In either case, technology has little effect until it is applied. Such applications are normally carried out within frameworks of complex social institutions, involving large numbers of individuals with diverse habits and motivations. These habits and motivations influence how any technology actually works in practice, just as, in turn, they are themselves influenced by past technological developments. This two-way interaction between technology and society is a dominant factor in determining the long-term effects of any new application.

If, as I believe we should, we reject a "technological imperative" which holds that anything which can be done should be done, then we must try to evaluate the effects of each proposed implementation of possible innovation in order to help decide whether or not it should be done. I will therefore consider some social factors that seem relevant to various approaches to the uses of materials in the future.

The Inertia of Habits and Social Institutions

The inflexibility of human habits and social institutions strongly influences the implementation of new technology, generally acting to delay it. A simple example is the time needed to train enough people to work the new technology. A related example, especially important in connection with the substitution of one material for another, is the difficulty of transferring workers or capital equipment from one industrial process to a replacement process. Since the interests of workers and capital owners are among the criteria to be considered when deciding about any new technology, this factor may—except in emergency situations such as wars—act to delay the introduction of substitutes beyond the point of economic viability.

This type of inertia, which basically stems from the inborn limitations of the human nervous system, is unlikely to be easily modified. However, it could be somewhat ameliorated through redistributions of income from those profiting by new technology to those losing by it. The delaying effects of social inertia could also be avoided to a certain extent through automation, inasmuch as it is presumably easier to discard obsolete machines than obsolete workers. In the context of future use of materials, it would appear that these human factors would tend to favor the development of new sources of old materials rather than the development of substitute materials.

Human inertia exacerbates another problem caused by the inertia in social institutions—namely, the problem of mobilizing resources to deal with situations that are not immediately evident. A current example is the agonizingly slow attempts being made to deal with the already foreseeable exhaustion of hydrocarbon sources of energy. Ideally, advanced warning of the necessity for a change in our energy base should prove very helpful. Because of the difficulty of changing work habits and capital equipment to new applications, a long lead time is necessary to prepare for such a transition. But even with such a lead time—or perhaps even because of it—it remains doubtful whether we will act with sufficient speed and purpose to develop new energy supplies.

Only an emergency such as a war seems able to stimulate the kind of group effort needed to effect a major transition, and the threats of future energy and materials shortages seem to constitute an insufficiently compelling emergency. If this is the case, the consequences for future sources of materials are evident. Without large amounts of available energy, we will be unable to produce materials at anything near the present rate, even from the high-grade ores we now use, let alone from the low-grade ores likely to be needed in the future. Furthermore, even if adequate energy does become available, the engineering research and manpower training needed to carry out any of the strategies I have outlined for future sources of materials will still require time.

I do not know the precise cause of this type of social inertia. A contributory factor is the pragmatic strain in American thought, which tends to deprecate planning, especially on a long time scale. Another factor is the periodic electoral process, which tends to narrow the horizons of government to four years or less. Within these constraints, perhaps the best we can do is to develop other institutions to provide the foresight needed to cope with distant crises. Such institutions should have inputs into the determination of short-run policy, so that this will have at least some component in the direction that will help deal with the long-range problems.

Social and Economic Costs of New Materials Technology

Some of the costs associated with each of the possible new ways of obtaining materials are evident, such as the costs of building new facilities to process low-grade ores or the development costs for technologies needed to substitute plentiful materials for scarce ones. Other costs are more subtle. If we are to obtain materials from low-grade ores or common rocks, sizeable tracts must be set aside to obtain the matrix and to deposit up to ten cubic kilometers of waste material annually. Neither the land nor sizeable areas of surrounding territory could be used for other purposes such as residential development or agriculture. This form of social cost may be easier to arrange in the United States than in more densely populated countries. But even here, voices are raised to oppose the transformation of any parts of the country into aesthetically displeasing forms. It is difficult, indeed, to predict the attitudes that may ultimately prevail toward this type of land use.

Yet another social cost of new materials technologies involves the perennial problem of the extent to which any living generation can be expected to act in the interests of future generations, and especially of remote descendants. How willing is a society to accumulate capital—necessary to set up the new technologies—as opposed to immediately consuming its national product? After all, materials shortages are probably some time off even if little is done to avoid them. Moreover, avoiding them will take substantial immediate efforts and sacrifices by many who would not personally suffer from the eventual shortages. Hence, there arise questions, both in ethics and in practical politics, as to whether costly efforts to stave off a materials crisis should and will be undertaken now. If we do choose to help alleviate posterity's materials problems, perhaps on the ground that we have done much to create the problems through our own use of materials, we will deny ourselves other things that might be had instead of the long-term development program. If we choose not to do so, the costs will be paid by our descendants in the form of less affluent lives. Still another alternative—to decrease our own use of materials in order to extend the period of availability of high-grade ores—would involve the cost of impoverishing our own lives. The willingness of people to accept such costs, or even to recognize their existence, remains uncertain, with evidence existing on both sides of the issue.[26] Whatever choices are made should be informed by as much knowledge of the various choices, and of their consequences, as possible.

Materials Use and New Modes of Civilization

Implicit in the foregoing discussion is the assumption that all future societies will be characterized by an intensity of energy and materials use similar to that which now obtains in the industrialized countries. Such a globalization of material affluence seems likely, albeit far from certain. Even if the energy and materials are readily available, the preferred way of life may conceivably take other directions which imply a per capita use of materials that is substantially less than that which presently characterizes the industrialized countries. Such a change has, of course, been called for by sundry environmentalists[27] and other admirers of the "natural life." But I think it unlikely that the particular road they advocate will be followed. Indeed, it seems more probable to me that other types of technology could open new possibilities that will decrease at least some of our materials and energy requirements.

One such technology, which I believe to be more characteristic of the late twentieth century than technologies that increase the use of materials or energy, is information technology, as exemplified by computers and by television. Peter Goldmark[28] has suggested that information and communications technology could substitute for a large part of the travel we now do and so lead to savings in transportation-related energy and materials uses. We might also, through computer storage and information processing, reduce our tremendous consumption of paper and also consumption of the most precious resource, people's time. It is well to remember, then, that materials use is not the only area in which technology may advance. Indeed, the most important changes in the supply and the demand for materials may result from technological developments quite outside that field.

Nor should the role that the use of materials resources plays in the overall pattern of civilization be exaggerated. Important changes in modes of civilization have occurred in the past, and will continue to occur, which are not mirrored in a growth or decline in the use of materials and energy. What society does with materials is a means of accomplishing what it thinks is important. The spectacular growth in energy and materials usage in this century is significant because of the beneficial changes that it has allowed in our lives, not because of the value of materials processing in itself. Since the future supply of materials and energy is only one of the elements that will enter into the determination of the course along which our civilization develops, the questions dealt with in this chapter should not be answered as if they were independent of the aims of future civilization. Only if we have some understanding of our aims can we hope to determine what the true needs for materials will be in the future and how reasonable it is to fill these needs.

The foregoing survey of prospects in materials technology suggests no insuperable obstacles to our meeting any reasonable needs for materials in the indefinite future, both in the United States and worldwide. Any scenario for the future will require planning and hard work—beginning now. Our present sources of materials and energy cannot be continued indefinitely. Indeed, we must begin the transition to alternative sources within the foreseeable future. It would seem prudent to make this transition in such a way that it need occur only once, after which new sources can be used indefinitely. The development of technology to extract materials from common rock, together with the development of substitutes for materials that cannot easily be obtained in this way, would represent significant initial steps. We would then be in a position to satisfy whatever materials needs the course of our civilization itself may require.

Notes

1. Hesiod, *Works and Days*, quoted in *Greek Poetry for Everyone*, ed. Lucas (Boston: Beacon Press, 1951).

2. The classification of prehistory into the Stone Age, Bronze Age, and Iron Age is due to C.J. Thomsen, *A Guide to Northern Antiquities* (1836).

3. Weinberg's views on a subject closely related to that of this book— future supplies of energy—are described in an article in *American Scientist* (July-August 1970): 412.

4. The views of Meadows and collaborators are described in *The Limits to Growth* (New York: Universe Books, 1972).

5. See the comments by Forrester at the First Franklin Conference, 1974, published in the *Proceedings of the Franklin Institute* (1975).

6. The most detailed statistics available to me concerning the sources, use, and disposition of materials are for the United States in the references given below. Of course, the United States is not typical in its use of materials, but it is perhaps indicative of the way other countries are evolving.

7. Data given in *Minerals Yearbook* (1971), Vol. 1, published by the U.S. Department of the Interior, Bureau of Mines.

8. Some values for the lifetime of materials in various uses are given in Table 4C.7 of *Materials Needs and the Environment, Today and Tomorrow*, the final report of the National Commission on Materials Policy.

9. A useful concept in this regard is that of an in-use pool of a material, or the amount of material currently bound in the form of artifacts in use. It has been estimated that the in-use pool of iron is about twenty times the yearly extraction of new iron, and the in-use pool of copper is about thirty times the yearly extraction of copper. The in-use pools of other materials are probably a substantially smaller multiple of current extraction.

10. See the discussion in the *Bulletin of the Atomic Scientists* (September 1972): 24, 27.

11. See the *Handbook of Chemistry and Physics*, 54th edition, P F – 184 (Cleveland: CRC Press, 1973).

12. These views are in agreement with those expressed by several other authors, including H. Brown in *The Challenge of Man's Future* (New York: Viking Press, 1954), and more recently, D.B. Brooks and P.W. Andrews, *Science* 185, no. 13 (1974). Different views have been expressed by T. Lovering in *Resources and Man* (W.H. Freeman and Co., 1967). See also the article by P. Cloud in the *Texas Quarterly* 11 (1968): 103.

13. For example, Meadows et al., *The Limits to Growth*.

14. Some relevant figures are given in *Minerals Yearbook* (1971), Vol. 1, Table 3, p. 18. The total volume of production of metals doubled from 1880 to 1892, i.e., in twelve years. The next doubling took thirteen years, the next took thirty-seven years, and there has not yet been another doubling. This increase in the time of successive doublings implies a growth for most materials that is slower than exponential. See also the figures for individual materials given in *Historical Statistics of the U.S..*, Bureau of the Census.

15. A detailed analysis of the energy requirements for obtaining these metals from various sources is given in a report by J.C. Bravard and C. Portal, ORNL-MIT132. I have used their analysis, extrapolated to lower concentrations, in constructing Table 8-4.

16. See, for example, articles in the *New York Times*, 2 April 1975.

17. The proposal is to create a national bank to finance long-term risk research on new and essential technologies, which cannot easily be financed by conventional means, but which needs longer term commitments than the normal political process can ensure. See the record of the Bar Association of New York City, December 1974.

18. For example, in "A Blueprint for Survival," *The Ecologist* 2 (1972).

19. Examples of this are the spinodal alloys, which are more uniform in microstructure than ordinary alloys and have better metallic properties. See the description by J.T. Plewes in *Metal Progress* (July 1974): 46.

20. See S.S. Brenner, "Metal Wiskers," *Sci. Am.* (July 1960): 64.

21. The possibility of high temperature superconductivity was proposed by W.A. Little, *Phys. Rev.* 134, A1416 (1964). Experiments have not yet confirmed this possibility.

22. A detailed study of superconducting power transmission lines is given by the Brookhaven Power Transmission Group in the report BNL 50320, National Tech Inf. Serv., 1972. I have used this report for the data in making the estimates below.

23. S. Wagner et al., *Applied Physics Letters* 26 (1975): 229, and *Applied Physics Letters* 25 (1974): 434.

24. L.W. Jones, *Science* 174, 367 (1971).

25. A good general summary of the properties of individual metals is given in R.B. Ross, *Metallic Materials* (London: Chapman and Hill Ltd, 1968). The gaps in our knowledge of the properties of many materials are noted in this book.

26. Uruguay and Japan are two contemporary examples of opposite national attitudes toward sacrificing present consumption for future goods.

27. See "A Blueprint for Survival."

28. P. Goldmark, in *Research Management* 15, 14 (1972).

Index

Abduh, Muhammad, 6
Agricultural Act of 1970, 23
Agricultural commodity market, 23;
loosening from political restrictions, 24
Agriculture, 21
Ajami, Fouad, xiv, xvi; his "Natives
and Prospectors: Arab Oil and
Competing Systems of Legitimization," ix-x
Alaskan pipeline, 52
Allende, Salvatore, 70
Antitrust actions, 51
Arabs, ix, x, xi; Arab-Israeli conflict,
73; Arab-Western encounter, 4-11;
critics of, 3-4; folklore of, 7; legitimacy of oil policies, 14; member-
ship in the Western system, 16-18;
nationalism of, 7-11; windfall
profits of, 13-14
Argentina, 47
Australia, 70, 72; and ocean resources,
117

Balfour Declaration, 7
Belaunde, 52
Belgium, 65
Bergsten, C. Fred, 17
Bethlehem Steel Corporation, 93
Biosphere, 133, 135
Birthrate: acceleration of, 21. *See also*
Population growth
Bolivia, 52; and French Bureau de
Recherches Geológiques et
Minières, 86
Bonaparte, Napoleon, x; invasion of
Egypt, 6
Bougainville Copper, Ltd.: in New
Guinea, 86
Boumedienne, 5
Brazil, 16, 17, 55, 76; accumulation of
large coffee stocks, 43
Bretton Woods Agreement, 50
Brown, Courtney, 77

Brzezinski, Zbigniew, 12
Burke-Hartke Bill, xii, 50
Butz, Earl, 23, 26

Caldwell, Lynton Keith, xvii; his
"Global Resource Transfers: a
Scientific Perspective," xv-xvi
Canada, 52, 70, 71, 72; and ocean
resources, 117
Carr, E.H.: his *The Twenty Years'
Crisis 1919-1939*, 4
Chile, 70; nationalization of copper
mining operation in, 85
China, 24, 30; trade with United
States, 25, 26
Christianity, 134; feud with Islam, 14
CIPEC: organization of copper
producing countries, 91
Colombia, 76
Commissariat a l'Energie Atomique:
and Niger, 86
Commodity Credit Corporation, 26
Commodity markets: international
commodity agreements, 41-42;
structuring international, 39-55
Common Market, European, 62
Communist Bloc, xi
Conant, Melvin A., 75-76
Concession contracts, 94-97; bargain-
ing model of, 86-88, 94-97; bargain-
ing power, 86-87; information base,
86-87; negotiating power, 86-87
Continental Oil Company: in Niger, 86
Control Data Corporation, 70
Cuban missile crisis, 26

DeBeers Mining Corporation: in
Lesotha, 86
DeGaulle, Charles, 62
Denmark, 65
Détente: American policy of, 23; and
the food crisis of the 1970s, 21;
implications of, 11; negotiations
related to, 28-29; Nixon-Ford
policy of, 29; promotion of, 24

173

Nixon, Richard M. (cont.)
commodity market, 23; and surcharge on imports, 28
Norway, 117

Ocean Resources. *See* Resources, ocean
October War, 11
Oil, ix, x, 75-76; Arab, 3-19; embargo against Western importers, 5, 49; politicizing of, 8; price in the Middle East, 52; struggle over prices, 4-5; as a weapon, 11-13
OPEC (Organization of Petroleum Exporting Countries), ix, xi, xiii, 13, 68, 71, 75, 76; ability to increase profits shared with private companies, 91; challenge of Western dominance, 18; creation of, 9; and inflation in Western Europe, 27; information sharing role of, 85-98; possession of offshore oil reserves, 116; shift in bargaining power due to successes of, 85; success of, 65
Organization for Economic Cooperation and Development, 90

Palestine Liberation Organization, 30
Palestinian Resistance Movement, 10
Palestinians, 9
Pan-Arabism, 8
Pennsylvania State University, 43
Persian Gulf, 8, 15
Peru, 48, 52; copper development agreements in, 85-86
Pestamina, 93
Pestel, Edward, 21, 135
Planck, 134
Plato, 134
Political economy: vs. science, 141-147
Population growth, ix, 143; and food production, 29; in Latin America, 22
Puritanism, 14

Qaddafi, 6; achievement of, 10
Qassem, 9

Realpolitik, 14
Resource flows: political economy of international, ix
Resource transfers, 131-147
Resources: distribution of, 144; limits of earth's, ix
Resources, ocean: amount and future importance of, 108-110; access, property rights and efficiency of exploitation of, 110-113; distribution of, 113-118; management of, 107-122; Truman Proclamation and, 107
Reston, James, 15
Riyadh, 11
Russell, Bertrand: his *Freedom vs. Organization*, 7

Sadat, Anwar, 10, 11
Saudi Arabia, 8, 17, 18, 48, 49
Savage, Richard I., 43
Science: application to resource policy, 137, 138, 139-140; lack of communication of knowledge, 134-136; vs. political economy, 141-147
Seabury, Paul, 13, 14
Servian-Schreiber, Jean Jacques, 62
Sierra Leone, 97
Smith, David, x, 131; his "Information Sharing and Bargaining: Institutional Problems and Implications," xiii-xiv
South Africa, 30, 49
South Korea, 16
Spain, 27
Spengler, 16
Suez, 8; Egypt's seizure of canal, 63
Sunkel, Osvaldo, 64
Surinam, 48, 93
Sykes-Picot Treaty, 7
Syria, 8, 10; defeat of, 11

Taiwan, 16

About the Contributors

Fouad Ajami is an assistant professor of politics at Princeton University. Articles and reviews by Ajami discussing the politics of the Middle East have appeared in *Foreign Affairs Issues, Society, Alternatives,* and the *Journal of International Affairs.*

Lynton Keith Caldwell is Arthur Bentley Professor of Political Science and professor of public and environmental affairs at Indiana University. He has served as a member of numerous national commissions on the environment including the National Commission on Materials Policy, which he represented at the United National Conference on the Human Environment in 1972.

Lowell Dittmer, assistant professor of political science at the State University of New York, Buffalo, became interested in resource questions through his investigation of the agrarian problems of the Peoples Republic of China.

Gerald Feinberg, professor of physics at Columbia University, is a theoretical physicist with a particular interest in the future. He is the author of numerous technical articles and books.

Peter P. Gabriel is a former Dean of the School of Management, Boston University, and has served as an advisor to the Government of Venezuela. He is the author of a number of articles appearing in *Columbia Journal of World Business* and *Journal of World Trade Law.*

Stephen Krasner, assistant professor of political science at the University of California at Los Angeles, formerly at Harvard University, has written in the field of political economy. His articles on the politics and trade of raw materials have appeared in *World Politics* and *Foreign Policy.*

Lennart J. Lundqvist is an assistant professor of political science at Uppsala University, Sweden and his interests focus on the administrative aspects of environmental management. He is a special consultant to *AMBIO, Journal of the Environment: Research and Management*, a publication of the Royal Swedish Academy of Science.

David N. Smith, assistant dean for international legal studies, Harvard Law School, is internationally known for his work on concessions contracts. His articles have appeared in the *Harvard International Law Journal, American Journal of International Law,* and *American Journal of Comparative Law.*

About the Editors

Gerald Garvey, a professor of politics at Princeton University, consults and writes in the field of energy policy. His books include *Energy, Ecology, Economy,* and *Nuclear Power and Social Planning* (forthcoming). He received the Ph.D. in political science from Princeton University and has taught at the Air Force Academy.

Lou Ann Garvey, Master of Princeton Inn College, Princeton University is a specialist in Latin American politics and in the world food trade. She received the Ph.D. in International relations from American University.

Center of International Studies: List of Publications

Gabriel A. Almond, *The Appeals of Communism* (Princeton University Press 1954)

William W. Kaufmann, ed., *Military Policy and National Security* (Princeton University Press 1956)

Klaus Knorr, *The War Potential of Nations* (Princeton University Press 1956)

Lucian W. Pye, *Guerrilla Communism in Malaya* (Princeton University Press 1956)

Charles De Visscher, *Theory and Reality in Public International Law*, trans. by P.E. Corbett (Princeton University Press 1957; rev. ed. 1968)

Bernard C. Cohen, *The Political Process and Foreign Policy: The Making of the Japanese Peace Settlement* (Princeton University Press 1957)

Myron Weiner, *Party Politics in India: The Development of a Multi-Party System* (Princeton University Press 1957)

Percy E. Corbett, *Law in Diplomacy* (Princeton University Press 1959)

Rolf Sannwald and Jacques Stohler, *Economic Integration: Theoretical Assumptions and Consequences of European Unification*, trans. by Herman Karreman (Princeton University Press 1959)

Klaus Knorr, ed., *NATO and American Security* (Princeton University Press 1959)

Gabriel A. Almond and James S. Coleman, eds., *The Politics of the Developing Areas* (Princeton University Press 1960)

Herman Kahn, *On Thermonuclear War* (Princeton University Press 1960)

Sidney Verba, *Small Groups and Political Behavior: A Study of Leadership* (Princeton University Press 1961)

Robert J.C. Butow, *Tojo and the Coming of the War* (Princeton University Press 1961)

Glenn H. Snyder, *Deterrence and Defense: Toward a Theory of National Security* (Princeton University Press 1961)

Klaus Knorr and Sidney Verba, eds., *The International System: Theoretical Essays* (Princeton University Press 1961)

Peter Paret and John W. Shy, *Guerrillas in the 1960's* (Praeger 1962)

George Modelski, *A Theory of Foreign Policy* (Praeger 1962)

Klaus Knorr and Thornton Read, eds., *Limited Strategic War* (Praeger 1963)

Frederick S. Dunn, *Peace-Making and the Settlement with Japan* (Princeton University Press 1963)

Arthur L. Burns and Nina Heathcote, *Peace-Keeping by United Nations Forces* (Praeger 1963)

Richard A. Falk, *Law, Morality, and War in the Contemporary World* (Praeger 1963)

James N. Rosenau, *National Leadership and Foreign Policy: A Case Study in the Mobilization of Public Support* (Princeton University Press 1963)

Gabriel A. Almond and Sidney Verba, *The Civic Culture: Political Attitudes and Democracy in Five Nations* (Princeton University Press 1963)

Bernard C. Cohen, *The Press and Foreign Policy* (Princeton University Press 1963)

Richard L. Sklar, *Nigerian Political Parties: Power in an Emergent African Nation* (Princeton University Press 1963)

Peter Paret, *French Revolutionary Warfare from Indochina to Algeria: The Analysis of a Political and Military Doctrine* (Praeger 1964)

Harry Eckstein, ed., *Internal War: Problems and Approaches* (Free Press 1964)

Cyril E. Black and Thomas P. Thornton, eds., *Communism and Revolution: The Strategic Uses of Political Violence* (Princeton University Press 1964)

Miriam Camps, *Britain and the European Community 1955-1963* (Princeton University Press 1964)

Thomas P. Thornton, ed., *The Third World in Soviet Perspective: Studies by Soviet Writers on the Developing Areas* (Princeton University Press 1964)

James N. Rosenau, ed., *International Aspects of Civil Strife* (Princeton University Press 1964)

Sidney I. Ploss, *Conflict and Decision-Making in Soviet Russia: A Case Study of Agricultural Policy, 1953-1963* (Princeton University Press 1965)

Richard A. Falk and Richard J. Barnet, eds., *Security in Disarmament* (Princeton University Press 1965)

Karl von Vorys, *Political Development in Pakistan* (Princeton University Press 1965)

Harold and Margaret Sprout, *The Ecological Perspective on Human Affairs, With Special Reference to International Politics* (Princeton University Press 1965)

Klaus Knorr, *On the Uses of Military Power in the Nuclear Age* (Princeton University Press 1966)

Harry Eckstein, *Division and Cohesion in Democracy: A Study of Norway* (Princeton University Press 1966)

Cyril E. Black, *The Dynamics of Modernization: A Study in Comparative History* (Harper and Row 1966)

Peter Kunstadter, ed., *Southeast Asian Tribes, Minorities, and Nations* (Princeton University Press 1967)

E. Victor Wolfenstein, *The Revolutionary Personality: Lenin, Trotsky, Gandhi* (Princeton University Press 1967)

Leon Gordenker, *The UN Secretary-General and the Maintenance of Peace* (Columbia University Press 1967)

Oran R. Young, *The Intermediaries: Third Parties in International Crises* (Princeton University Press 1967)

James N. Rosenau, ed., *Domestic Sources of Foreign Policy* (Free Press 1967)

Richard F. Hamilton, *Affluence and the French Worker in the Fourth Republic* (Princeton University Press 1967)

Linda B. Miller, *World Order and Local Disorder: The United Nations and Internal Conflicts* (Princeton University Press 1967)

Henry Bienen, *Tanzania: Party Transformation and Economic Development* (Princeton University Press 1967)

Wolfram F. Hanrieder, *West German Foreign Policy, 1949-1963: International Pressures and Domestic Response* (Stanford University Press 1967)

Richard H. Ullman, *Britain and the Russian Civil War: November 1918-February 1920* (Princeton University Press 1968)

Robert Gilpin, *France in the Age of the Scientific State* (Princeton University Press 1968)

William B. Bader, *The United States and the Spread of Nuclear Weapons* (Pegasus 1968)

Richard A. Falk, *Legal Order in a Violent World* (Princeton University Press 1968)

Cyril E. Black, Richard A. Falk, Klaus Knorr and Oran R. Young, *Neutralization and World Politics* (Princeton University Press 1968)

Oran R. Young, *The Politics of Force: Bargaining During International Crises* (Princeton University Press 1969)

Klaus Knorr and James N. Rosenau, eds., *Contending Approaches to International Politics* (Princeton University Press 1969)

James N. Rosenau, ed., *Linkage Politics: Essays on the Convergence of National and International Systems* (Free Press 1969)

John T. McAlister, Jr., *Viet Nam: The Origins of Revolution* (Knopf 1969)

Jean Edward Smith, *Germany Beyond the Wall: People, Politics and Prosperity* (Little, Brown 1969)

James Barros, *Betrayal from Within: Joseph Avenol, Secretary-General of the League of Nations, 1933-1940* (Yale University Press 1969)

Charles Hermann, *Crises in Foreign Policy: A Simulation Analysis* (Bobbs-Merrill 1969)

Robert C. Tucker, *The Marxian Revolutionary Idea: Essays on Marxist Thought and Its Impact on Radical Movements* (W.W. Norton 1969)

Harvey Waterman, *Political Change in Contemporary France: The Politics of an Industrial Democracy* (Charles E. Merrill 1969)

Cyril E. Black and Richard A. Falk, eds., *The Future of the International Legal Order.* Vol. I: *Trends and Patterns* (Princeton University Press 1969)

Ted Robert Gurr, *Why Men Rebel* (Princeton University Press 1969)

C. Sylvester Whitaker, *The Politics of Tradition: Continuity and Change in Northern Nigeria 1946-1966* (Princeton University Press 1970)

Richard A. Falk, *The Status of Law in International Society* (Princeton University Press 1970)

Klaus Knorr, *Military Power and Potential* (D.C. Heath 1970)

Cyril E. Black and Richard A. Falk, eds., *The Future of the International Legal Order.* Vol. II: *Wealth and Resources* (Princeton University Press 1970)

Leon Gordenker, ed., *The United Nations in International Politics* (Princeton University Press 1971)

Cyril E. Black and Richard A. Falk, eds., *The Future of the International Legal Order*. Vol. III: *Conflict Management* (Princeton University Press 1971)

Francine R. Frankel, *India's Green Revolution: Political Costs of Economic Growth* (Princeton University Press 1971)

Harold and Margaret Sprout, *Toward a Politics of the Planet Earth* (Van Nostrand Reinhold 1971)

Cyril E. Black and Richard A. Falk, eds., *The Future of the International Legal Order*. Vol. IV: *The Structure of the International Environment* (Princeton University Press 1972)

Gerald Garvey, *Energy, Ecology, Economy* (W.W. Norton 1972)

Richard Ullman, *The Anglo-Soviet Accord* (Princeton University Press 1973)

Klaus Knorr, *Power and Wealth: The Political Economy of International Power* (Basic Books 1973)

Anton Bebler, *Military Rule in Africa: Dahomey, Ghana, Sierra Leone, and Mali* (Praeger Publishers 1973)

Robert C. Tucker, *Stalin as Revolutionary 1879-1929: A Study in History and Personality* (W.W. Norton 1973)

Edward L. Morse, *Foreign Policy and Interdependence in Gaullist France* (Princeton University Press 1973)

Henry Bienen, *Kenya: The Politics of Participation and Control* (Princeton University Press 1974)

Gregory J. Massell, *The Surrogate Proletariat: Moslem Women and Revolutionary Strategies in Soviet Central Asia, 1919-1929* (Princeton University Press 1974)

James N. Rosenau, *Citizenship Between Elections: An Inquiry Into The Mobilizable American* (Free Press 1974)

Ervin Laszio, *A Strategy For the Future: The Systems Approach to World Order* (Braziller 1974)

John R. Vincent, *Nonintervention and International Order* (Princeton University Press 1974)

Jan H. Kalicki, *The Pattern of Sino-American Crises: Political-Military Interactions in the 1950s* (Cambridge University Press 1975)

Klaus Knorr, *The Power of Nations: The Political Economy of International Relations* (Basic Books 1975)

James P. Sewell, *UNESCO and World Politics: Engaging in International Relations* (Princeton University Press 1975)

Richard A. Falk, *A Global Approach to National Policy* (Harvard University Press 1975)

Harry Eckstein and Ted Robert Gurr, *Patterns of Authority: A Structural Basis for Political Inquiry* (John Wiley & Sons 1975)

Cyril E. Black, Marius B. Jansen, Herbert S. Levine, Marion J. Levy, Jr., Henry Rosovsky, Gilbert Rozman, Henry D. Smith, II, and S. Frederick Starr, *The Modernization of Japan and Russia* (Free Press 1975)

Leon Gordenker, *International Aid and National Decisions: Development Programs in Malawi, Tanzania, and Zambia* (Princeton University Press 1976)

Carl Von Clausewitz, *On War*, edited and translated by Michael Howard and Peter Paret (Princeton University Press 1976)

Gerald Garvey and Lou Ann Garvey, eds., *International Resource Flows* (Lexington Books, D.C. Heath 1977)